EASTER
(Påsk)

August Strindberg

EASTER

Translated by
Gregory Motton

OBERON BOOKS
LONDON

First published in this translation in 2005 by Oberon Books Ltd
(incorporating Absolute Classics)
521 Caledonian Road, London N7 9RH
Tel: 020 7607 3637 / Fax: 020 7607 3629
e-mail: oberon.books@btinternet.com
www.oberonbooks.com

Cover illustration: Andrzej Klimowski

ISBN: 1 84002 555 7

Printed in Great Britain by Antony Rowe Ltd, Chippenham.

Translator's Note

The fashion these days is for versions. The Oxford Stage Company has gone against this trend and commissioned this translation. In the current climate that is almost to be considered a bold step in itself. In this translation from the Swedish, I have kept as close as I can to the meaning and style of the original language. I'm not sure what English audiences expect Strindberg to be, but my guess is that they would be surprised if they were to read him in his original language. I hope this translation has captured something of his way of writing.

In theatre, the authors we select from the past tend to be those who at least seem to be in favour of, let us say, certain developments since their death. They are writers who seem to share the values, for example, of the artistic establishment of the day, and to disapprove of their opponents. In theatre, whenever the writer doesn't quite fit what we want him to be, we simply remake him in our own image. We can set the play somewhere else, dress the play up in different clothes, adjust the meaning of the text until it says something we want it to say, make it 'about' something that it wasn't about – alter it until it coincides with what we happen to think at that particular time. It's called 'making it relevant to today' – and I think it's what they mean when they say that every age has its own Shakespeare. Whenever do we see a writer who is regarded highly, who *doesn't* seem, however subtly, to offer his approbation to the orthodxy of the day? If we did we might even think the production was strange and out-of-date. Don't expect, too often, to see a play produced that seems to oppose the views of the Management.

This is something we should especially bear in mind when we go to see productions of dead *foreign* writers, because when translation is involved, there is a further opportunity to alter the writer to our own design. Because it is obvious that a translation cannot be exactly right, this is taken to mean that inaccuracy is as valid as accuracy, taking liberties becomes the same as trying to be faithful. In other words – if the truth is hard to find, we may as well lie. In this way each age uses the writers of the past to reinforce its delusions about itself.

In the case of Strindberg, we like to think of him as the radical innovator, the rebel waving his approval to today's (artistic or other) establishment, that thinks of *itself* as radical and innovative. I would only say, from my reading of Strindberg, that if he seems to be waving anything in our particular direction, it is very likely his fist.

Gregory Motton, 2005

Characters

FRU HEYST [1]

ELIS [2]
her son, a teacher

ELEONORA [3]
her daughter

KRISTINA
Elis' fiancée

BENJAMIN [4]
school pupil

LINDKVIST

Pronunciation
1. *Fru* as in 'flu', *Heyst* as in 'heist'
2. Pronounced Eehlis
3. Five syllables: El-e-o-nor-a
4. Ben-yameen

This translation of Easter was first performed by Oxford Stage Company on 17 March 2005 at Nuffield Theatre, Southampton, with the following cast:

ELIS, Bo Poraj
KRISTINA, Katherine Tozer
FRU HEYST, Sally Edwards
BENJAMIN, Nicholas Shaw
ELEONORA, Frances Thorburn
LINDKVIST, Edward Peel

Director, Dominic Dromgoole
Designer, Michael Taylor
Lighting Designer, Mark Doubleday
Sound Designer, Fergus O'Hare

The whole of the foreground consists of a glass veranda on the ground floor, furnished as a living room. In the centre, a large door leading onto the garden which has a fence and a gate to the street. On the other side of the street, which together with the house is on a hill, can be seen a low garden fence of a garden which slopes down towards the town. The background shows the treetops from this garden, showing the green leaves of spring. Above that is a church tower and the gable of a grand house.

The windows of the veranda, which occupy the full breadth of the stage, are provided with curtains of a pale yellow floral cretonne, and can be drawn closed. A wall mirror hangs on a window frame up stage right, to the left of the door; below the mirror is a day calendar.

To the right of the upstage door is a large desk with books, writing materials and telephone. To the left of the upstage door is a dining-table, a stove with mica windows in the door, as well as a sideboard. To the right is a sewing table with a lamp. Beside this, two armchairs. There is a ceiling light.

Outside, on the street there is a gas lamp.

To the left in the veranda is a door into the rest of the apartment; to the right, a door to the kitchen.

The action takes place over two days.

ACT ONE

Maundy Thursday.

Music before this act: Haydn, 'Sieben Worte des Erlosers', Introduction, Maestoso Adagio.

A ray of sunlight shines diagonally across the room from the left reaching one of the chairs by the sewing table. On the other, unlit chair, sits KRISTINA threading tapes into a pair of newly ironed Venetian blinds.

ELIS: (*Comes in wearing an overcoat, unfastened, carrying a large bundle of documents, which he sets on the desk. Then he takes off his overcoat and hangs it up, left.*) Good afternoon, my friend!

KRISTINA: Hello, Elis!

ELIS: (*Looks about him.*) Winter windows removed; floor scrubbed, clean curtains… Yes, it's spring again! And they've cut up the ice, the catkins are in bloom down by the river… Yes! It's spring. And I can hang up my winter overcoat… You know, it's so heavy (*He weighs it in his hand.*) it's as if it has soaked up all the drudgery of winter, the sweat of anxiety and the dust of school… Oh!

KRISTINA: And now you've got the school holidays!

ELIS: Easter holidays! Five glorious days to enjoy, to breathe, and to forget!

He stretches out his hand to KRISTINA, and then sits in the armchair.

No, the sun has returned… It went away in November, I remember the day it disappeared behind the brewery, just across the street… Oh that winter! That long winter!

KRISTINA: (*With a gesture to the kitchen door.*) Hush, hush, hush!

ELIS: I shall be quiet, and I shall be happy that it is over and done with… Ah, the good kind sun… (*He rubs his hands together, and pretends to take a shower*) …I want to bathe in the sunshine, and wash in the light after all this dark dirt…

KRISTINA: Hush, hush!

ELIS: I think peace will return, I think our misfortunes have ended.

KRISTINA: Why do you think that?

ELIS: Well, partly because, when I walked past the cathedral just now, a white dove flew along: she landed on the pavement and dropped a twig, which she'd been holding in her beak, right at my feet.

KRISTINA: What kind of twig was it?

ELIS: Well, it couldn't very well have been olive, but I think it was a sign of peace, and I feel just now a kind of holy, sun-filled calm… Where's mother?

KRISTINA: (*Indicates the kitchen.*) In the kitchen!

ELIS: (*Silent. Closes his eyes.*) I can *hear* that it's spring! I can hear that the winter windows have been taken out. Do you know how? The rumbling of the carriage axles mainly… But what's that? The woodpecker is hammering. And they're hammering down in the boatyard, and it smells of paint from the steamboats, from the red lead.

KRISTINA: Can you smell it all the way from here?

ELIS: Here? True, we are *here*, but I was *there*, up in the north, where our home is… How have we ended up in this dreadful city, where everyone hates each other, and where you are always alone? Yes, it was bread that led the way…but alongside the bread were all the misfortunes: father's crime and our little sister's illness; – Do you know if mother has been able to visit father in the prison?

KRISTINA: I think she's been there today in fact.

ELIS: What did she say?

KRISTINA: Nothing, she just talked about something else.

ELIS: One thing is better anyway; After the verdict there was certainty and a kind of calm, once the newpapers stopped writing about it. A year has passed now; in one more year he'll be free, and we can start again.

KRISTINA: I admire your patience in suffering.

ELIS: Don't! Don't admire anything in me, because I have only faults! So now you know! If only you'd believe it!

KRISTINA: Suffering for your own faults is one thing, but these are someone else's!

ELIS: What are you sewing?

KRISTINA: The kitchen blinds of course, silly!

ELIS: It looks like a bridal veil… In the autumn you will be my bride, won't you?

KRISTINA: Yes, but let's think about the summer first.

ELIS: Summer, yes! (*Takes out his cheque book.*) You see, I already have the money in the bank! And when school breaks up, then we can go off back to the north, to our own country – to Mälaren.* The cottage is already in order, just as it was when we were children. The lime trees are still there; The logs for firewood are there

* Pronunciation: *Mä* as in 'air'

13

under the weeping willows... Oh if only it were summer, and I could swim in the lakes! This family's dishonour has clung to my body and my soul – I need a lake to wash it off in!

KRISTINA: Have you heard anything from your sister, Eleonora?

ELIS: Yes, poor thing, she's anxious. She writes letters that tear me apart. She wants to get out and come home, of course, but the governor of the institution refuses to let her go. He says she does things that could lead to prison. I feel terrible pangs of conscience because I voted for her to be committed.

KRISTINA: My dear friend, you reproach yourself for everything, but in this case it was a good deed, to give her treatment, the poor girl!

ELIS: It's true, what you say, and I think things are calmer this way. Yes, it's as good as it can be for her. When I think of how she went around here overshadowing any shred of happiness; how her fate oppressed us like a nightmare and drove us to despair, then I'm selfish enough to feel a relief that is quite like happiness. And the greatest unhappiness I can imagine now, is to see her come through that door. That's the kind of a wretch I am!

KRISTINA: That's how human you are.

ELIS: While at the same time... I suffer, at the thought of her agonies, and my father's.

KRISTINA: Some people seem to be born to suffering...

ELIS: Poor you, ending up with a family like this one, doomed from the outset...condemned.

KRISTINA: Elis! You don't know if it's a test or a punishment.

14

ELIS: What it is for you, I don't know, because you're without blame, if anyone is.

KRISTINA: The tears of the morning are the joys of the evening. Elis, maybe I can help you overcome this...

ELIS: Do you think mother has a white scarf?

KRISTINA: (*Worried.*) Are you going out?

ELIS: I'm going to a dinner. Petrus defended his thesis yesterday, as you know, and he's having a dinner party today.

KRISTINA: And are you going?

ELIS: You mean I should keep away, because he turned out to be such an ungrateful pupil?

KRISTINA: I don't deny his treachery upset me – he promised you to quote from your dissertation, but then stole from it instead! He never gave his source.

ELIS: Oh, that's so common, I'm just happy to know it was my work.

KRISTINA: Did he invite you?

ELIS: It's true, he hasn't. It really is strange, he's been talking about this dinner party for years, it was taken for granted that I would be invited. I've talked about it to other people. If I'm not invited now, it's a public snub. I don't care, it's not the first time, and it won't be the last.

Pause.

KRISTINA: Benjamin's late. Do you think he'll pass his examination?

ELIS: I should certainly hope so, with top marks in Latin!

KRISTINA: He's a good boy, Benjamin.

ELIS: Unusual, but a bit of a dreamer. You know, don't you, why he is staying with us?

KRISTINA: Is it because…

ELIS: Because my father embezzled his trust money, along with that of so many others. You see Kristina, this is the terrible thing; I have to see these fatherless, robbed boys about the school, suffering the humiliation of being non-paying pupils. And you can imagine through what kind of eyes they look at me. I have to keep thinking of their suffering to be able to forgive them for their cruelty.

KRISTINA: I think your father is probably better off than you!

ELIS: Probably!

KRISTINA: Elis, we were going to think about the summer, not about the past.

ELIS: The summer, yes. – You know I woke up last night with the student song in my head; it went:

'Yes I'll follow the happy winds
to the birds, the birch and limes I love,
to the lakes and the valleys once again,
to see them as they were when I was young.'

He stands up, moved.

Shall I see them again? Will I ever get away from this dreadful city, from Ebal, the hill of banishment to see Gazarim once again?

Sits by the door.

KRISTINA: Yes! You shall!

ELIS: But do you think I'll see *my* birches again, and the lime trees, as I saw them before? Don't you think the same black veil will lay upon them, as it has done upon the whole of life and nature here, ever since that day…

He points to the armchair which is now in the shadow.

You see! Now the sun has gone!

KRISTINA: It will come back, and it will stay longer.

ELIS: That's true; the days are drawing out and the shadows are shortening.

KRISTINA: We are moving towards the light, Elis, believe me.

ELIS: Sometimes I think so, and when I think of the past and compare it with the present, I'm happy. Last year you weren't there – you'd left me and broken off our engagement! You know, that was the worst of all. I literally died, bit by bit; but when you came back – I was alive again. Do you remember why you left?

KRISTINA: No, I don't remember, and now it seems as if there was no reason. Something prompted me to leave; and so I left, as if I was walking in my sleep. When I saw you again, I woke up and was happy!

ELIS: And now there'll be no more leaving, because if you left now, I really would die! Here comes mother! Don't say anything; indulge her in her deluded world, where father is a martyr, and all his victims rogues.

FRU HEYST: (*In from the kitchen, peeling an apple; speaks in a friendly manner, somewhat foolish.*) Good afternoon to you my children! Do you want the apple soup cold or warm?

ELIS: Cold, little Mamma.*

FRU HEYST: That's good, my boy, you always know what you want, and say so, but Kristina doesn't. You've learnt

* Not like the French, but something like the English 'Mummer', without the 'r' sound

17

it from your father; he always knew what he wanted and what he was doing, and people don't like that, and that's why things went badly for him. But his day will come, and he'll be justified and the others condemned! Wait now; what was I going to say? Oh yes! Do you know Lindkvist has moved here? Lindkvist, the biggest rogue of all.

ELIS: (*Stands up, he is disturbed.*) Has he moved here?

FRU HEYST: Yes he lives right across the road.

ELIS: Then we'll see him go past every day. That too!

FRU HEYST: Let me speak to him just once! He'll never show his face again. I know his little ways!… Well, Elis, how did it go for Petrus?*

ELIS: It went well.

FRU HEYST: I can imagine it did. When will you present your thesis?

ELIS: When I can afford it, Mamma.

FRU HEYST: When I can afford it! That's not a proper answer!… And Benjamin? Has he passed his examinations?

ELIS: We don't know yet; but he'll be here soon.

FRU HEYST: Well, I don't really like Benjamin, he goes about as if he thinks he has rights here…but we'll rid him of that idea!… A nice boy though. Also there was a parcel for you, Elis. (*Goes out the kitchen door and returns with a parcel.*)

ELIS: The way mother keeps track of everything and follows it all; I think sometimes she's not as foolish as she makes herself out to be.

* Pronounced 'Peertrus'

FRU HEYST: Here's the parcel! Lina took it in.

ELIS: A present! I'm afraid of presents – I was given a box of street cobbles once. (*Puts the parcel on the table.*)

FRU HEYST: I'll go back out to the kitchen now. – Isn't it too cold to have the door open?

ELIS: Not at all, Mamma.

FRU HEYST: Don't hang your overcoat there, Elis, it looks untidy!… Well, Kristina, are my curtains ready?

KRISTINA: In a few minutes Mamma.

FRU HEYST: Now, Petrus I do like; he's my favourite… Are you going to the dinner, Elis?

ELIS: Well, I should think so, yes!

FRU HEYST: Well, why did you say you wanted the apple soup cold, when you're going out? You're such a muddle, Elis. It's all that business with Petrus I suppose… Close the doors when it gets too cold, so you don't catch colds. (*Goes out right.*)

ELIS: Dear kind old lady!… And always Petrus… Do you think she means to embarrass you by mentioning him?

KRISTINA: Me?

ELIS: You know how old women get these ideas, these dreamed up notions.

KRISTINA: What's that present you've got?

ELIS: (*Tears open the packet.*) A twig for lent…

KRISTINA: Who from?

ELIS: Anonymous!… Well, it's innocent enough, I'll put it in water, and it can bloom like Aaron's rod. 'Birch…as in

the moments of my youth'… So, Lindkvist has turned
up.

KRISTINA: What does he want?

ELIS: It's him we owe the most money to.

KRISTINA: But you don't owe any debt to him.

ELIS: Yes, all for one and one for all; we all do; the family's
name is disgraced.

KRISTINA: Change your name.

ELIS: Kristina!

KRISTINA: (*Sets aside her work, which she has now finished.*)
Thank you Elis. I just wanted to test you.

ELIS: But you mustn't tempt me… Lindkvist is a poor man
and needs his money… Wherever my father has been is
like a battlefield strewn with dead and wounded… And
mother thinks he's the victim!… Would you like to come
out for a stroll?

KRISTINA: Go and look for the sun? Gladly!

ELIS: Do you understand this, Our Saviour suffered for our
sins, and yet we have to carry on paying for them. No-
one pays for me!

KRISTINA: But if someone paid for you, would you
understand…?

ELIS: Yes, then I'd understand! Hush! Here comes
Benjamin. Can you tell if he looks pleased?

KRISTINA: (*Looks out through the door upstage.*) He's walking
so slowly… Now he's stopped by the fountain… He's
bathing his eyes…

ELIS: That too!

KRISTINA: Wait now…

ELIS: Tears, tears!

KRISTINA: Patience!

*

BENJAMIN comes in, friendly, respectful, but distressed. He is carrying a few books and a briefcase.

ELIS: Well, how did it go in the Latin?

BENJAMIN: It went badly.

ELIS: May I see your paper? What did you do?

BENJAMIN: I wrote *ut* in the indicative, even though I knew it was the subjunctive.

ELIS: Then you are lost. How could you?

BENJAMIN: (*Submissive.*) I can't explain it… I knew how it ought to be, I wanted to put the right thing, and wrote the wrong thing. (*Sits down at the table, defeated.*)

ELIS: (*Sinks down at the desk and reads from BENJAMIN's briefcase.*) Yes, here it is, the indicative! Oh my God!

KRISTINA: (*Strained.*) Well, better luck next time: life is long, so dreadfully long!

BENJAMIN: Yes, it is.

ELIS: (*Sad but without bitterness.*) It's all come at once! – And you were my best pupil, what can I expect from the others? – My reputation as a teacher is lost! I won't get any more pupils, and then, everything collapses. (*To BENJAMIN.*) Don't take it too badly…it's not your fault…

KRISTINA: (*With the greatest of effort.*) Elis! Courage, courage! For God's sake!

21

ELIS: Where should I get courage from?

KRISTINA: Where you used to get it.

ELIS: It's not the same as it used to be! I seem to be in disfavour.

KRISTINA: It is a blessing to suffer wrongfully...don't let yourself be fooled into impatience... Stand the test, because it is only a test, I can feel that it is...

ELIS: Can a year for Benjamin become shorter than three hundred and sixty-five days?

KRISTINA: Yes, a glad heart shortens time.

ELIS: Kiss it better, as one says to children!

KRISTINA: Be a child then and I can kiss it better... Think of your mother...how she bears everything!

ELIS: Give me your hand; I'm sinking!

KRISTINA stretches out her hand to him.

Your hand is shaking...

KRISTINA: I hadn't noticed...

ELIS: You're not as strong as you pretend to be...

KRISTINA: I don't feel any weakness...

ELIS: Why can't you give me any strength then?

KRISTINA: I don't have a surplus of it.

ELIS: (*Looks out through the window.*) Guess who's coming now?

KRISTINA: (*Looks out through the window, falls to her knees, devastated.*) It's too much!

ELIS: The creditor, who can take our furniture whenever he likes. Lindkvist, who has moved here so he can sit like a spider in the web keeping watch over the flies...

KRISTINA: Run away!

ELIS: (*Gets up.*) No, not that... When you're weak I grow strong... Now he's coming along the street... He's already cast his evil eye upon his prey...

KRISTINA: Move back, at least!

ELIS: No, he amuses me... He seems to brighten, as if he has seen the quarry in the trap... Come on!!... He's counting the steps to the gate and he's seen from the open door that we are at home...but now he's met someone, he's stopped to talk... He's talking about us, he's looking this way...

KRISTINA: As long as he doesn't meet your mother here, she's bound to provoke him with her bitter words. Try to prevent that, Elis!

ELIS: Now he's shaking his stick, as if to say, 'There will be no mercy in place of justice here!'... He unbuttons his overcoat to show that he hasn't yet taken the clothes off our backs... I can read his lips... What should I answer him?... 'My good sir, you are right! Take it all, it belongs to you!'...

KRISTINA: That's all you should say.

ELIS: Now he's laughing! But a kindly laugh, not a nasty one! Maybe he isn't so cruel, even though he does want his money!... If only he would come *now*!...and stop his blessed talking. Now his stick is in motion again...they always have sticks, these people who have debts outstanding...and leather galoshes that go 'slosh, slosh, slosh', just like a cane in the air... (*Lays KRISTINA's hand on his heart.*) Can you feel how my heart is beating?... I

23

can hear it myself, like an ocean liner in my right ear...
Well, God, now he's saying goodbye...and now the
galoshes, 'slosh, slosh, slosh', like the Easter twigs. But
he's got ornaments hanging on his watch chain! So he
can't be that hard up! They always have ornaments made
of red cornelian, like old meat they've scraped out of
their neighbour's backbone... Listen to those galoshes...
'Slosh, wolves, rage, slosh, slosh.' Look out! He can see
me! He can see me!... (*Leans out into the street.*) ...He
greets me first! He smiles! He's waving his hand...and...
(*Falls back to the desk, crying.*) He's gone past.

KRISTINA: Thanks be to God!

ELIS: He went past...but he'll be back!... Let's go out into
the sun.

KRISTINA: And the dinner with Petrus?

ELIS: Since I'm not invited yet, I will keep away. Besides,
what would I do there amongst all that merry-making?
To meet a faithless friend! I'd only suffer on his behalf,
so as not to be injured on my own.

KRISTINA: Thank you for staying with us!

ELIS: I prefer it, as you know!... Shall we go?

KRISTINA: Yes, this way

They go out left.

ELIS: (*As he goes past BENJAMIN, he pats him on the head.*)
Courage, lad.

BENJAMIN hides his head in his hands.

(*Picks up the Easter twig from the table and puts it behind the
mirror.*) It wasn't an olive branch the dove brought, it was
birch. (*Goes out.*)

*

ELEONORA comes in from upstage; a sixteen-year-old girl with plaits. She carries a yellow daffodil in a pot. Without seeing or letting on that she sees BENJAMIN, she takes a water jug from the sideboard and waters the flower, then puts it on the dining table, sits by that table herself, directly facing BENJAMIN, she looks at him and imitates his gestures.

He looks at her, surprised.

ELEONORA: (*Indicates the daffodil.*) Do you know what *that* is?

BENJAMIN: It's a daffodil, obviously… But who are you?

ELEONORA: (*Friendly, with sadness.*) Well, who are you?

BENJAMIN: My name is Benjamin and I am staying here in Fru Heyst's house.

ELEONORA: Aha! My name is Eleonora and I am the daughter here.

BENJAMIN: How strange, no-one has mentioned you.

ELEONORA: They don't speak of the dead.

BENJAMIN: Dead!

ELEONORA: Officially speaking, I am dead, because I did a very wrong thing.

BENJAMIN: You?

ELEONORA: Yes, I have embezzled trust money – and it didn't matter so much, because ill-gotten gains ought to perish – but for my father to be left with the blame and sent to prison, that, you see, cannot be forgiven.

BENJAMIN: You speak so strangely and so beautifully… And I've never thought of my inheritance as ill-gotten.

25

ELEONORA: We mustn't bind people, we must release them.

BENJAMIN: Yes, you've freed me from the worry of having been swindled.

ELEONORA: Then you have come of age!

BENJAMIN: Yes and it's my unhappy lot to be stuck with these poor people sitting out their debt.

ELEONORA: You mustn't use harsh words, because then I shall leave; I am so soft, I cannot endure anything harsh. And so, you are suffering this, all on my account?

BENJAMIN: All on your father's account.

ELEONORA: It's the same. He and I are the same person… (*Pause.*) I've been very ill… Why are you so sad?

BENJAMIN: I have suffered a setback.

ELEONORA: Are you sad because of that? 'The birch and punishment gives you wisdom, beat him with the rod and save his soul from hell…' What setback have you had?

BENJAMIN: I have failed my Latin examination – even though I was absolutely certain of passing it.

ELEONORA: I see, you were so absolutely certain, that you bet on it!

BENJAMIN: I did as well!

ELEONORA: I thought so. There you see, that's what you get for being so sure.

BENJAMIN: Do you think that was the reason?

ELEONORA: Of course it was. Pride comes before a fall.

BENJAMIN: I'll remember that next time.

ELEONORA: That's right: 'The sacrifice that pleases God is the broken spirit.'

BENJAMIN: Are you a believer?

ELEONORA: Yes I am, and if you speak ill of God, my benefactor, then I shan't sit at the same table as you!

BENJAMIN: How old are you?

ELEONORA: For me there is no time and place; I am everywhere at every time! I am in my father's prison, and in my brother's schoolroom, I am in my mother's kitchen and in my sister's shop far away in America. When it goes well for her and she sells something, then I feel her joy, and when it goes badly then I suffer, but most of all I suffer when she does wrong. Benjamin, you're called Benjamin because you are the youngest of my friends...well, all people are my friends...will you let me adopt you so I can suffer for you too?

BENJAMIN: I don't really understand the words you're saying, but I think I understand the thought behind it. And now I want what you want!

ELEONORA: Do you want to start by not judging people, even if they are convicted criminals...

BENJAMIN: Yes, but I want a reason for it. I've studied philosophy you see!

ELEONORA: Oh have you! Then you can help me understand these words of a great philosopher. This is what he says: 'Those that hate the righteous shall be desolate.'

BENJAMIN: According to all logic it means, that you can be sentenced to commit a crime...

ELEONORA: And the crime itself is a punishment.

BENJAMIN: That is truly deep. It sounds like Kant or Schoepenhauer!

ELEONORA: Don't know them.

BENJAMIN: In what book have you read it then?

ELEONORA: In the Holy Book.

BENJAMIN: Really? Is there that kind of thing in there?

ELEONORA: What an ignorant and badly brought up child you are! If only I could instruct you.

BENJAMIN: Little girl…

ELEONORA: But there's definitely no harm in you! You look more good than bad… What's your Latin teacher's name?

BENJAMIN: Lektor Ahlgren!*

ELEONORA: I shall remember that… Oh, now my father is in great pain! They are being cruel to him!

She stands still as if she is listening.

Can you hear that singing in the telephone wires?… It's the harsh words which the soft lovely red copper wires can't bear… When people slander one another in the telephone, then the copper wires complain, and accuse… (*Harshly.*) …and every word is written in the book…and at the world's end, comes the reckoning!

BENJAMIN: You're so severe!

ELEONORA: Not I, not I! How could I ever dare to be severe? Me? Me?

She goes over to the stove and opens the lid; takes out some torn sheets of a letter on white paper. BENJAMIN stands

---

* Pronunciation: 'Arl-grien' (last syllable as in the name 'Ian')

and looks at the papers, which ELEONORA arranges on the table.

(*To herself.*) How people can be so thoughtless as to put their secrets in stoves… Wherever I go, I always go straight to the stove! But I never misuse it, for I would never dare, because that would give me so much pain!… What's this now? (*Reads.*)

BENJAMIN: It's Licentiate Petrus, writing to arrange a meeting with Kristina… I've been waiting for this for a long time!

ELEONORA: (*Puts her hands over the papers.*) Ha! You! What have you been waiting for! Tell me, you wicked person, who only thinks ill of others! This letter brings only good… I know Kristina, she's going to be my sister-in-law. And the point of this meeting is to avert a disaster for my brother Elis… Will you promise me you'll keep silent, Benjamin?

BENJAMIN: I don't think I'd dare mention it!

ELEONORA: That's what unjust people do who know secrets, 'Professing themselves to be wise they become fools'… But what's it got to do with me!

BENJAMIN: Yes, why are you so curious?

ELEONORA: Well, you see that's my illness, I have to know everything, otherwise I become anxious…

BENJAMIN: Know everything?

ELEONORA: It's a fault that I can't overcome. But I still know what the starlings say.

BENJAMIN: They can't talk can they?

ELEONORA: Haven't you heard starlings that have been taught to speak?

BENJAMIN: Yes, ones that have been taught.

ELEONORA: Well then, starlings can learn to talk. Now there are some that teach themselves, autodidactic ones... They sit and listen, of course without us realising it, and then they just copy us. I heard just now, when I arrived, two of them in the walnut tree, sitting talking.

BENJAMIN: You're funny aren't you? So what did they say then?

ELEONORA: Well, 'Petrus,' said one of them. 'Judas!' said the other. 'They're just the same,' said the first. 'For shame!' said the other. But have you noticed how the nightingales only sing in the garden of the deaf and dumb people's house next door?

BENJAMIN: Yes, I've heard that. Why do they?

ELEONORA: Because those who can hear don't hear what the nightingales are saying, but the deaf and dumb, they do hear.

BENJAMIN: Tell me some more stories!

ELEONORA: If you're nice.

BENJAMIN: How nice?

ELEONORA: Well, you must never pick me up on everything I say. Never say, 'Oh you said this and then you said that...' Shall I talk some more about the birds? There is a wicked bird called the Rat Buzzard; as you can tell by the name, he lives on rats. But because he is a wicked bird it has to be difficult for him to catch the rats, and so he only has to say a single word and it sounds like a cat saying 'meow!' So when the Rat Buzzard says 'meow!' the rats go and hide... But the buzzard doesn't understand what he is saying himself – and he often has to go without food, because he is nasty – Do you want to hear some more? Or shall I talk about flowers?... Do you know, when I was ill I was allowed to take a medicine from henbane, which has the effect of making the eye into a magnifying glass... Belladona, on the other hand, makes everything look smaller... Anyway, now I can see further than everyone else, and I can see the stars in daylight.

BENJAMIN: But the stars aren't out are they?

ELEONORA: You're so funny! The stars are always out...and now I'm sitting facing north and I can see Cassiopeia which looks like a 'W' and is in the milky way... Can you see it?

BENJAMIN: No, I can't.

ELEONORA: Take note of that, one person can see what another can't... Don't be so sure, then, of what your own eyes tell you... Now, I was going to talk about this flower on the table here... It's a daffodil which is most at home in Switzerland... It has a bulb which has drunk the sunlight, which is why it is yellow and can soothe pain... I went past a florist's, just now, saw this and wanted to give it to my brother Elis... When I tried to go in through the door I found it was closed... Apparently someone was being confirmed today... Since I had to have the flower, I took out my keys and tried them... And imagine! My door key fitted... I went in... Well, do you understand the silent language of flowers? Each scent expresses a whole collection of thoughts, and these thoughts overwhelmed me; and with my magnifying eye I saw into their shop as no-one else had done. And they spoke to me of their sorrows which the foolish gardener had caused them – I don't say he was cruel, because he was only thoughtless!... Then I put a krona along with my card on the counter, and took the flower and left.

BENJAMIN: So thoughtless! What if they notice the flower has gone and don't find the money?

ELEONORA: That's true, you're right!

BENJAMIN: Money can get lost, and if they only find your card, then you are done for!

ELEONORA: But no-one could imagine that I wanted to take anything?

BENJAMIN: (*Looks pointedly at her.*) Couldn't they?

ELEONORA: (*Looks at him.*) Oh! I know what you mean! Like father, like daughter! How thoughtless I've been!… Well! What must be must be. (*Sits down.*) Let it happen then!

BENJAMIN: Can't this be sorted out?

ELEONORA: Shsh! Talk about something else!… Lektor Ahlgren!… Poor Elis! Poor all of us! But it is Easter and we must suffer. There's a concert tomorrow isn't there? And they're playing Haydn's 'Seven Stations of the Cross!' 'Here is Your Son.' (*She cries into her hands.*)

BENJAMIN: What illness did you have?

ELEONORA: It's not fatal, it's to the greater glory of God. 'I looked for good and evil came unto me, when I waited for the light, there came darkness!'… What was your childhood like, Benjamin?

BENJAMIN: I don't know. Not very nice. And yours?

ELEONORA: I never had one. I was born old… I knew everything when I was born, and when I learned something it was just like remembering. I knew mankind's…thoughtlessness and foolishness when I was four years old, and that's why people were horrible to me.

BENJAMIN: Everything you are saying, I feel as if I have thought it too.

ELEONORA: You probably have!… Why did you think my my coin would probably get lost in the florists?

BENJAMIN: Just because the most infuriating things always seem to happen!

ELEONORA: You've noticed that too!… Hush! Someone's coming. (*Looks upstage.*) I can hear…that it is Elis!… Oh how nice!… My only friend on earth!… (*She darkens.*) But…he's not expecting me! And he won't be happy to see me. No, he won't. Definitely not! – Benjamin! Benjamin, put on a friendly face and a glad heart when my poor brother comes. I'll go in here, and you can prepare him for my arrival. But no harsh words, because they hurt me so much, you hear me! Give me your hand!

BENJAMIN gives her his hand.

(*Kisses the top of his head.*) There! Now you are my little brother! God bless and protect you!

She goes out left and in passing she strokes the sleeve of ELIS's overcoat.

Poor Elis!

*

ELIS comes in from upstage, worried.

FRU HEYST comes in from the kitchen.

ELIS: Ah, there you are, Mamma!

FRU HEYST: Is it you? I thought I heard a stranger's voice.

ELIS: I have some news! I met our lawyer in the street.

FRU HEYST: And?

ELIS: The case will go to the Court of Appeal…and to save time I have to read through all the minutes of the case.

FRU HEYST: Then you must do it soon.

ELIS: (*Indicates the documents on the desk.*) I thought that was all over. Now I have to go through the whole of the Passion again! – All the accusations, all the testimonies, all the evidence! All over again!

FRU HEYST: Yes, but then he will be released by the Court of Appeal.

ELIS: No, no, mother, he has confessed!

FRU HEYST: Yes, but there might be a technicality, that's what the lawyer said when I spoke to him last.

ELIS: He just said that to comfort you.

FRU HEYST: Aren't you going out to dinner?

ELIS: No.

FRU HEYST: Now you've changed your mind again!

ELIS: Yes!

FRU HEYST: It's very bad of you.

ELIS: I know but I'm being thrown around like shingle between the breakers.

FRU HEYST: I'm sure I heard a strange voice just now, one that I recognised – But I must have heard wrong. (*Points to his overcoat.*) That coat shouldn't be hanging there, I said! (*Goes out right.*)

ELIS: (*Moves to the left; sees the daffodil on the table. To BENJAMIN.*) Where did that flower come from?

BENJAMIN: A young lady brought it.

ELIS: Young lady? What's all this? Who was it?

BENJAMIN: It was…

ELIS: Was it…my sister?

BENJAMIN: Yes.

ELIS: (*Sinks down at the dinner table. Pause.*) Did you speak to her?

BENJAMIN: Oh yes!

ELIS: Oh God, how much more of this!… Was she unpleasant to you?

BENJAMIN: Her? No, she was nice, very nice!

ELIS: Odd!… Did she talk about me? Was she very angry with me?

BENJAMIN: She said you were her best and only friend on this earth…

ELIS: What an incredible transformation!

BENJAMIN: And when she left, she stroked your overcoat, there, on the sleeve.

ELIS: She left? Where did she go?

BENJAMIN: (*Points to the door, left.*) In there.

ELIS: So she's in there?

BENJAMIN: Yes.

ELIS: You look very happy and friendly, Benjamin.

BENJAMIN: She spoke so prettily to me…

ELIS: What did she talk about?

BENJAMIN: She told me stories, and then there was a lot about religion…

ELIS: (*Gets up.*) And that made you happy?

BENJAMIN: Yes!

ELIS: Poor Eleonora, so unhappy herself and yet she makes others happy! (*Goes left, reluctantly.*) God help me!

ACT TWO

Good Friday.

Music before this act: Haydn, 'Sieben Worte', Largo No. 1, Pater Dimitte Illis.

Same set as before, but the curtains are drawn and illuminated from outside by the street lamps. The room light is lit; on the dinner table is a small oil lamp. There is a fire in the stove.

At the sewing table sit ELIS and KRISTINA unoccupied. At the dinner table sit ELEONORA and BENJAMIN reading opposite one another, with the lamp between them. ELEONORA has a shawl over her shoulders.

All of them are dressed in black; ELIS and BENJAMIN have white cravats.

On the desk are the case documents spread out. On the sewing table stands the daffodil. On the dinner table is an old ornamental clock.

Now and again the shadow of a passer-by can be seen on the curtain.

ELIS: (*In a half-whisper to KRISTINA.*) Good Friday! What a long long day! And the snow has settled on the paving stones like straw outside the house of a dying man; every noise has ceased – except the bass of the organ, which I can hear even from here…

KRISTINA: Mamma has gone to Evensong…

ELIS: She darent go to high mass, because the looks people give her hurt her too much.

KRISTINA: These people are strange; they expect us to keep away, they think it's appropriate…

ELIS: Yes, quite rightly perhaps…

KRISTINA: For the fault of one, the whole family is banished…

ELIS: Yes, that's the way it *is*.

ELEONORA pushes the lamp over towards BENJAMIN so that he can see better.

(*Indicates ELEONORA and BENJAMIN.*) Look at those two!

KRISTINA: Isn't it lovely!… And they get along so well together!

ELIS: What a joy that Eleonora is so calm. If only it would last!

KRISTINA: Why shouldn't it?

ELIS: Because…happiness doesn't usually last very long! I'm afraid of everything today.

BENJAMIN pushes the lamp over towards ELEONORA so that she can see better.

KRISTINA: Look at them!

ELIS: Have you noticed how changed Benjamin is? That dull stubbornness has given way to a peaceful kind of submissiveness…

KRISTINA: Just think, how sweet she is in her whole being – one doesn't want to use the word beautiful!

ELIS: She has brought an angel of peace with her. It goes about invisibly breathing a quiet calm.

KRISTINA: Do you think Eleonora has recovered now?

ELIS: Yes, if only she didn't still have this exaggerated sensitivity. She's sitting there reading Christ's Passion, and sometimes she cries.

KRISTINA: Well, I remember we did that too in school, on Wednesdays during Lent…

ELIS: Not so loud, she hears so well!

KRISTINA: Not now she won't, she's miles away!

ELIS: Have you noticed how Benjamin has acquired something noble and worthy in his expressions?

KRISTINA: It's the suffering; happiness makes everything banal.

ELIS: Maybe it's more likely to be…love! Don't you think those two young…

KRISTINA: Hush, hush, hush…don't touch the butterfly's wings, or it'll fly away.

ELIS: They're probably just looking at one another and pretending to read, they're not turning any pages, from what I can hear.

KRISTINA: Hush!

ELIS: See, now she can't control herself any longer…

ELEONORA gets up, goes on tip-toes to BENJAMIN and puts her shawl over his shoulders. BENJAMIN puts up a mild resistance, but submits; then ELEONORA goes and sits back down and pushes the lamp over to his side.

KRISTINA: She doesn't even know how kind she is! Poor Eleonora.

ELIS: (*Gets up.*) Now I must go back to my documents.

KRISTINA: Can you see any point in all this reading?

ELIS: Only one: to keep Mother's hope alive! But even though I too am only pretending to read, the words stick like thorns into my eyes. The witnesses' testimonies, the amounts of money, father's confessions, like this: 'The accused admits in tears,' ...so many tears, so many tears. And these papers...with their official stamps that remind you of forged notes or prison keys; and the ribbons and the red seals...like Jesus' five wounds they are...and the sentencing, which never ends, the endless torment... The stuff of Good Friday... Yesterday the sun shone, yesterday we went out to the country, in our thoughts... Kristina... Imagine if we have to stay here this summer!

KRISTINA: We'd save a lot of money, but it would be very miserable!

ELIS: I wouldn't survive it... Three summers I've spent here...and it's like a grave. In the middle of the day when you see the long grey road winding like a trench...not a soul, not even a horse, or dog...but out of the drain covers come the rats, while the cats are on their summer holidays...and behind the curtains sit the few people who are left behind, spying on their neighbour's clothes... 'Look at him, he's got his winter clothes on!'... and on their neighbour's worn down heels, and on their neighbour's faults... And from the poorer quarters crawl the cripples, who had hidden themselves until now, people without noses and ears, wicked people and unhappy ones... And they sit along the promenades sunning themselves, just as if they have occupied the city...where before beautiful and well-dressed children played to the sounds of their beautiful mothers' encouraging words, now prowl the ragged multitudes, scolding and tormenting one another...this was on a midsummer's day two years ago.

KRISTINA: Elis, Elis! Look forwards, forwards!

ELIS: Does it look any brighter there?

KRISTINA: Let us believe so!

ELIS: (*Sits by his desk.*) If it would only just stop snowing out there! Just so that one could get out and go for a walk!

KRISTINA: My dear friend, yesterday evening you wished the darkness would come back, so that we would be hidden from view… 'The dark would be so nice, so comforting,' you said, 'It would be like a roof over our heads.'

ELIS: Then you see, the suffering is as great whichever way… (*Reads his papers.*) The worst thing about this trial, though, is the close questioning about my father's way of life…it says we held glittering parties… One witness says, that he drank!… No, it's too much! I can't bear it anymore!… But I have to anyway…unto the end… Aren't you cold?

KRISTINA: No, but it certainly isn't warm!… Isn't Lina home?

ELIS: She's gone to confession, as you know.

KRISTINA: Mamma will be home soon won't she?

ELIS: When she comes home, I'm always afraid she will have seen so much, and heard so much…and all of it pain.

KRISTINA: Your family is unusually gloomy.

ELIS: That's why only gloomy people have wanted to keep company with us. The happy ones have shunned us.

KRISTINA: That was Mamma.

ELIS: Don't be impatient with her, Kristina.

KRISTINA: Oh no. It's harder for her than for any of us. But I don't understand her.

ELIS: She hides her shame as well as she can, and that makes her hard to understand. Poor mother!

*

FRU HEYST: (*Comes in dressed in black, with Psalm book and handkerchief* in her hand.*) Good evening, children.

ALL: (*Except BENJAMIN who greets her silently.*) Good evening Mamma dear.

FRU HEYST: You're all dressed in black as if you were in mourning!

Silence.

ELIS: Is it still snowing?

FRU HEYST: Yes, it's sleet! It's cold in here… (*Goes to ELEONORA and strokes her.*) Well, my chick, you are reading and studying I see. (*To BENJAMIN.*) And you aren't doing so bad either!

ELEONORA takes the mother's hand and puts it to her lips.

(*Supresses her gesture.*) There my child, there, there…!

ELIS: You went to Evensong, Mamma.

FRU HEYST: Yes, and it was the rector, I don't like him.

ELIS: Did you see anyone you know?

FRU HEYST: (*Sits down beside the sewing table.*) It would have been better if I hadn't met anyone!

ELIS: Then I know who…

FRU HEYST: Lindkvist! And he came up to me…

ELIS: So cruel, so cruel.

FRU HEYST: Asked, how I was…and, imagine my horror, he asked, if he could pay us a visit this evening.

ELIS: On Good Friday?

FRU HEYST: I was speechless! And he interpreted my silence as agreement! (*Pause.*) He could arrive any minute!

ELIS: (*Gets up.*) Here? Now?

FRU HEYST: He said that he wanted to give us some papers, and it was urgent.

ELIS: He wants the furniture.

FRU HEYST: But he looked so peculiar... I couldn't understand him!

ELIS: Well, let him come. He has right on his side, and we have to submit. We must receive him in a suitable manner, when he comes.

FRU HEYST: As long as I don't have to look at him!

ELIS: Well, you can stay in the other room...

FRU HEYST: But he mustn't be allowed to take the furniture. How would we live if he took everything? We can't live in empty rooms! Can we!

ELIS: The foxes have their dens, the birds have their nests... There are homeless people living in the woods.

FRU HEYST: That's where rogues should live, but not decent folk.

ELIS: (*At his desk.*) I'm reading, Mamma!

FRU HEYST: Did you find any mistakes?

ELIS: No, I don't think there are any.

FRU HEYST: But I met the public notary just now, and he said that there could have been a technical fault, a partial witness, an unproven statement, or a contradiction, maybe you haven't read carefully enough!

ELIS: Yes, I have, Mamma, but it's so tiresome…

FRU HEYST: Listen now, I met the public notary just now, – oh yes, I already told you that – and he told me about a break-in that took place here in town yesterday, in broad daylight.

ELEONORA and BENJAMIN start.

ELIS: Break-in? Here? Whereabouts?

FRU HEYST: In the florists on Klostergatan.* But it was all very strange. Apparently, the shopkeeper closed his shop to go to church, where his son…or maybe it was his daughter, was being confirmed. When he came home at about three, or maybe it was four, but that doesn't really matter…well, the shop door was open and flowers were missing, quite a few flowers, in particular a yellow tulip, which he first noticed was missing.

ELIS: A tulip! If it had been a daffodil then I would have been worried.

FRU HEYST: No, it was a tulip, that's quite certain. Well, now the police are involved.

ELEONORA has stood up, as if she wants to speak, but BENJAMIN goes to her and whispers something.

Imagine, Easter Thursday, when the young people are being confirmed, to break in to a shop…the whole town is full of scoundrels! That's why they put innocent people in gaol!

ELIS: Is no-one suspected?

FRU HEYST: No. But he must have been a strange thief, because he didn't take anything from the till…

KRISTINA: Oh if only this day were over!

* Kloster-gatan (pronounced 'gahtan'): cloister-street

FRU HEYST: And if Lina would come home!... Yes, well I heard about Petrus' dinner yesterday. The Lord Lieutenant himself was there!

ELIS: That surprises me, since Petrus was always supposed to be against the Lord Lieutenant's party!

FRU HEYST: He must have changed his mind then.

ELIS: He's not called Petrus for nothing, I can see that.

FRU HEYST: What have you got against the Lord Lieutenant?

ELIS: The man is an obstruction. He obstructs everything; he obstructed the high school; he obstructed target-practice for the youth cadet corps; he wanted to obstruct the innocent cyclist, as well as those lovely summer camps for children... And he has obstructed me!

FRU HEYST: I don't understand all that...and I don't care either. Anyway the Lord Lieutenant made a speech and Petrus thanked him...

ELIS: ...moved I imagine, and then denied his teacher and said, 'I do not know this man.' And the cock crowed once more! Isn't the Lord Lieutenant called Pontius, and has the surname Pilate?

ELEONORA moves as if she wants to talk but calms herself.

FRU HEYST: You shouldn't be so bitter, Elis. People are people, and you have to put up with them.

ELIS: Hush! I can hear Lindkvist coming!

FRU HEYST: Can you hear that in the snow?

ELIS: I can hear his stick against the stones, and his leather galoshes... Go now, Mamma!

FRU HEYST: No, now I want to stay, I'll tell him!

ELIS: Please, Mamma, go! It's too painful!

FRU HEYST: (*Stands; shaken.*) Cursed be the day I was born!

KRISTINA: You mustn't blaspheme!

FRU HEYST: (*With an expression of magnanimity.*) 'Is not destruction for the wicked and a strange punishment for the masters of iniquity?'

ELEONORA: (*With a cry of anguish.*) Mamma!

FRU HEYST: My God, why have you forsaken me! And my children! (*Goes out left.*)

*

ELIS: (*Listens to the street outside.*) He's stopped!... Maybe he thinks this is inappropriate...or just too cruel!... But he probably doesn't think so, the man who wrote such dreadful letters! They were always on blue paper. I have never been able to see blue writing paper since, without shaking.

KRISTINA: What do you intend to say, what do you intend to suggest?

ELIS: I don't know! I've lost all presence of mind and ability to think... Should I fall on my knees before him, beg him for forgiveness... Can you hear him? I can't hear anything except the blood rushing in my ears.

KRISTINA: Let's think what could be the worst that could happen; he takes everything...

ELIS: Then, the landlord comes and wants a deposit, which I cannot raise... He wants a deposit, because the furniture is no longer security for the rent.

KRISTINA: (*Behind the curtains, looking out into the street.*) He isn't there anymore! He's gone!

ELIS: Oh! You know, Mamma's indifference and her submissiveness annoy me more than her anger.

KRISTINA: Her submissiveness is just put on, or imagined. There was something of the lioness in her last words… Did you see how she seemed to get bigger?

ELIS: You know, when I think of Lindkvist, I see him as a good-natured giant, who only wants to scare children. How come I think of that now?

KRISTINA: Thoughts come and go…

ELIS: What joy, not to have been at that dinner yesterday… I would most definitely have made a speech against the Lord Lieutenant…and that would have ruined everything for all of us. What luck!

KRISTINA: You see!

ELIS: Thank you for the advice. You knew your Petrus alright!

KRISTINA: My Petrus!

ELIS: I mean, my Petrus! Look, here he is again! God help us!

On the curtain can be seen the shadow of a man approaching hesitantly. The shadow grows gradually larger and becomes enormous. Everyone becomes highly anxious.

The Giant! Look, the giant, come to eat us up!

KRISTINA: Just smile at it, like in the stories!

ELIS: I can't smile anymore!

The shadow grows smaller and disappears.

KRISTINA: Look at that stick of his, you're bound to smile!

ELIS: He's gone. I can breathe again. Now he won't come back until tomorrow! Oh!

KRISTINA: And tomorrow the sun will be shining, because it's the day of resurrection, the snow will be gone and the birds will be singing.

ELIS: Say more! I can *see* what you describe.

KRISTINA: Elis, if you could only see into my heart, see into my thoughts, my good intentions, my innermost prayers, Elis, now when I... (*Stops herself.*)

ELIS: What? Tell me.

KRISTINA: Now, when I...ask something of you.

ELIS: Tell me!

KRISTINA: It's a test! Think of that, it's a test, Elis!

ELIS: A test? Testing? Well what is it?

KRISTINA: Let me...no, I don't dare! It might not work!

ELEONORA listens.

ELIS: Why are you tormenting me?

KRISTINA: I might regret it; I know!...let it be so! Elis, let me go to the concert this evening.

ELIS: What concert?

KRISTINA: Haydn's 'Seven Stages of the Cross', in the cathedral.

ELIS: Who with?

KRISTINA: With Alice.

ELIS: And?

KRISTINA: Petrus.

ELIS: Petrus?

KRISTINA: See, now your face darkens!… I've changed my mind now, but it's too late!

ELIS: It certainly is late! But explain yourself.

KRISTINA: I did warn you that I couldn't explain myself, that's why I asked for your unlimited trust!

ELIS: (*Mildly.*) Go! I trust you; but it still hurts just as much, that you seek the company of that traitor.

KRISTINA: I understand that. But it's just a test.

ELIS: That I can't pass!

KRISTINA: You will!

ELIS: I want to but I can't! – You shall go anyway.

KRISTINA: Give me your hand.

ELIS: (*Extends his hand.*) Here.

The telephone rings.

(*Speaking in the telephone.*) Hello!…no answer!… Hello!… All I can hear is my own voice!… Who's there… How strange! I can hear my own words like an echo!

KRISTINA: That happens sometimes.

ELIS: Hello!… This is horrible! (*Rings off.*) Go now Kristina. No explanations, no conditions. I will pass the test!

KRISTINA: If you do, then all will be well with us.

ELIS: I will…

KRISTINA goes out right.

Why are you going out that way?

KRISTINA: I have my clothes out there. So! Farewell for now! (*Goes.*)

ELIS: Farewell my friend! (*Pause.*) For ever! (*Staggers out left.*)

*

ELEONORA: God help us, what have I done now? The police are looking for the wrong person, and if I'm discovered – poor Mama, and Elis!

BENJAMIN: (*Childishly.*) Eleonora, you must say that I did it!

ELEONORA: You? Can you bear someone else's guilt? You're only a child.

BENJAMIN: It's easy, if you know you are innocent.

ELEONORA: One must never fool people!

BENJAMIN: Well, then let me telephone the florists and explain how it is.

ELEONORA: No, I have done wrong, and I will be punished by having to worry. I have made them afraid of break-ins, and now its my turn to be afraid.

BENJAMIN: But if the police come?

ELEONORA: That will be difficult…but it will just have to be! Oh if only this day were over! (*Goes to the clock on the table and starts to wind round the hands.*) Please clock, go a little faster! Tick, tock, ping, ping, ping! Now it's eight o'clock! Ping, ping, ping…now it's nine! Ten! Eleven! Twelve!… Now it's Easter Saturday! The sun will come up soon, and we can write on the Easter eggs. I'm going to write this: 'Satan has desired to have you, so that he may sift you like wheat, but I have prayed for you.'

BENJAMIN: Why do you hurt yourself so much Eleonora?

ELEONORA: Me? Hurt? Benjamin, think of all the flowers that have bloomed, the blue anemones and the snowdrops that have been stuck in the snow all day and all night, freezing in the dark. Imagine how they must suffer! The night time must be the worst, when it's dark, and they get afraid of the dark and can't run away…and they stand there waiting for it to be day. Everything, everything suffers, but the flowers most of all! And the migrating birds that have arrived! Where will they sleep tonight?

BENJAMIN: (*Childishly.*) They sleep in hollow trees of course, you know that!

ELEONORA: There aren't enough hollow trees for all of them! I've only seen two hollow trees here in the parks, and the owls live there of course, and they kill small birds… Poor Elis, thinking Kristina has abandoned him; but I know she'll be back.

BENJAMIN: If you know, why don't you say?

ELEONORA: Because Elis must suffer; everyone has to suffer today, on Good Friday, so that they can remember Jesus on the cross.

The sound of a police whistle can be heard from outside.

(*She jumps up.*) What was that?

BENJAMIN: (*Gets up.*) Don't you know?

ELEONORA: No.

BENJAMIN: It was the police.

ELEONORA: Ah!... Yes it sounded like it, like when they were coming to arrest father...and I was ill! And now they're coming to get me!

BENJAMIN: (*Stands between ELEONORA and the upstage door, facing it.*) No, they can't take you, I'll defend you, Eleonora!

ELEONORA: That's nice of you Benjamin, but you mustn't...

BENJAMIN: (*Looks out through the curtains.*) There are two of them!

ELEONORA tries to push BENJAMIN away but he puts up a mild resistance.

Not you, Eleonora – I wouldn't want to carry on living!

ELEONORA: Go and sit down child, go and sit in that chair.

BENJAMIN obeys relectantly.

(*Looks out from the curtains, without hiding.*) It was just two men. O we have so little faith. Do we think God would be so cruel, when I haven't done anything wrong, only acted thoughtlessly... It serves me right. Why did I doubt?

BENJAMIN: But tomorrow he's coming, the one who wants to take the furniture.

ELEONORA: Let him come! And we can go out! Away from it all...all the old furniture, that father collected for us, and which I have seen here since I was a little child! Yes, you shouldn't own anything that binds you to this earth. Go out onto the stony roads and roam with blistered feet – the road leads upwards, that's why it's hard...

BENJAMIN: Now you are tormenting yourself again, Eleonora!

ELEONORA: Let me!... But do you know what I'll find it hardest to part with? That mantel clock, there. It was there when I was born, and it has measured out my hours and days... (*She lifts the clock from the table.*) Can you hear, he is beating like a heart...exactly like a heart...and he stopped the moment grandpa died, he was with us even then. Good bye little clock, I hope you'll stop again soon!... Do you know he used to speed up when there was unhappiness in the house, just as if he wanted to get through that time as quickly as possible, for *our* sakes, of course! But when there were happy times, then he slowed down so that we could enjoy it for longer. That was this nice clock. But we had a nasty one too...that one has to hang in the kitchen now. It hated music, and whenever Elis played the piano it started to strike, we all noticed it, not only me; and that's why she has to hang in the kitchen, because she was nasty! But Lina doesn't like it either, because it isn't quiet at night,* and she can't use it to time the eggs...because they always end up hard boiled, Lina says. Now you're laughing.

BENJAMIN: What am I meant to do?...

ELEONORA: You're a nice boy Benjamin but you ought to be serious. Think of the birch, there behind the mirror!

BENJAMIN: But you talk so funnily, I have to smile...and why should we cry all the time?

ELOENORA If we don't cry in the vale of tears, where should we cry?

BENJAMIN: Hm!

ELEONORA: You just want to smile all day, and that's why you've been allowed to. But I only like you when you are serious. Remember that!

BENJAMIN: Do you think we'll get through all this, Eleonora?

ELEONORA: Yes, most things will sort themselves out, once Good Friday is over, but not everything. Today birch, tomorrow Easter Eggs. Today snow, tomorrow thaw. Today death, tomorrow resurrection!

BENJAMIN: How wise you are.

ELEONORA: Yes; I can already feel that the weather is clearing up, the snow is melting…you can smell melting snow in here already…and tomorrow the violets will bloom against the south wall. The clouds have lifted, I can feel that when I draw breath…oh I know so well when it's open all the way to the heavens!… Go and open the curtains, Benjamin, I want God to be able to see us.

BENJAMIN gets up and obeys her instruction; moonlight falls into the room.

Do you see the full moon? It's the Easter moon. So now you know, the sun is still there, even if it is the moon that shines.

*

ACT THREE

Easter Eve.

Music before this act: Haydn, 'Sieben Worte', No. 5, Adagio.

Same set as before, but the curtains are opened. The same view outside as before except that there is an atmosphere of grey weather: the upstage doors are closed.

ELEONORA is sitting before the stove and holding a bunch of blue anemonies in front of her.

BENJAMIN in from the right.

ELEONORA: Where have you been all this time, Benjamin?

BENJAMIN: That wasn't long!

ELEONORA: I've missed you!

BENJAMIN: Where have you been then, Eleonora?

ELEONORA: I've been to the market square, and bought some blue anemonies, and now I am going to warm them, because they were frozen, poor little things.

BENJAMIN: Where's the sun?

ELEONORA: Behind the mist; there are no clouds today, its just sea mist, it smells of salt…

BENJAMIN: Did you see if the birds were still alive out there?

ELEONORA: Yes, and not one of them falls to the ground unless God wills it. But on the square, there are dead birds.

*

ELIS: (*Comes in from the right.*) Has the newspaper arrived?

ELEONORA: No, Elis!

ELIS walks across the stage, then, when he is in the middle of the stage, KRISTINA comes, from the left.

KRISTINA: (*Not noticing ELIS.*) Has the newspaper arrived?

ELEONORA: No it hasn't arrived.

KRISTINA walks across the stage to the right, past ELIS, who goes out to the left, without them seeing one another.

Ush! It's gone so cold! Hate has entered the house! As long as there is love you can endure anything, but now ush! So cold!

BENJAMIN: Why did you ask for the newspaper?

ELEONORA: Don't you understand? It's because it will say in there, all about...

BENJAMIN: What?

ELEONORA: Everything! The burglary, the police, and more besides...

*

FRU HEYST: (*Comes in from the right.*) Has the newspaper arrived?

ELEONORA: No, Mamma dear!

FRU HEYST: (*Goes out again, right.*) Tell me first, when it comes!

*

ELEONORA: The newspaper, the newspaper! – Oh if only the printing press had broken or the editor was ill…no, I mustnt say that! You know, I was with father last night…

BENJAMIN: Last night?

ELEONORA: Yes, in my sleep…and I was in America with my sister… She had sold something for thirty dollars and that means she made a profit of five.

BENJAMIN: Is that a lot or a little?

ELEONORA: It's quite a lot.

BENJAMIN: (*Slyly.*) Did you see anyone you know, when you were at the market?

ELEONORA: Why do you ask that? You mustn't be sly with me, Benjamin: you want to know my secrets, but you can't.

BENJAMIN: And you think you can find out mine, in the same way.

ELEONORA: Can you hear the buzzing in the telephone wires? That means the newspaper has come out; and now people are telephoning each other: 'Have you read it?'; 'Yes, I've read it!'; 'Isn't it dreadful?'

BENJAMIN: Isn't what dreadful?

ELEONORA: Everything! Life itself is dreadful! But we have to be satisfied anyway!… Think of Elis and Kristina; they like each other, but they hate each other just as much. The thermometer drops when they walk across the room. She went to the concert yesterday, and today they aren't talking to one another… Why? Why?

BENJAMIN: Because your brother is jealous.

ELEONORA: Don't say that word! What do you know anyway, other than that it's an illness, and consequently a punishment. One must not touch wicked things, because then you get covered in it! Just look at Elis; haven't you noticed how changed he is, since he started reading those documents…

BENJAMIN: About the trial?

ELEONORA: Isn't it as if all the badness there has oozed into his soul and shines out through his face and eyes. Kristina can feel it, and so that she doesn't get touched by his badness she makes herself armour out of ice. Oh! Those papers; if only I could burn them! Wickedness and falseness stream out of them. Therefore, my child, you must keep the wicked and the unclean away from you, from your lips, and your heart.

BENJAMIN: You notice everything don't you!

ELEONORA: Do you know what's in store for me if Elis and the others find out it was me who bought that daffodil in that unusual way?

BENJAMIN: What will they do to you?

ELEONORA: I will be sent back…there, where I have come from, where the sun doesn't shine, where the walls are white and bare, like in a bathroom, where all you can hear is weeping and moaning, where I have wasted a whole year of my life!

BENJAMIN: Where do you mean?

ELEONORA: Where people are tormented, worse than in prison, where the unblessed live, where there is anguish, and despair keeps watch night and day, and from where no-one ever returns.

BENJAMIN: Worse than prison, where do you mean?

ELEONORA: In prison you are judged, but there you are condemned! In prison you are examined and questioned, there they don't ask you any questions!... Poor daffodil, you are to blame; I meant so well, and did so wrong!

BENJAMIN: But why don't you go to the florists and say, 'This is how it was'? You're exactly like a lamb going to be slaughtered.

ELEONORA: When it knows it *must* be slaughtered, it doesn't complain, and doesn't try to run away. What else can it do?

*

ELIS: (*Comes in left with a letter in his hand.*) Hasn't the newspaper arrived yet?

ELEONORA: No, my dear brother.

ELIS: (*Turns around, talks into the kitchen.*) Lina, go and buy a newspaper will you.

FRU HEYST comes in left.

ELEONORA and BENJAMIN are frightened.

FRU HEYST: Leave the room a moment will you children, please.

ELEONORA and BENJAMIN go out left.

*

FRU HEYST: Did you get a letter?

ELIS: Yes.

FRU HEYST: From the institution?

ELIS: Yes.

FRU HEYST: What do they want?

ELIS: Eleonora back.

FRU HEYST: They can't have her! She's my child!

ELIS: My sister!

FRU HEYST: What do you mean?

ELIS: I don't know, I can't think any more.

FRU HEYST: But I can!… Eleonora, that child of sorrow, has brought joy to us here, not of this world though; her anxiety has been turned into peacefulness that she spreads all around her. Mad or not! For me she is wise, she knows how to carry life's burden better than I do, than we do. Besides, Elis, am I in my right mind? Am I in my right mind to think my husband was innocent? I knew after all that it was proved over and over again with solid, reliable proof; and that he had confessed himself!… And you, Elis, are you in your right mind when you don't see that Kristina loves you? When you think she hates you?

ELIS: It's a peculiar way to love.

FRU HEYST: No! Your coldness freezes her inside, and it's you who hates. But you're wrong, and that's why you must suffer.

ELIS: How can I be wrong? Didn't she go out with my faithless friend yesterday evening?

FRU HEYST: Yes she did, and with your knowledge. But why did she go? Well, you ought to be able to guess!

ELIS: No, I can't.

FRU HEYST: Well! Then you'll have to carry on as you are!

*

The kitchen door opens, and a hand passes out the newspaper, which FRU HEYST receives and gives to ELIS.

ELIS: This is the only real disaster. With her I could bear the others! But now my last support is snatched away, and down I fall!

FRU HEYST: Fall then, but fall well, so you can get up again!… What is the news in the paper?

ELIS: I don't know, I'm afraid of the newspaper today!

FRU HEYST: Give it to me, I'll read it.

ELIS: No, wait a moment…

FRU HEYST: What are you afraid of, what are you expecting?

ELIS: The very worst.

FRU HEYST: It has already happened so many times… And you child, if you knew my life!… If you had been there when I saw your father slide into ruin, wishing I could have warned those poor people he took down with him!

ELIS: What was his downfall? I've never understood it.

FRU HEYST: Pride, like all of us.

ELIS: Why should we have to suffer for his wrong-doing when we are innocent?

FRU HEYST: Be quiet! (*Pause during which she takes the newspaper and reads.*)

ELIS, worried, stands still at first then paces up and down.

What's this?… Didn't I say that it was a yellow tulip that was stolen from the florists?

ELIS: Yes, I remember that clearly.

FRU HEYST: But here it says…a daffodil!

ELIS: (*Horrified.*) Does it?

FRU HEYST: (*Sinks down into a chair.*) It's Eleonora! O God! O my God!

ELIS: So it's not over.

FRU HEYST: Prison or the institution!

ELIS: It's impossible that she can have done it, impossible!

FRU HEYST: And now the family's name will be dishonoured again!

ELIS: Does anyone suspect her?

FRU HEYST: It says suspicions point in a certain direction…it's easy to see which direction.

ELIS: I'll speak to her.

FRU HEYST: (*Gets up.*) Speak nicely to her! I can't bear anymore!… She's lost…we won her back , now she's lost again… Speak to her! (*Goes out right.*)

ELIS: Oh! (*Goes to the door, left.*) Eleonora my child! Come, I want to talk to you!

ELEONORA: (*Comes in, her hair is down.*) I was putting my hair up.

ELIS: Leave it be!… Tell me, little sister, where did you get this flower?

ELEONORA: I took it…

ELIS: Oh God!

ELEONORA: (*With bowed head, crushed, her arms crossed over her chest.*) But I put the money next to…

ELIS: So you paid?

ELEONORA: Yes and no. It's always so annoying…but I haven't done anything wrong…I only meant well…do you believe me?

ELIS: I believe you, my dear; but the newspaper doesn't know you're innocent!

ELEONORA: Dear Elis, then I must suffer that too… (*She bows her head, so that her hair hangs forwards over her face.*) What will they do with me now? Let them!

BENJAMIN: (*In from the left, beside himself.*) No, you mustn't touch her, she hasn't done anything. I know because it was me, me, me! (*He cries.*) I did it!

ELEONORA: Don't believe him…it was me.

ELIS: What am I to believe; who am I to believe?

BENJAMIN: Me! Me!

ELEONORA: Me! Me!

BENJAMIN: Let me go to the police…

ELIS: Hush, hush…

BENJAMIN: No, I want to go, I want to go…

ELIS: Quiet child! Mamma's coming.

*

FRU HEYST: (*Comes in, very upset, takes ELEONORA in her arms and kisses her.*) Child! Child! My beloved child! You are here with me and you are staying here with me!

ELEONORA: You are kissing me, mother. You haven't done that for many years. Why now?

FRU HEYST: Because now...because now, the florist is outside and he says he's sorry he has caused so much aggravation...the missing money has been found and your name...

ELEONORA: (*Runs into ELIS's arms and kisses him; then she throws her arms around BENJAMIN's neck and kisses his forehead.*) You good child, wanting to suffer for me! How could you want to suffer for me?

BENJAMIN: (*Shy, childish.*) Because I like you so much, Eleonora.

FRU HEYST: Get dressed now, children and go out into the garden. The weather's clearing up.

ELEONORA: Oh, the weather's clearing up! Come Benjamin. (*She takes his hand; they go hand in hand out left.*)

*

ELIS: Can we throw the birch on the fire now?

FRU HEYST: Not yet! There's a little more to come.

ELIS: Lindkvist?

FRU HEYST: He's standing out there, but he's very peculiar, and strangely mild; the only thing is, he's so talkative, and he talks so much about himself!

ELIS: Now that I've seen a ray of sunlight, I'm not afraid to meet the giant. Let him come!

FRU HEYST: Don't provoke him... Providence has put our fates in his hands, and the Meek...well, you know what happens to the Proud!

ELIS: I know!… Listen, those galoshes, 'wolf, wolf, wolf'! Does he intend coming in with those on? Why not? It's his carpet and his furniture…

FRU HEYST: Elis, think of us! (*Goes out right.*)

ELIS: I will, mother!

*

LINDKVIST comes in from the right. An elderly, serious looking man with a dreadful appearance. He has grey hair with a toupee; his fringe is combed right back and the hair at his temples is cut to a very high line. Large black bushy eyebrows, small short clipped black sideburns. Round glasses with black hornrims, a large Cornelian charm on his watch-chain: a cane in his hand. Dressed in black with a fur; a top hat in his hand, high boots with leather galoshes that squeak. When he comes in he looks fixedly at ELIS, with curiosity, and remains standing throughout.

LINDKVIST: Lindkvist is the name!

ELIS: (*Defensively.*) Heyst is mine! Do sit down.

LINDKVIST sits on a chair to the right of the sewing table and looks hard at ELIS.

Pause.

Can I be of service?

LINDKVIST: (*Formally.*) Ahem! – I had the honour yesterday evening to give notice of my intended visit; but on closer reflection I found it to be inappropriate on a holiday to discuss business matters.

ELIS: We are most grateful…

LINDKVIST: (*Sharply.*) We are *not* grateful! Well. (*Pause.*) In any case, the day before yesterday I had occasion to visit the Lord Lieutenant… (*Pauses, and looks to see the impression his words have upon ELIS.*) Do you know the Lord Lieutenant?

ELIS: (*Nonchalantly.*) I haven't had the honour!

LINDKVIST: Then you shall have the honour!… We spoke of your father!

ELIS: I can well believe it!

LINDKVIST: (*Takes out a paper and puts it on the table.*) And I was given this paper.

ELIS: I have expected this a long time. But before we go any further, may I be allowed to ask a question?

LINDKVIST: (*Abruptly.*) Go on.

ELIS: Why don't you leave this paper with the solicitor? That way we avoid, at least, the long and painful execution.

LINDKVIST: I see, young man!

ELIS: Young or not, I am not asking for mercy, only justice!

LINDKVIST: I see! No mercy, no mercy! – Look at this paper I have put on the edge of the table here! Now I shall put it back in my pocket again!… So you want justice! Only justice! Now listen my old friend, once upon a time I was robbed in a very unpleasant way, of my money! When I wrote to you a good-natured letter asking how much time you needed, you answered discourteously! And you treated me as if I was a usurer, robbing widows and fatherless children, notwithstanding the fact that I was the robbed party. But, being wiser, I contented myself with answering your discourteous invective with a courteous but sharp reply! You recognise my blue writing paper, don't you? I can have it stamped to authorise distraint and seizure of goods when I want to, but I don't necessarily want to! (*He looks about the room.*)

ELIS: Be my guest, the furniture is at your disposal!

LINDKVIST: I wasn't looking at the furniture! I looked to see if your mother is here. She loves justice just as much as you do, I should think!

ELIS: I hope so!

LINDKVIST: Good!... You know, if this justice that you value so highly would have its way, then your mother, as witting accomplice to criminal actions, would have suffered Man's justice!

ELIS: Oh no!

LINDKVIST: Oh yes, and it's not too late for that either!

ELIS: (*Stands up.*) My mother!

LINDKVIST: (*Takes out another blue paper and lays it on the table.*) You see, now I am putting this paper on the edge of the table, and it really is blue...but still with no stamp.

ELIS: Good God! My mother! Everything is coming full circle.

LINDKVIST: Yes, my young lover of justice, everything is coming full circle, everything!... That's how things can go... If I would now ask myself this question: Anders Johan* Lindkvist, born to poverty and privations, and labour, do you have the right, in your old age, to rob your children, mark that *your children,* of their means of support, which you have purposefully, and with care and through privations, saved penny for penny? What will you, Anders Johan Lindkvist do, if you are to be just? You robbed no-one, but if you object to having been

* Pronunciation: Andersh Yohan

robbed, then you can no longer live in this town, because no-one will want to visit the house of an unmerciful man, who demanded what was due to him! You see then, that there is a mercifulness that goes against justice, and above it!… That is Grace!

ELIS: You are right, take it all! It belongs to you!

LINDKVIST: I have the right, but I don't dare to use it!

ELIS: I shall think of your children and I shall not complain!

LINDKVIST: (*Puts the paper back in his pocket.*) Good, then we can put this blue paper back in my pocket!

ELIS: I'm sorry…do they really intend to prosecute my mother?

LINDKVIST: Now, let us go to the next step first!… You don't then, know the Lord Lieutenant personally?

ELIS: No, and I don't want to know him!

LINDKVIST: (*Takes out the blue paper again.*) None of that, none of that! The Lord Lieutenant, you see, was an old friend of your father's, and he wants to get to know you! Everything comes full circle, everything. Don't you want to pay him a visit?

ELIS: No!

LINDKVIST: The Lord Lieutenant…

ELIS: Can we talk about something else?

LINDKVIST: You must be polite to me, because I'm defenceless…since you have opinion on your side, and I have only right on mine. What have you against the Lord Lieutenant? He doesn't like bicycles and high schools, that is a peculiarity of his. We don't really have to respect peculiarities, but we can look past them and keep to the important matters, between one person and another. And in life's big crises we have to take one another with all our faults and weaknesses, swallow each other, the wheat along with the chaff!... Go and see the Lord Lieutenant!

ELIS: Never!

LINDKVIST: Is that the kind of man you are?

ELIS: (*Decisively.*) Exactly that kind!

LINDKVIST: (*Gets up and bows, walks across the room in his squeaking boots, waving his blue paper.*) That's bad! That's bad!... Well, then I'd like to start from another end... Some vengeful person has tried to bring charges against your mother. You can prevent it.

ELIS: How?

LINDKVIST: Go and visit the Lord Lieutenant.

ELIS: No!

LINDKVIST: (*Goes and takes ELIS by the shoulders.*) Then you are the most wretched person I have ever met in my life... And now I shall go myself to your mother!

ELIS: Don't go!

LINDKVIST: Will you visit the Lord Lieutenant then?

ELIS: Yes.

LINDKVIST: Say it once more, and louder!

ELIS: Yes!

LINDKVIST: There, that's that sorted out. (*Leaves the blue paper.*) Here is *that* paper!

ELIS receives the paper without reading it.

Now to item number two, which *was* number one… (*They sit as before.*) You see, if we meet each other halfway the road is half as long!… Number two… My claim upon your home!… Yes, have no illusions, because I neither can nor want to give away my family's property! I will take out my claim unto the last penny.

ELIS: I understand.

LINDKVIST: (*Sharply.*) Aha! You understand that?

ELIS: I didn't mean any offence…

LINDKVIST: No, I see that. (*Lifts up his glasses and looks fixedly at ELIS.*) …The wolf! The angry wolf! The whip, the whip and the meat-red Cornelian; the giant who doesn't eat children, only scares them! I shall scare you out of your minds! The value of every last stick of furniture shall be extracted. I have the inventory here in my pocket, and if one single article is missing, then you'll be in a police cell, where neither sun nor Cassiopeia will shine! Yes I can eat children and widows when I am provoked. And opinion? Bah! Opinion!… I can simply move to another town!

ELIS has no answer.

You had a friend, Petrus was his name, Petrus Holmblad.* He studied languages and was your pupil. But you wanted to make some kind of prophet out of him… Well, he was unfaithful: the cock crowed twice, didn't it?

ELIS remains silent.

Human nature is unreliable, like matter and thought: Petrus was disloyal, I don't deny it, and I don't defend him. On that point! But the human heart is bottomless and in it lies gold and filth and whatever else. Petrus was a disloyal friend, but a friend just the same!

---

* Pronunciation: Holm-blahd

ELIS: A disloyal...

LINDKVIST: Disloyal, maybe but a friend just the same! This disloyal friend has, unbeknownst to you, done you a great service of friendship.

ELIS: That too!

LINDKVIST: (*Moves closer to ELIS.*) Everything comes full circle, everything!

ELIS: Everything bad, yes! And good is replaced by bad!

LINDKVIST: Not always; the good also comes around again! Believe me!

ELIS: I have no choice, otherwise you'll torment the life out of me!

LINDKVIST: Not your life, but I shall squeeze your pride and your wickedness, out of you!

ELIS: Carry on!

LINDKVIST: Petrus has done you a service, I said.

ELIS: I don't want any favours from that man!

LINDKVIST: Ah there we are again!... Listen to me! Through the offices of your friend Petrus, the Lord Lieutenant has been persuaded to put himself out for your mother! So you shall write a letter to Petrus to thank him. Promise!

ELIS: No! Anyone else in the world but not him!

LINDKVIST: (*Moves nearer.*) Then I shall squeeze you again... Listen, you have money in the bank!

ELIS: Well, what does that concern you? I am not responsible for my father's debts!

LINDKVIST: Don't say that! Don't say that! Weren't you present eating and drinking while my children's money was being squandered in this house? Answer!

ELIS: I can't deny it.

LINDKVIST: And since the furniture doesn't cover the debt, then you can write out a cheque at once for the rest – You know the amount.

ELIS: (*Reduced to nothing.*) That too?

LINDKVIST: That too! Off you go, write!

ELIS stands up, takes out his cheque book and writes at the desk.

Write it out to me or to be cashed.

ELIS: It's not enough anyway.

LINDKVIST: Then you will have to go out and borrow the rest. Every penny shall be paid!

ELIS: (*Passes the cheque to LINDKVIST.*) There, everything I have. That's my money for the summer, and for my bride. More I do not have to give you!

LINDKVIST: Then you'll have to go and borrow it, I said.

ELIS: I can't!

LINDKVIST: You'll have to find someone who'll go bail for you.

ELIS: There isn't anyone who will go bail for a Heyst.

LINDKVIST: I shall now put it to you as an ultimatum. Thank Petrus, or pay out the full amount!

ELIS: I don't want to have anything to do with Petrus.

LINDKVIST: Then you are the most wretched person I know! By just a simple courteous act you could save your mother's house and the money for your bride's upkeep, and you don't do it! You must have motives you're not telling me about! Why do you hate Petrus?

ELIS: Kill me, but don't torture me any longer!

LINDKVIST: You're jealous of him!

ELIS shrugs his shoulders.

That's the way it is! (*Gets up and walks about the room. Pause.*) Have you read the morning paper?

ELIS: Yes, worse luck!

LINDKVIST: All of it?

ELIS: No, not all of it!

LINDKVIST: Aha!… Then you don't know that Petrus is engaged?

ELIS: No I didn't know that!

LINDKVIST: Nor to whom? Guess!

ELIS: How…

LINDKVIST: He is engaged to a young lady called Alice. It was decided last night at a certain concert, where your fiancée acted as go-between.

ELIS: Why was it such a secret?

LINDKVIST: Don't two young people have the right to keep their hearts secrets from you?

ELIS: And for their happiness I had to suffer this agony?

LINDKVIST: Yes! Those who suffered for your happiness!… Your mother, your father, your fiancée, your sister… Sit down, let me tell you a very brief story.

ELIS sits reluctantly. During the previous and the following scene the weather has been slowly brightening outside.

It was forty years ago! I came to the capital as a youth, alone, unknown and without acquaintances, to seek employment. I had only one riksdaler,* and it was a dark evening. Since I didn't know a cheap hotel, I asked passers-by, but no-one answered. At the height of my despair, a man came and asked why I was crying! – for I was crying. I told him my need, and he turned out of his way and took me to a hotel, and comforted me with kind words. I went in through the entrance hall, and the glass door of a shop opened and hit my elbow, and the glass broke. The shop owner was uncontrollable. He said he wanted instant payment or he would call the police. Imagine my despair with a night on the streets facing me! – The well-intentioned stranger, who saw the incident, intervened, went to the trouble of calling the police, and saved me!... That man – was your father!... So everything comes full circle, even good things. And for your father's sake... I have cancelled my debt... Therefore, take this paper, and keep your check! (*Gets up.*) Since you have difficulty saying thank you, I shall go at once, probably because I find it embarrassing to be thanked. (*Approaches the door upstage.*) Go instead to your mother at once and free her from her worry! (*With a deprecating gesture to ELIS who tries to approach him.*) Go!

ELIS hurries out left.

The upstage door opens. ELEONORA and BENJAMIN come in, calm but serious; they stop when they see LINDKVIST and are afraid.

Well, little ones, come in, don't be afraid... Do you know who I am?... (*With an assumed voice.*) I am the giant who scares children! Wooah! Wooah!... But I'm not very

* Pronunciation: reeks-dahler

74

frightening! – Come here Eleonora! (*Takes her head between his hands and looks her in the eyes.*) You have your father's kind eyes; he was a good man – but weak! (*Kisses her forehead.*) There!

ELEONORA: Oh! He speaks well of my father! Can anyone think well of him?

LINDKVIST: I can, ask your brother, Elis.

ELEONORA: Then you can't surely mean us any harm?

LINDKVIST: No, my beloved child!

ELEONORA: Well, help us then!

LINDKVIST: Child I cannot help your father out of his punishment, nor Benjamin in his Latin exam…but the other matter has already been dealt with. Life doesn't grant you everything, and nothing is free. Therefore, you must help me, will you?

ELEONORA: What can a poor creature like me do?

LINDKVIST: What day is it today? Take a look.

ELEONORA: (*Takes down the calendar from the wall.*) It's the sixteenth.

LINDKVIST: Well, before the twentieth you must make your brother Elis pay a visit to the Lord Lieutenant, and write a letter to Petrus.

ELEONORA: Nothing else?

LINDKVIST: Oh my child, but if he fails to do it then the giant will come and say Whooah!

ELEONORA: *Why* will the giant come and scare the children?

LINDKVIST: To make them behave!

ELEONORA: That's true! The giant is right! (*Kisses LINDKVIST on the sleeve of his furcoat.*) Thank you, kind giant!

LINDKVIST: You must call me Herr Lindkvist, you know!

ELEONORA: No, it's such an everyday name...

LINDKVIST: Goodbye children, now you can throw the birch on the fire!

ELEONORA: No, it must stay where it is, children are so forgetful.

LINDKVIST: How well you know children, little one! (*Goes.*)

ELEONORA: We *shall* go to the country, Benjamin! In two months time! Oh I hope they pass quickly! (*She tears pages from the day calendar and strews them into the ray of sunlight that crosses the room.*) See how the days pass by! April, May, June! And the sun shines on them all! Look!... Now you must thank God, who helped us get away to the country!

BENJAMIN: (*Shyly.*) Can't I do it quietly?

ELEONORA: Yes you can do it quietly! Because now the clouds are gone and it can be heard up there!

*

KRISTINA has come in from the left and stopped. ELIS and FRU HEYST come in from the right, KRISTINA and ELIS go to one another with amicable expressions on their faces, but the curtain falls before they meet.

End.

JANET JACKSON'S
YORKSHIRE

First published in Great Britain in 2021 by Cancan Press
Copyright © Becky Papworth, 2021

The right of Becky Papworth to be identified as the Author
of the Work has been asserted by her in accordance with the
Copyright, Designs and Patents Act 1988.

A CIP catalogue record for this title is available from the
British Library

Paperback ISBN: 978-1-7397948-0-4
eBook ISBN: 978-1-7397948-1-1

JANET JACKSON'S
YORKSHIRE

B&B

Becky Papworth

For Eleanor & Lizzie

'A good laugh is sunshine in the house.'

WILLIAM MAKEPEACE THACKERAY

THE BEGINNING BIT

How would I describe Lavender Cottage? You'd never know from the outside quite how big the garage cottage is. It has a pitched, red slate roof you can actually touch if you stretch high enough – useful when clearing the gutters – and a small, pale green, uPVC door, which looks like wood, with two square casement windows either side. The duck-egg linen curtains in the windows are ones I knocked up myself. (Well done, Janet.) They look decent, as long as you don't interrogate the hems too closely. They're not straight, plus I ran out of green and white cotton, so I went with a navy blue zigzag stitch. Hopefully it looks deliberate, like something Kirstie Allsopp might run up in a quiet morning.

Once through the door, you're straight into a huge living room. It has a giant, triangular beam framing it and is full of light from the two windows. What surprises everyone, as they wander through, is that when you step up into the kitchen the place suddenly doubles in height. A staircase leads up to a large double bedroom next to a family-sized bathroom. All in all, it's a small cottage rather than a simple B&B. Somewhere you can spread out, unlike your usual double room with a kettle and two Bourbons on a tray. An unfinished granny flat is what we were told it was when we bought the house, but it's more of a double-height extension – the latter added in haste when the land behind it got sold to developers to build another house.

After my ex-husband, Franklin, left – and once he'd finally got round to evacuating his mountain of hobby motorbikes and the pick-up-sticks of discarded tools (*how many spanners does one man need?*) – I spent weeks of my life in here, staring at the concrete block walls of the extension where they butt up to the original red-brick garage, trying to imagine what it could be. It had loops of electric wire slung around in mid-air and a large pit in the floor filled by an oily puddle.

I, Janet Jackson, Hebden Bridge born and bred, was *sooo*

miserable. I spent far too long brooding, and feeling sorry for myself, after the marriage went down the plughole. Then, thankfully, something clicked around my birthday. I was forty after all. I was nearly forty-one! It was time to stop staring at the garage walls and do something. Three years and £25,000 in loans and remortgages later, using every spare hour and one stress-induced kidney stone later, the conversion from oily garage to bed and breakfast cottage accommodation is complete.

In fact, lovely reader, it's been finished for three months now. The next challenge is to do something with it. And I will. A hundred per cent I will... soon as I pluck up enough courage and take some time off from my job. I am a receptionist at Valley Dental in Hebden Bridge, where I organise appointments, look after our patients, keep an eye on the fish and sell a lot of TePe interdental brushes.

I mean, what do I know about running a B&B? Zero.

Mind you, having said that, here is a list of my skills – I can: get stains off sofas, empty bins, mop up teenage tears and console errant sisters on their hopeless love affairs. I know a good cotton sheet over a polyester mix. I like flowers – no, I don't, I *love* flowers, all kinds – and I grow them wherever I can. I'm confident at answering a phone and can be quite good at organising a diary. All of the above will come in handy when running a B&B. In my day-to-day life though, I like things steady; boring, even. Too much change is unsettling. The truth is I like to be prepared, which is why I always have a blanket and a can of Pringles in the boot of the car. Note to self: I really should check the date of those Pringles.

What really worries me is that if I take the leap into opening a bed and breakfast, it could all end in embarrassment and failure. What if I get it all completely wrong? Do I really want to put myself through that? I'll try. *Forget 'try', Janet, you've got to do it.* The bank balance is screaming for help.

I pick up a pen and a piece of paper and write on my to-do list: *Open B&B.* There it is, in writing. That means I've got to do it. I'm bound to learn something interesting along the way. OK, OK, let's do it. Here we go.

Step one. Make decision to open Janet Jackson's Yorkshire B&B... tick!

CHAPTER 1

It's a busy Monday in Hebden, and I am already thirty minutes into my lunch hour. I've had to wait twenty minutes in the sandwich shop called Cheese Please, as a very indecisive bunch of young women, their T-shirts declaring they are *craftivists engaged in the art of gentle protest*, are holding up the queue. I feel like leading a gentle protest myself when one of them changes her mind for the fifth time about whether she is having crumbly Lancashire or apricot Wensleydale in her cheese salad baguette.

I eat my sandwich – beetroot, feta and rocket, twist of black pepper, granary sliced – on the hoof, risking indigestion, as I pick my way through the crowds for the annual Hebden Bridge Arts Festival. It's a hugely popular two weeks, especially with families, and creates havoc with the parking. I arrive at Hebden's only design-print-cum-stationery business with the witty name of TH*INK*, to collect business cards for the cottage.

'*How* much?' It's £137.00 plus VAT! I try to say I've been waiting six weeks and it's double the original quote, but Ray is so stressed. His purple ponytail is shooting out at all angles, held in place by what looks like a chopstick.

'You know Gwen who does my filing?' he tells me distractedly. 'Well, she's packed it all in to live with Lance – you know, the big bloke with the Dutch barge from the rowing club?'

I don't, but I nod to be helpful, then subtly step back from the counter to avoid my eyes watering from the impact of his breath which is pure coconut vodka. I recognise it from when my sister Maureen passed out last Christmas.

'I'm still getting on top of the orders. He's had three wives, y'know.'

No, I didn't know that. I didn't have a flipping clue. I nod again and smile in the hope it might speed things up. The cards look nice. I'm really pleased with the little painting I did of the cottage on the front.

They are meant to fold like a mini card, but Ray explains, 'I didn't have time, not for the price.'

So they come flat in the boxes. I spend an hour, between appointments and enquiries in Valley Dental, where I'm the hardest working receptionist in the teeth business, attempting to fold them up. With two partners, three hygienists and an aquarium full of neon tetras it can be crazy busy in here at the best of times. I manage to make four useable ones. I wonder if I'll have enough with two thousand of the things. How long is this going to take me?

At the end of the afternoon, I pack up and drive home with the cards. I wish someone else would cook occasionally. I'm struggling with a lumpy cheese sauce for a lasagne when Chloë comes in. She's my sixteen-year-old daughter and takes after her dad, Franklin, with legs almost twice the length of mine and an eyebrow permanently arched. She takes one look at the business cards and notices something I've missed.

She says, 'Lavander is spelt wrong. It should be L-a-v-e-n-d-e-r.'

Although her eyes roll as she says it, it's not out-and-out venomous. I think the little talk we had about trying to be nicer to each other has had an impact. After the meal, which we call 'tea' up here in the North of England, I decide that rather than get the cards printed again I'm going to get the sign remade for the front of the garage at a cost of £48. 'Lavander' with an 'a' gives it an edge, a little touch of uniqueness, I decide.

Have got to stop calling my B&B '*the garage*'.

Wrist pain flares up tonight from repetitive folding action. After six hours, I now have at least sixty cards that are useable. I plan to put the first ten into Hebden Bridge Tourist Information tomorrow. EXCITED!

I am up ridiculously early and can't decide if it's giddiness or the strong Earl Grey I had last night. It doesn't matter, *this is the day*. I, Janet Jackson, no relation to The Jackson Five (that I know of), am stepping into the unknown and boldly scattering my business cards out into the world, ready to accept an influx of enquiries and finally make enough money to pay off my loans and possibly contribute to a teeny-tiny pension. Thrilling stuff.

The morning unravels when Maureen chastises me for bringing the *Daily Mail* into the house. I try to hide it under the fruit bowl, but she has laser detection when it comes to the *Mail.* I explain that it has a free seed offer, but she goes on and on.

'It's the ultimate in misogyny, guilty of printing outrageous, sordid, unverified, sexual copy to humiliate and degrade women.'

She goes on to mention women I don't know, from TV shows I've never heard of. I attempt to move her gently off the subject and remind her that her rent's now two months late. She gets very overwrought.

'You know the workshops have not taken off yet,' she says. 'A new business takes time to grow.'

I try to be encouraging and mention a part-time job for a care worker that I've seen advertised in the *Courier.*

She takes a deep breath and says through gritted teeth: 'If you're going into town, can you pick me up some gingerbread vodka? I've a new recipe I want to try.'

Maureen is a challenge. She's three years older than me and has lived with me for the last four years. Once Franklin had gone, she decided I needed her support and, as I was too defeated and distracted to really register what was going on, she quickly installed herself in the loft conversion and became a permanent fixture. I love her, she's my only sibling – extremely entertaining, the life and soul of any party – but it's always a knife-edge between her natural *joie de vivre* and a meltdown.

I hear the door slam, which means Chloë has gone to school, and Maureen, barely dressed in a tie-dyed scarf, is watching me vacuum up the chain of hairballs Harvey the cat has deposited along the hall. I can't leave it, otherwise I'll only have it to do when I come home. Maureen doesn't do cleaning; it makes her depressed.

Hebden is a nightmare to park in. I like a busking saxophonist as much as the next person, but when you're trying to get somewhere and a six-foot man is jigging randomly around, wielding a huge instrument like a lunatic, well, it makes navigating the cobbles a worry. I head straight for Hebden Tourist Office, where Catherine Purdy is hovering behind the counter. Since she's had all new veneers done, she does a lot more smiling. It's a shame it's one of those smiles that can easily double for a grimace. The festival is obviously attracting the great and the good. I'm certain that's Carol

Vorderman buying a tea towel, but I'm behind her, so I wouldn't stake my life on it. When the shop finally goes a bit quiet, I approach the counter.

'Hello, Catherine, it's Janet Jackson. You know, from Valley Dental? I'm setting up a little B&B. Would you mind displaying my cards with your local accommodation list, please?'

Well, she handles my card like it's a tatty dandelion head she's found in a Jane Packer centrepiece.

'I'm afraid we don't just *put out* cards. It's reputational, you see. Do you have a website?'

'Not really. Not yet, no.'

'Oh. Well, that's not going to work for us. We have to see recommendations online before we'd ever consider in-store promotion.'

She hands me back my card and, feeling like a popped balloon, I hunt about for the cheapest thing I can buy – a recycled Hebden Bridge eraser – and go for a mooch in Help the Aged, which is where I bump into Shelley Finnigan. She's in the surgery so often with her recurring gingivitis that over the years we've become friendly.

We do all the general chit-chat, parking nightmares, GCSE stress, etcetera, and then out of the blue she says, 'I've got my son's wedding coming up next weekend. Is your cottage finished yet?'

I'm gobsmacked. An enquiry for the cottage! I explain that Barry the builder has finally got round to fixing the ceiling where his foot went through it while doing the insulation and Ted the plumber has replaced the mini boiler for the second time, so yes, the cottage is finally ready.

She explains that her house is bursting with relatives and 'I cannot *stand* my sister', so would I be able to put the latter and her family up? How much was it, and how many could I squeeze in at a push?

I'm not really thinking straight and say, 'Thirty-five pounds, bed and breakfast?' and she jumps straight in and says, 'Yes, I'll take it.'

I give her one of the cards.

'It looks lovely. Did you do the drawing? Clever thing. What an unusual spelling of lavender. I'm so glad I've bumped into you, Janet.'

I walk around Hebden in a daze. What has just happened? What do I need to do now? I buy an extra four-litre carton of milk and a bar of Dairy Milk. So excited. The cottage has its first booking. This is it.

Janet Jackson, you own a B&B!

· ·

TIPS FOR RUNNING A B&B

Think carefully about the name of your B&B. Remember spellcheck is a thing.

Maybe make a plan about how you advertise your B&B ahead of opening.

Do you really need little cards printing? Do a budget.

Remember that friendly little chat you had with the woman down the market about your plans? Well, sometimes that chit-chat can pay off. Just saying.

CHAPTER 2

Booking No. 1: The Turners

Shelley rings after tea and confirms the booking. There are five of them: her sister Frances Turner, husband Mike Turner, and three sons, Patrick, Toby and Jack staying at the cottage next Friday and Saturday! I decide I'll need two days off from work to get the place ready.

I ring and leave a message about booking holiday off next week with one of the partners, Tony Friar. Ten minutes later I get a text, a terse *OK* and a frown emoji. I worry for a minute or two but needs must. I've worked there a long time, and I never take a day off. I also remind myself that Tony is never happy. He's only smiled once in three years and that was to show off the effects of his Invisalign brace to a customer. Maybe I should have tried the other partner, Miles. Handsome, sporty, arrogant Miles barely notices I exist. Though maybe he will do when there's no toilet paper in the downstairs loo, the fish are starving, and my replacement books him in with Mrs Fulcher (of whom more anon).

The days quickly tick by, and I'm so relieved to finally be off work and able to concentrate on the cottage. I am having a nightmare with the blinds I bought off eBay. They are not official Velux, having come from www.alotlike.com, and the one upstairs refuses to pull down. I have to wedge it in and will have to pretend that it usually works. I ask Maureen if she could give me a hand cleaning the cottage this morning.

'Later, maybe. Right now I need to lie down. I've felt nauseous ever since the guilty verdict on *Judge Rinder*.'

Chloë says to me, as she is leaving for school, 'If you want to get good reviews, you will like need to leave like a welcome basket of good stuff for like the guests for when they like arrive.'

I haven't stopped thinking about what Catherine Purdy said about the importance of reviews. I decide Chloë is right and this basket might make the difference between *Reasonable night* and *Fantastic, highly recommend.*

By the afternoon, I've been four hours cleaning in the cottage and decide I need a break. Throwing caution to the wind, well, cash to the wind, I go to the speciality shop in Hebden, called So Up Market. It's a nightmare to park, again. I usually avoid the artisan deli until the sales on Boxing Day. As it is, I decide I need to impress and spend £18 on Rum Gumbo preserve, lapsang souchong leaf tea and Pamukkale coffee.

I bump into Maureen in there, who has a good look in the basket and makes me feel terrible when she pays for a packet of sunflower seeds with a plastic bag of two pence pieces. I tell her I am thinking about making the guests one of my fruit cakes. She says to me that winning 4th Prize for my Victoria sponge in the Todmorden Show Baking Competition is nothing to be ashamed of, though I do come away feeling it definitely *is* something to be ashamed of. Sometimes it's hard to have Maureen as a sister.

Shelley leaves a message tonight.

'Hello, love. Y'know my sister's a real pain? Well, she's got a new puppy and is insisting that she brings it with her. Is that OK with you?'

I haven't replied to the phone message yet. I don't know if we accept pets or not at Lavander Cottage. Harvey the cat is fairly territorial; he gave me six lashes on the back of my hand yesterday for not feeding him fast enough.

That night, I dream I'm being suffocated in a duvet cover while running from a pack of angry dogs wearing braces. I think I'm panicking a bit. I don't really know anything about running a B&B. I keep telling myself that that's what this weekend is for, and I will know a whole lot more on Sunday. But what if the Turners hate it? What if they give me bad reviews? Or I forget something really important?

I notice a tiny stain on the white linen cover on the cottage sofa, so I have it soaking and on the line for two hours. I bleach the toilet three times, wash the windows twice and put all my best glasses, my Royal Crown Derby tea service, the wingback chair, the DVD player, the Poole plates and the best silver cutlery all into the cottage before

I decide the silver cutlery is probably too much and take it back home. I pull my John Lewis sheepskin rug out of my bedroom and put it in the bedroom upstairs. My best Designers Guild cushions from my living room go on the sofa-cum-bed downstairs. What with there being five of them staying, I get Argos to deliver two fold-down beds at £89.00 each, and ordered two sets of single bed linen and two single duvets in addition to the two sets of double bed linen and duvets I already supply for the double bed and the sofa bed. The fold-down beds are sprung so they should be comfortable. I daren't do the maths. I've now spent every last penny of next year's Christmas money.

By the time Friday arrives, I am exhausted. I am still cleaning when Shelley's sister Frances, her enormous three teenage sons, Patrick, Toby, Jack and silent husband Mike and a loud cockapoo called Conor turn up at 9.30 a.m. Frances does not seem very impressed with the accommodation.

The only nice thing she says is, 'Isn't that a lovely sheepskin rug?' just as Conor rolls himself up in it and begins chewing the edges. I've already had to gently shoo him off the sofa bed downstairs but Frances says, 'Don't bother, he's not house-trained.'

I think about my cushions and gulp.

I wander over later with the welcome basket and she gives it a good rummage.

'Thank you. What time is breakfast?'

I say, 'Breakfast is served at nine, and I'll be in to take your order at eight.'

'No, sorry, we have to leave at eight thirty to get to the venue, so could we have breakfast at seven instead? I don't want to risk getting the full works on my dress. It's Coast and cost me over £200. I'm such a messy eater. Patrick is vegetarian, by the way, so he'll have Linda McCartney's and don't even think about giving any of us tomatoes, as Jack is severely allergic. Do you mind Conor playing in the garden? What's the Wi-Fi code?'

Wi-Fi. Blood drains from my head. I feel like I've been punched.

'I... it's playing up a little bit today. Leave it with me.'

I panic and ring Chloë.

'Chloë! Wi-Fi, Wi-Fi, we've no Wi-Fi! That's it! They'll give us bad reviews.'

'Mum, calm it! It's OK. We've got a good signal. Go to Currys and get a booster plug. It'll extend in . Sorry, Mum, I should've said. I thought they'd all hotspot.'

I've no idea what she's on about, but I get straight into the car and fly into Halifax at top speed. I nearly hit 40 mph on the ring road. I race into Currys, which is huge, and get out of puff trying to find a Wi-Fi section. Eventually I get some help choosing a plug and then head to the counter, where the young man there is so distracted dancing to electronic music it's only when I accidentally knock over a stand of gift cards that he serves me.

Thank God, Shelley pops round to say hello to her sister and to check on everything. I am getting a bit emotional reading the instructions for the plug. She takes one look at it and plugs it into my socket at the back door whilst I close my eyes and secretly pray for it to send stuff over into the cottage. We realise it's working when a teenager bursts out of the door wielding his iPhone like an Olympic torch and asks for the code.

Then it's time for Chloë to return from school. She says hello to Frances's oldest son – 'His name's Jack' – on the drive, runs upstairs and comes down ten minutes later in her favourite bright pink body-con minidress and offers to take breakfast orders.

I say, 'Great,' and ask her if she could take round a couple of plastic bags and drop a hint about Conor's deposits on the lawn.

Apparently, Maureen and Chloë tell me over supper, I should have told the guests not to arrive until after 2 p.m. How come they know this stuff? I feel like the least qualified person to be running a B&B. Whilst we're chatting, I realise I haven't actually visited a B&B in three years. The last one was a weekend at Rhyl, and it was awful – not very clean, uncomfortable bed, greasy breakfast.

'Did you bum-star them?' Chloë gives me a hard stare.

'What?'

'Leave a bad review.'

'I didn't leave a review of any kind.'

'It's a moral obligation to review for the sake of others if not yourself.'

Maureen pipes up, 'I think I'd make a good hotel inspector, I've excellent taste.'

'Go for it. What training do you need?'

Maureen tuts at me. 'I'm daydreaming, Janet, daydreaming, not looking for an Open University course.'

I'm tempted to say all sorts of things, but now is not the time for a tussle with Maureen. I'm off to bed, as I've a very early start tomorrow.

I'm up at practically dawn, prepping. I feel a little nauseous, as I'm plating up the fifth full breakfast before 6.30 a.m. And when my eyes start stinging, I remember that I haven't changed the filter in the extractor since moving in here, thirteen years ago. I have to stand outside the back door to breathe in normal air before continuing with the twelfth fried egg. Neither Maureen nor Chloë are up in time to help with the food.

Carrying the plated breakfasts from my house over to Lavander Cottage is a process that needs some refining. I almost slip on a Conor deposit on the drive whilst delivering the third breakfast. To avoid treading it into the carpet in the cottage, I have to shout from the door for someone to 'Come and get it!'

By the time they actually hear me, get to the table and then eat it, the beans have gone cold. Apparently they are expecting a continuation of the full waitress service, so I run back with a microwaved Tupperware container full of beans, but Frances is back to explain the disaster I've caused.

'The whole bloody thing's exploded on Patrick as he's taken the lid off. We're having to soak his shirt now. He's only got one shirt good enough for a wedding and that's covered in bean juice!'

After that, I leave them to it. I don't know what the early breakfast was about, since they don't leave for the wedding until 10 a.m., all in a screaming panic. I then spend the afternoon in the garden cleaning up after Conor.

Chloë comes over to me, as I am scooping.

'When are they going?' she demands.

'Tomorrow.'

'What time?'

'I have no idea.'

She rolls her eyes and returns ten minutes later with her iPad showing me a guestbook on the web from a local B&B.

'Look, Mum, it has like a welcome pack, with the Wi-Fi code, and like departure and arrival times and like a list of things to see and do in the Hebden Bridge area.'

I am mortified. It's so obvious. How totally unprofessional not to have a welcome pack. This is the sort of thing that will be mentioned in a review:

A welcome pack would have been useful. We didn't know where anything was, or how anything worked in the cottage.

I decide Catherine Purdy was so right not to put my cards out. I've no idea what I'm doing. I need a welcome book. With stuff in it. I need to go into Hebden, but then have a moment of clarity. How do I avoid the crowds? It's the last day of the arts festival and that can be pandemonium. Last year, I had completely forgotten about it and inadvertently got trapped in the crush of toddlers trying to see Mr Bloom. I was pushed into the decorated tree trail and ended up having to have a plastic diplodocus cut out of my hair, learning the hard way that I do not have the ears for a short bob.

I take the view that trying to park is going to use up too much time, so I haul my trusty old Raleigh Wayfarer bike out from the shed. On the cycle path, I try to avoid braking because of the high-decibel screech my brakes emit every time I put on any pressure, so I reach speeds that are pushing me way out of my comfort zone. I've become a nervous cyclist ever since I got my bike wheel trapped in the tramline outside M&S in Manchester. I actually managed to bring the tram system to a complete halt whilst two drivers and a large crowd helped me get it free. Anyway, I brave the route, freewheeling at tremendous speed, and get to Hebden in mere minutes. I have no trouble parking – oh, the joy – and it's definitely the right decision. The town is a chaos of tourists, buskers and loud, dancing robots – but I am able to use my bike like a shield to part the ways.

Although I'm on a mission to get sorted, I can't help becoming distracted by the plaintive voice of this young man singing in the square as if his life depended on it. He's pockmarked and wizened, like an old man, but is only in his early to mid twenties, and I stop to listen to him for a moment.

'Druggie,' I hear someone say in a disparaging way.

I look at the young man and think that might explain his

shambolic, worn-out appearance. Yet he still has the voice of a melancholy angel. He sounds so tragic, as he sings the Beatles' song 'Blackbird', that I find myself welling up as I listen to him. At least I think that's why – until I realise the burger van has just thrown on a load of fresh onions and there's a breeze.

I wrench myself away and push the bike through the crowds to TH*INK*, where I peer through the window and see that Ray is deep in conversation with a customer. I overhear the words 'Dutch barge' and 'Lance'. The woman visibly sighs with relief when I walk in. There is no guest book as such in stock, but there is a large notebook at £8.49. Ray offers me a five per cent discount because it features a calendar from 2015. I thank him and he sighs.

'Have you heard about Gwen?'

I don't know what comes over me. I take his hands in mine, look him in the eye and say, 'Gwen has gone. It's time to move on, Ray.' It's as good a way as any to bring Ray to a sudden stop, and I ping my card to pay and rush out before he can engage brain-mouth gear.

On the way home, I pick up speed on the bike, racing along the canal ever so slightly out of control and, at one point, nearly collide with a Jack Russell. To be fair, the dog appears without warning from under a bridge, and I am ruthless in my approach; it's a case of me or him and a body of water. I am home in a flash, even after the feisty altercation with the pensioner dog owner.

I write in the front page of the notebook with my best pen:

Welcome to Lavander Cottage
Arrival time 2 p.m. and departure time 11 a.m.

I can't decide if I can go into the cottage now they are officially renting it. Would I be trespassing? I dilly-dally by the door for ages when Chloë spots me.

'What are you doing, Mum?'

'I don't know if I'm allowed back in to put this welcome book in?'

'Welcome book?'

'The book you suggested, to say guests must leave at 11 a.m.'

'Janet, just open the bloody door.' It's Maureen, who appears wrapped in a United States flag, wearing sequin flip-flops and smoking what looks like a cigar.

With the two of them giving me the hard stare, I unlock the door to Lavander Cottage and sidle in. I try not to notice the mess everywhere and place the guest book discreetly open by the door on the little welcome table with the bowl for keys.

I am so tired that by 4 p.m. I have a bath and get into my nightie. Unusually for her, Maureen offers to do me a spinach omelette for tea. I refuse, as I've spoilt myself on parkin. I am in bed with a headache tablet soon afterwards. What a day. Alarm set for 6 a.m.

I wake up at 2 a.m. when I hear voices. I can't understand where they are coming from, then realise it's the Turners coming back from the wedding. I lift the blind surreptitiously so I can see out.

It seems Mike Turner is not the strong, silent type after all. His shirt is undone to his waist, displaying grey, frothy chest hair, and he bellows at high volume: 'Frances, admit you never loved me.'

'Shut up, Mike.'

'I won't shut up.'

'Mike, you're drunk. Come to bed.'

Chloë comes in bleary-eyed at this point, and we decide to watch from her room which has much the better view. Mike really is tanked up and in full flow.

'I am not drunk. I'm the most sober I have ever been. I can see clearly for once in my life.'

'Mike, you're talking shite.'

'No! I know the truth. You wouldn't have married me if you hadn't been pregnant with Patrick. Deny it! You can't 'cos it's true, that's why... and you can't handle the truth.'

'Mike, I am not going to talk to you while you're quoting Tom Hanks films and acting like a dick. You'll wake everyone up.'

'I don't care. This is my life. And it's not Tom Hanks, it's Jack Nicholson, my favourite actor. Or don't you care? That's who Jack is named after. Do you *ever* listen to me?'

'Not unless I have to. Now, honest to God, you've lost it, just come to bed.'

'How do I know? Come on, ask me: how do I know? Jack isn't mine, that's how I know.'

'Mike, you have had eight pints and three gin and tonics. You were humming "Bat Out of Hell" when they said their vows. You are not right in the head.'

'Oh, aren't I? Oh, aren't I? So how do you explain that nose?'

'Give me strength. I'm off to bed.'

At this point, Frances slams the door on Mike, who huddles on the doorstep for ten minutes, before Patrick lets him in. Chloë turns to me once he has gone inside and when it's been quiet for a couple of minutes.

'I'm not sad about you not being with Dad any more, y'know, Mum?' she tells me. 'I'm sort of over it. I know you weren't, like, happy and that's important.' Then she hugs me, the first proper hug in months.

I realise I don't get many proper hugs. I'd forgotten what the sensation of being touched and squeezed actually feels like. It's lovely, and I need it. I don't realise how much. I well up a bit. Everything is obviously getting to me and being disorientated with going to bed early and being woken up in the middle of the night.

'Thank you, love,' I say emotionally. 'That means everything to me.'

I hug her back and it takes some persuading to make me let go. She holds me at a distance and smiles and kisses my forehead. I am way too tired to really take it in. She is almost saying, I think, that she forgives me for divorcing Franklin. I thought she'd hold it against me forever. She adores her dad. It is a moment to treasure, cut short by the sound of a smash coming from Lavander Cottage.

'I hope that isn't my Royal Crown Derby.'

We laugh at that and head back to bed. I collapse onto the pillow, only for Harvey the cat to wake me up at a quarter past five, wanting to be let out. I daren't risk ignoring him after he left a deposit on the chopping board last week. If he pulls that stunt again and Health and Safety happened to visit this morning, that'd be it, I'd be done as an establishment due to a risk to human health. Front cover, *Hebden Bridge Times*: 'Cat Filth at B&B'. I must have dozed back off after letting him out, because I struggle when the alarm goes off at six and wake up convinced that I am in prison doing time for poisoning pedigree dogs.

By the time I get myself going and am downstairs, I have a real panic on when I realise Maureen has used all the eggs. I shout to her to come and get me some replacements, but there's no response, so I rush down to the Co-op where Benedict, the manager, who must be eighty-five, is pushing a cage of fresh bread around with the energy and vitality of a man on death row. I feel sorry for him until I glimpse a reflection of myself in the fridge door. In my bobbly fleece, baggy leggings and my dirty Ugg boots, with no make-up on and my hair in a scrunchie, I realise I look like his cellmate. I bag a reduced pack of button mushrooms and a first-press *Mail on Sunday*. Once home, I put a ton of foundation on and even a smear of lipstick. I hide the *Mail* under a pile of bills, where I can guarantee Maureen will *never* look. I cook off twelve eggs and sixteen rashers of bacon, a dozen mushrooms and twenty-four slices of fried bread. I stick it all in the oven on number 1 and tap gently on the cottage door.

No answer.

I go back inside and, nearly gagging on the smell of crispy bacon, I open all the windows and doors to let the fumes out and put my coat on for warmth. I risk a sit-down and a cup of tea with the *Sunday* magazine. The next thing I know, Chloë is waking me up.

'Mum, what are you doing? You're asleep. Will you sign my school planner for the next six weeks?'

She plonks it in front of me with a chewed-up biro and then she microwaves and eats two full breakfasts. God knows what we'll do with the rest. I suppose we can have them for lunch. I'm just finishing signing Week 6 when Maureen wafts into the kitchen wrapped in what looks like a toga made of kitchen foil.

'Still subscribing to your fascist propaganda, Janet?'

'And good morning to you too, Maureen,' I say and look down. The *Mail* magazine is under the planner, open at page 8. She leans over me as if I am in a World War II interrogation scene and stabs the headline with an immaculate coral fingernail.

'Oh, look at that riveting headline. "Kerry Katona puts on a busty display as she flaunts" – note the word "flaunts" – "her six-stone weight loss in a sizzling scarlet jumpsuit". So judgmental, I despair. Why oh why, do women do this to each other?'

Chloë comes over to look. 'I like her jumpsuit.'

I focus properly on the photograph for the first time and agree. 'Yes, it's a lovely shade of red, really suits her colouring.'

Maureen sighs. 'I give up. Have the happy family gone? It's well past time for them to leave.'

'Mmm. Yes,' I say vaguely. 'Want some breakfasts? There are lots of them in the oven.'

'The car is still in the drive.'

'Is it? Oh.' I am caught in the glaring headlight stares of Maureen and Chloë. I shrug, too tired to fight back. 'Maybe they're still here then.'

Chloë and Maureen exchange looks. Chloë huffs out and bangs on the cottage door. After five minutes of an increasingly threatening drum roll of knocks, Patrick, bleary-eyed, opens it.

'Afternoon, are your mum and dad up? We have another booking for Lavander Cottage, so unless they want to pay for another night, we need you out in fifteen minutes so we can get on and turn it around... You hear me? Now, do you want me to write it down or are you OK to pass that on?'

Well, Frances comes out ten minutes later. She is wearing dark glasses and carrying Conor the dog and wearing a polo neck with tartan pyjama bottoms. Mr Turner thanks me for a lovely stay, says he's left the money on the table and pushes the boys into the car. Chloë waves them off in hot pants and a vest after exchanging Snapchat details with Jack.

We all three stand there politely like servants on *Downton Abbey*, waving off the lord and lady, and the moment they are out of sight, we pelt into the cottage.

When we get inside, I gulp because it looks like the 'after' photograph at a crime scene. Towels are thrown everywhere, and the sheepskin rug is on the sofa in tatters, covered in dog hair. There is a dent in the plaster in the living room, the shape of which, it turns out, fits the broken mug on the draining board; the sink is full of washing-up and the bin is overflowing with giant, empty bottles of Coke. The almost-Velux blind in the bedroom is hanging at half mast and there is a fuchsia-coloured lipstick stain on two of the pillowcases.

As I tidy up, I find three brand-new toothbrushes, wrapped and untouched, and a half used tube of Crabtree & Evelyn rose hand cream that I give to Maureen. No sign at all of the wicker welcome basket, which I was planning to reuse. On the kitchen table, under the fruit bowl, is £140.

'One hundred and forty pounds?' Maureen was raging.

'Maybe I didn't make myself clear to Shelley.'

'They saw you coming.'

'I told her thirty-five pounds each.' I work it out: for two nights for five people that makes £350. I've been swindled.

'Did you say that?'

'No, I just said thirty-five. They must have assumed children don't count.'

'Children! They were six-foot louts. You must have spent thirty-five quid on bacon alone, trying to feed the bloody lamp posts.'

'Hmm,' Chloë puts in. 'How much have you spent, Mum?'

'I'm not sure. I got the mushrooms half price.'

I crack on with stripping the beds, which is energetic work. Maureen traipses after me, going on and on about them taking advantage of me. I offer her £30 to help me clean the place, and she reluctantly picks up the towels. Chloë tuts in exasperation and, ten minutes later, is on her phone quoting examples of prices for B&Bs in the area.

'Mum, thirty-seven pounds, *per person*, per night, is like the average, and then it's like five pounds extra average for a dog.'

'Well, that's good to hear, and at least I know for next time.'

Quite frankly, I don't know if there will be a next time.

My linen sofa cover looks a bit ragged with what looks like a Coke stain on the arm. I bleach it for two hours and then wash it by hand and hang it out to dry. I beat the sheepskin rug to try and get out the dog hair, then attempt to darn it where it has three holes chewed in it.

This evening, Chloë comes and finds me in bed, where I'm hunkered down, hours before anyone else. She is carrying a cup of peppermint tea for me, and the guest book. She opens it and points to the first entry on page two. It reads:

3 April, Turner family. Reasonable night.

'Well done, Mum. You've done it. Your first review.'

I don't know what to say. I definitely feel a little glow. Not sure what it is: pride, satisfaction, disbelief? I've done it. The first booking.

I am dog-tired, we definitely need a new filter in the extractor, washing is slung everywhere, with every doorway draped with a faceful of damp sheet or a duvet cover. I'm not rich. I can't say I loved it, but it wasn't a complete disaster.

My own B&B. It's a start.

. . . .

TIPS FOR RUNNING A B&B

Have clear arrival and departure times, and pass this information to the guests *before they arrive.*

Have a guest book repeating all this information.

What are you going to charge? Check out the competition and agree with guests *before they arrive.*

Don't forget Wi-Fi and don't assume they will all be hotspotters.

These tips are so obvious it's embarrassing. I hope it's useful to learn from my mistakes.

And by the way, say NO to puppies.

CHAPTER 3

Maureen has a new boyfriend, and we are no longer allowed to call her Maureen. Only 'Mitzi' will do. I remember this happening once before when she went through a stage of trying to force our mother to go with her to family therapy. Maureen had decided that Mother's decision to call her Maureen was tantamount to abuse.

'When I was born, Tammy Wynette was in the charts, Elkie Brooks was famous, Dusty Springfield, Kiki Dee, Aretha was big. Why couldn't you imbue me with some joy and creativity and recognise the creative spirit that was in front of you?' my sister whined.

Her words were always going to fall on deaf ears. Mother was a Yorkshire farmer's daughter who expressed any feelings she had through animal husbandry. I never saw her cry. The nearest she ever got to tears was when a cow she really liked gave birth on Christmas Day. The fact she called the calf Cher really did for her and Maureen's relationship. When Mum refused to go to therapy with Maureen, my sister changed her name by deed poll to Mitzi, even when our mother tried to explain that she had named her after Maureen Evans, the Welsh pop star. Our mother's favourite song, it turned out, was 'Like I Do', recorded by Maureen Evans in the 1960s when Mum was still young.

Mitzi was having none of it. She'd never heard of Maureen Evans. No one had. I got used to it eventually, but by then Mother had died, Maureen/Mitzi had moved into my house, there was no man on the scene, and my sister simply got bored of correcting me. That was when we reverted to Maureen and Janet.

Well, Mitzi is back, and with it, I hope, a bit of va-va-voom, as Maureen's chanting sessions once a week with a couple of women she met at the Gin Café are not bringing much to the bread bin. I know she's hit a crisis point when she comes out of the latest session looking broken.

'We're mid chant, and they start arguing about a woman they both fancy who's led them both a merry dance and has now declared herself bi and moved in with the landlord at the White Swan.'

'Have you considered using your teaching degree? Or maybe retraining?'

She thanks me for my support in a loud, sarcastic way, slams the door and goes into town. Apparently, this is when she meets Peter. He is working in Hebden as the new librarian.

Maureen announces the new regime whilst we're having tea, a home-made spicy tomato soup with sourdough cheese croutons. Who am I kidding? They're not dainty little croutons – they're whopping great clumps of cheese on toast.

A self-important voice announces amidst the slurping and crunching: 'Could you please support me going forward in my new relationship by referring to me only as Mitzi.'

'I'll try, Maureen,' I say.

Chloë laughs.

It's another stressful day at Valley Dental. Mrs Fulcher is in with her four children for check-ups.

Tony is seriously unhappy they've been booked in with him and is on the verge of chastising me when I remind him, 'I was away on the day the booking went in the diary, Tony.'

It goes as badly as we all anticipated. Mrs Fulcher starts whimpering before they even get through Tony's door and that sets all the kids off. I suggest lollipops to try and placate them but that gets Jillian the hygienist's back up.

'We're a dental practice, Janet, we can't be advocating the use of lollipops.'

After ten minutes of deafening racket, I get a call from Tony.

'Shoot round to Something Sweet and pick up five drumstick lollies and make it snappy.'

It seems to calm down after that and, an hour and twenty minutes later, the Fulchers have finally left the building. I am busy enjoying my home-made, warmed-up carbonara lunch and looking at HebWeb, checking out holiday cottages in the area, when Miles, the other partner dentist, wanders past. He's back from his daily run around the park.

'That smells nice, Janet.'

'Oh sorry, is it too much? It's home-made carbonara.'

'Not at all. It looks and smells delicious.'

'I'll bring an extra portion next time.'

'Ooh, yes, please. I can't remember the last time I had a home-made carbonara.'

He is quite good-looking, Miles. Least, that's what the hygienists think. In a snog, marry, kill we did one Christmas, Miles was everybody's 'snog'.

'Thank you for not giving me the Fulchers. Did you hear all that racket? For a filling!'

'Yes, ridiculous. Tranquilliser dart next time.'

Miles laughs. 'How's your new bed and breakfast doing?' he asks.

I choke on a bacon chunk. It's the first really personal question he has asked me in eight years of working here.

'Fine, thank you,' which is a lie, but I am in such a state of shock and my eyes are watering with the strain of trying to avoid spitting the chunk out. I go for a tissue in my bag, in case I do have to put the chunk somewhere, and find a cottage business card that I hand to him. He turns it over in his hand and looks at me.

'Well done, Janet.'

I don't know what to say. It has taken me three years and three months, every spare penny and every spare hour to convert the garage. I suppose in some way, in those three words, he is acknowledging all that. I feel a little surge of pride that, yes, Janet Jackson, you have done something to be proud of.

'Thank you,' I squeak, the chunk really getting to me. He puts the card on the reception counter, and I leave it there all afternoon.

As soon as I get in, I drive Chloë to White Rose Shopping Centre in Leeds. Her excuse to drag me away from my plan to divide the geraniums is that she needs new school shoes. The reality seems to be that she needs to spend a lot of my money in the food court on smoothies and paninis and buying expensive Lush bath bombs and make-up that I would never dream of buying for myself.

On the way back, the M62 is jammed as always at Birstall. Chloë wants to know what the huge, colourful rainbow sticker says on a car quite a way in front, in another lane ahead of us. I nudge and manoeuvre our way towards it, and it's only as we get behind it that we can clearly read it. It says, *I Love Bum Sex*. We are both a bit shocked and don't talk much after that. She puts in her headphones, and I listen to a repeat of *Money Box* on Radio Four.

I am finally enjoying the first relaxing day in a while. Maureen, or should I say Mitzi, is going out again with Peter, which means there'll be none of her friends chanting in the living room. The couple are taking a trip to the Gordon Rigg Garden Centre, to buy some bulbs for Peter's window boxes, and are then planning to have a spot of lunch at the café. I have to say Maureen must be really taken with Peter, because she has never expressed any interest in gardening before. And eating lunch at a café is something Maureen has done maybe once or twice in her adult life, usually with me, in desperation to use the toilet when we've been on a day out. Maureen's diet has always been a cocktail of booze and cigarettes with the odd bowl of soup and an omelette at a push. She prefers bars and pubs and sees cafés as 'the refuge of the fleece wearers'.

I wave her off and try not to look too thrilled to see her leave the house. Once she's safely gone, I rush to read the *Mail* I've hidden in a copy of *Prima*.

I've given myself a day with nothing in it except to maybe try a new fruit cake recipe.

I've got my hot chocolate and a ginger thin biscuit, paper open at page 16 with some gardening tips from Monty Don, when Chloë bursts in unexpectedly in her school uniform and says, 'I've been sick, I'm sent home. I'm not like well.'

I think about leaving her in her bedroom for five minutes, to see if she feels any better, but decide I am being selfish. Monty can wait. I make her a cup of tea, open her bedroom door and get knocked backwards by the plumes of powerful incense smoke that pour out of the room. She is hanging out of the window, obviously flustered, and shouts at me.

'I need my space, do you mind? Can you try knocking?'

I apologise and then struggle to put the cup of tea down. Every surface is covered with pens, clothes, broken glass, mirrors, make-up, toiletries, books, pictures and discarded iPhone chargers. I eventually put it in her hand and then retreat downstairs.

I return five minutes later (knocking first) with an apron, pan scrubbers and a pair of Marigolds, determined that what she needs is a nice clean room to relax in, even though she is adamant, 'I only cleaned it this morning!'

I collect, on a first pass, sixteen plates, eight cups – six of them featuring hard mould – then fill a bin bag with R Whites lemonade bottles, six Simple make-up cleanser bottles, a small mountain of used cotton wool pads and nine bags from a Doritos Tangy Cheese multipack of tortilla chips. Her duvet cover is acrylic painted with a dolphin design and the carpet in front of the full-length mirror features what I think is a new rug but turns out to be make-up smears.

I explain, as calmly as possible, that I don't have the money to replace the carpet or the duvet cover and she needs to take more care of her things. And, by the way, can I see her school planner, please?

Well, she explodes. Apparently I am 'always freaking her out' with my controlling ways, and she throws the planner across the room in my direction, knocking over the lava lamp she got for Christmas, which smashes dramatically into a luminous green mess on the floor. She puts her hand to her mouth, takes a picture of the smashed lamp and then promptly bursts into tears. I attempt to comfort her, though her hair is lacquered so stiff it makes close contact a bit of a challenge. We are welded in an awkward half hug position when I get a phone call from the school telling me Chloë has been excluded for a week for getting caught smoking.

Tea is a tense affair. Chloë is mute throughout. I agonise for twenty minutes trying to work out what is the right thing to do about her smoking. I ring my friend Victoria, who has four grown-up children and twelve grandchildren ranging from the ages of two to twenty-one. She knows exactly what to do.

Chloë looks shocked when I deliver her instructions.

'Removal of phone for one week, official grounding for two weeks and a pocket money ban for a month.'

Chloë cooperates but is silent in protest, whilst Peter, who has invited himself for tea, has a lot to say for himself. I imagine it must be something to do with the fact that he's so quiet at the library during the day. That or nerves, because I mention my love of gardening and he is off. Have I ever grown auriculas? Do I rate hydrangeas? How long has it taken me to create the borders? How he likes my mixture of annuals, and tells me that my *Dicentra spectabilis* (bleeding heart) was the best he'd ever come across.

Maureen is looking seriously peeved when we touch on his love of herbaceous perennials, so I hurry in with the lemon drizzle cake I baked earlier today, hoping it might bring this conversation to a speedy end.

He takes one mouthful and says, 'Wow, that is so deliciously moist.'

At this point, Maureen excuses them both from the table and the next thing I hear is the front door slamming, a car driving away and the sound of a bath running.

I'm listening to Jeremy Vine the next day about the impact a Russian cyberattack could have on the government's new NHS software, and it makes me wonder if they'll ever get round to my bunion. I can't remember how long I've been on the list. Long enough for me to give up on my lilac court shoes.

I feel a bit low today, having finally gone through my bank statements. I've had no enquiries about the B&B, and I'm overdrawn thanks to the expense of having the Turners to stay. I go into the cottage to mooch and am plumping up the cushions when Chloë finds me.

'I need your password so I can override the parental settings on the laptop.'

I'd forgotten I owned a laptop. It's nice to see Chloë, who has been in self-imposed solitary confinement since the phone call from her school. If it wasn't for the mystery disappearance of the packet of Chunky KitKats, I would have forgotten she was in the house. As she's not allowed out in school time, as part of her exclusion rules, she's taken to walking around with no make-up on in her panda onesie. She looks like my little Chloë again, and I give her a big cuddle, even though I am still trying very hard to be cross with her.

'What's up, Mum?' she asks. 'You like look miserable.'

She's caught me off guard, so I blurt out the truth. 'I'm disappointed we've had no other people come to the cottage since the Turners.'

She looks at me with one eyebrow raised and then says patiently, 'Mum, nobody *knows* about the cottage. Nobody! Six people, who've now visited, know about the cottage.'

She's right, of course. I just don't know what to do about it.

Back home, we open the laptop and have a good laugh trying to guess my password, coming up with possible ones dating back to 2014, which was when I bought it. We eventually narrow the list down to:

Clooneyno (George got married)

Chloë (my first, favourite and only daughter)

mooseloose (something about the Scotland referendum)

Fuengirola (where me and Franklin went on honeymoon)

carbonara (my favourite food)

icebucket (I didn't do the challenge in the end)

Wicked (the best musical of all time)

It turns out to be 'ChloëRose'. I'd included her middle name.

Later, I reclaim the laptop and have a browse at other local bed and breakfasts. Having hosted just one family in Lavander Cottage, even though it was chaotic and the money was not enough and they were noisy and they took the welcome basket and the dog pooed everywhere, we're set up and ready for guests, at least. We've got through that hurdle, and surely it can't be that bad again, can it? Maybe it's time to advertise in the *Hebden Bridge Times*. Or hand some cards out? Yes, that is a good plan.

I'm stewing on all this when I hear Chloë racing down the stairs. She's wearing nicotine patches provided by Maureen and she's 'feeling hyped', apparently. She gives me a hug and asks if she can have £10.

'I can't wait to get back to school on Monday. They're going on a geography trip to Lightwater Valley to study landscape design.' The theme park is in Ripon, and it's home of Europe's longest roller coaster – the 'Ultimate'. I can't help wondering if a ride on said 'Ultimate' will be included in the cost of the trip.

It's lovely to see her enthusiastic about school. Hopefully this rebel phase is a blip and she's going to knuckle down now. I tell her to take £10 from my purse, as I need to get on and sort out the downstairs loo which is blocked again. I fill a large bucket full of hot water, kneel on a stool for balance and empty the water in stages into the toilet bowl. On the third pour, there is a vacuum rush of bubbles, as the wet wipes I suspect Chloë of flushing down it dislodge, and it's clear. Hallelujah!

It's been a long day. As I'm getting wearily into bed, Maureen pops her head round my bedroom door. She says she's having a breakthrough. It's a rare lunar eclipse tonight and she can feel it working its magic. I congratulate her and light a lavender, lemon and verbena candle to try and block out the memory of the sight and smell of the toilet bowl.

When I wake up next morning, I find a note under my bedroom door. Maureen is requesting a meeting. This is only ever bad news. The eclipse has brought her to some conclusions, apparently. Dreading it, I binge on a pack of Viennese whirls with my first cup of tea. She is suggesting 6 p.m. tomorrow and is strangely silent all day. It's spooky, as if she's storing up words. I wonder if it's anything to do with Peter? He popped into Valley Dental yesterday. I raved on about Mitzi this and Mitzi that and when I'd finished he said, 'I loved your lemon drizzle, Janet, was it the Jamie Oliver recipe? It's the open gardens weekend in Cragg Vale. Are you going?'

I smiled and said I wasn't sure, and pretended to be busy on the computer, accidentally printing out twenty-five copies of Mrs Cassidy's hygienist appointment reminders for Monday.

It's a gorgeous, bright, dry Saturday. A golden sun washes across the valley and gives everything a glow. Out in the garden, waves of double narcissi and alliums are leaning into the sunlight, a reward for the few hours I spent planting bulbs last season. I patrol the beds, trying to remember what fresh shoot belongs to which plant, as they wrestle with each other for space.

Chloë appears all dressed up and excited at her first day of freedom. 'Can we do something?'

We drive up to Hollings Stables and collect some manure. Chloë is horrified when I climb to the top of the steaming dunghill to locate the rotted down black stuff. She complains bitterly when I put some bags on the back seat.

'Mum, that absolutely stinks! This is my first time outside in six days and it's not what I had in mind when I said I wanted a trip out.'

I placate her with a mango crushed ice smoothie and a double cheese panini from Costa. The day passes pleasantly deadheading and mulching, but I haven't forgotten about my sister's demand for a meeting... the thought of which casts a shadow over the sun.

Maureen arrives at the kitchen table at ten past six. She's wearing a pinstripe business suit, making me feel very out of place in my *Work Less, Garden More* T-shirt, chino shorts and Crocs. She explains she wants to put a proposition to me. All sorts of things run through my mind. Faking her death for insurance purposes looms largest for some reason. I have been reading a lot of *Best* magazines left behind at the surgery, and this kind of thing crops up a lot when people run into debt.

My sister takes a deep breath and says she knows she's had a lot of career changes over the years, and how some had worked, and some had not.

I spend a moment considering Maureen's career changes. These have included a dog-walking service, for which she was given an ASBO – an antisocial behaviour order – by Calderdale Council and banned from continuing. Within the first month, sixteen people had complained about the multiple dog foulings she refused to pick up along the Hebble canal path. Next, she had a vintage stall in Hebbleroyd Antiques Centre that she struggled to fill with enough items to cover her rent because she wanted to keep everything she bought. At one stage, we ended up with forty-six glass clowns in the living room. There were so many of them that she had them seated on the sofas, which made it hugely unsettling trying to flop down and watch *Emmerdale* with any degree of comfort.

And let's not forget the eBay shop selling ancient coins, the phone line tarot card reader and the mindfulness coach, all short-lived, supposedly money-making sidelines. The kundalini chanting was the current and probably the least successful of all her schemes in recent memory.

Maureen said solemnly that she recognised that she needed to get practical and, of all her plans, she thought this new one was definitely the way forward – *if* her family were behind her and 'prepared to give me the support I need'.

I gulp. Support for Maureen is usually expensive.

At this point in proceedings, Chloë totters into the kitchen. She is wearing so much make-up that she looks almost unrecognisable. In huge heels and with her hair piled on top of her head she is nearly six feet tall and appears to be in her early thirties. What's more, her dress is so tight I'm sure I can see her heartbeat. I can hear her over the other side of the kitchen counter rummaging in the crisp basket.

'Seriously?' she whines. 'Salt and Vinegar Snaktastic? Can we please stop shopping at Lidl?'

Ignoring her niece, Maureen draws a deep breath and says in a long sentence without pausing once: 'If you would allow me to move into the cottage I've been looking at jobs and I could apply to foster some children at £429 a week and then I could pay you some rent easily make enough to pay bills and begin paying off some debts, your gut reaction?'

I wrestle with my face to keep it as neutral as I possibly can. I concentrate very hard on the paintwork that needs touching up on the skirting boards behind her. When was the last time I actually painted them? It was probably over ten years ago now.

Then the thoughts pour in. Maureen? Foster children? I remember when Chloë was born, my sister gagged when I breastfed the baby for the first time. Not at any point in the last fifteen years has Maureen shown Chloë, or any other child, any affection whatsoever. And yet, to give my sister her due, as the aunt of a teenage girl she has shown more potential. She and Chloë both fancy Cillian Murphy in *Peaky Blinders*, they both like a recipe in a book called *Modka Mocktails*, and they have been sharing nicotine patches for the last week, so I suppose she's mellowing with age.

I struggle for words. I want to support Maureen, I really do. But let her move into Lavander Cottage? Really? What about all my plans for financial security that the cottage represent, the debt to get it finished, the years trapped behind the desk at Valley Dental reception going on for ever and ever, looming in front of me? I involuntarily have a coughing fit trying to think about what to say when Chloë pipes up.

'Oh, Mum, don't say yes to that after I've just done your website. The cottage is live from tomorrow on HebWeb. Don't tell me I've wasted my time!'

I shake my head and then nod in the hope I might look like I have any clue what she is talking about.

'Mum, say we're doing the website or I'll be really peed off. It's taken me all week.'

'No, love, of course we're doing the website.'

'Great. Don't wait up. Greg's mum's gonna drop me off. Bye.'

I have no idea who Greg is. I had no idea about the website. I had no idea she was going out. Has the grounding at home expired? I can't remember how long we said. I don't know if I still want to run the B&B business. What I do know though, is that if I'm ever to have any money again, I cannot let Maureen move in.

'Sorry, Maureen, I... We're in the middle of plans for the cottage.'

She sighs, goes to the fridge and pulls the spoon out of the bottle of cava I watched her open this morning, pours herself a large one and gives me a tiny glass. She chinks the glasses together.

'Congratulations.'

Part of me wonders if I need to wait to see if she drinks from the glass first, just in case she's poisoned it.

'I didn't know you had plans. Well done, sis,' she says, and then there's a pause.

I smile nervously, not knowing what's coming. The pause goes on and on. I feel as if I'm in a Russian roulette game... and then it comes.

She throws back her drink, looks me right in the eye, and with a big tear rolling down her face, she says, 'Oh Janet, Peter and I have split up. I'm such a complete and utter mess-up.'

I grab her a bit of kitchen roll, she falls into my arms and, in giving her a hug, I remember that feeling, that need to feel loved.

· ·

TIP ON TEENAGE DAUGHTERS CAUGHT SMOKING

(punishment courtesy of Victoria)

Removal of phone for one week, official grounding for two weeks and a pocket money ban for a month.

. . . .

TIP ON SISTERS

Boyfriends come and go. *Never* express an opinion.

. . . .

TIPS ON PASSWORDS

Try to keep a list somewhere safe. Sorry, of course you do that already.

CHAPTER 4

Booking No. 2: Nick & Fergus

There's an early knock on the door, and I open it to Jim the postman. He hands me the post, says, 'Hi, Janet,' then gyrates and pouts and sings '*The best things in life are free*' very badly and at some volume. It distracts me from what I'd actually been thinking about, which is that today is the anniversary of my divorce. It's now three years since I became Janet Jackson again instead of Mrs Munroe. It's strange to think that it's an anniversary I can only share with Franklin. I know he won't remember it. Nothing personal – the man struggles to recall his own shoe size.

I try to forget it myself, but the date's lodged there, like the enormous, beige vinyl suitcase stuck under the eaves that we used for a holiday in Tenerife before Chloë was born. It was too heavy to carry and too sweaty to handle, and it was never used again. No wonder no one can ever be bothered to go through the faff of getting covered in ancient dust, pulling it out and getting rid of the monstrous thing. It's shameful really, leaving something up there to rot. Not that it will rot. Plastic is killing the oceans. Of course, I wouldn't dump the suitcase in the sea or anything. It's hard to reach the sea from here, as a matter of fact. Does Rochdale Canal eventually reach the sea? It meets the river at Sowerby Bridge, I believe. I'm a fully paid-up member of the Canal and River Trust, or at least I was a couple of years back. It's probably expired. Note to self: *must check that*. At that time, I went for Youth Hostel membership as well, hoping Chloë and I would take some trips away after we did Keswick one Easter and it rained for sixty-four hours solid...

I'm lost in memories for a few moments before rallying and thinking that I really should get under those eaves one of these days and recycle the suitcase. Thinking it through, I doubt there's a chemical out there that could penetrate that beige vinyl. Humans put a lot of effort into making rubbish things last a long time. I am startled by that thought, since it really does sum up my marriage.

It turns out that Chloë was making it up about the website. She lets me know why.

'Mum, Auntie Maureen is lovely, but she's a flake. You're too soft with her. Rented out, that cottage has the potential to give me like the two foreign holidays a year I richly deserve. Are we like going on holiday this year or what?'

'I've not planned anything. I'm sorry, love, I can't really afford it, not with the cottage and everything.'

Chloë sighs and pulls the laptop towards her, saying, 'You can make it up to me next year, somewhere hot with a pool. Right, let's get it on HebWeb before Auntie Maureen starts persuading you to let her live in it again.'

So Chloë gets to work taking and uploading photos of Lavander Cottage, and she tells me to hurry up and write some blurb to go with them. I look at the cards for inspiration.

Lavander Cottage self-catering for up to four people
in the heart of Hebden Bridge.
Contact J. Jackson on 01422 825104

I turn the cards over and over in my hand. What to put? How much to charge? Do I even want this? What's the point of going through all that expense, all that worry, all that *effort* of getting the garage converted if I just let it sit there? It's been so much of a journey, and now I'm at the end I don't know what to do.

'I hate cooking breakfasts,' I blurt out.

'Cool. Self-catering cottage. Much better.'

So, just like that, the decision is made. No breakfast. I realise I've been carrying that worry like a strapping great backpack along the boggy bits of the Pennine Way. This cottage is going to buy Chloë and me a holiday next year. Maybe we'll even allow my sister to come. I get writing. And by the way, I won't get roped into having families of five people here any more. They simply trash the place.

Lavander Cottage is a pretty dwelling in the lovely village of
Hebbleroyd, 10 minutes' walk from the popular tourist town of

Hebden Bridge. It is newly decorated, with a spacious bathroom and separate kitchen. Its large double bedroom and comfy sofa bed in the living room, with single beds available, make it suitable to sleep up to four easily. A TV and DVD player are supplied, with DVDs and some access to Wi-Fi. Oil-filled radiators keep it cosy. Cost: £37.00 per person, per night without breakfast. Although Lavander Cottage is close to beautiful countryside, Leeds and Manchester are only 40 minutes away. We do NOT accept pets. Contact Janet at JJackson65@googlymail.com

Chloë gives it the thumbs up, presses a few more buttons and we're live! It's £27.00 a year to host our site and ours goes straight to the top of the listings on the accommodation page!

I sit in all day waiting for a response, eating through a giant bag of Furrows – cheese and pickled onion crisps – and watching the international athletics. I remember one year when Usain Bolt came third in the 100 metres and got a standing ovation. It was his last race, and he was retiring at the age of thirty. I felt so sorry for the people getting first and second. What was the point of beating the fastest man in the world, if he only had to get third and the crowd still preferred him? That's the power of personality.

I've never been troubled by personality. I mean, I've never overpowered anyone, or a room, or an event with my charisma. Not that I know of. Except maybe for that one time at the PTFA ladies' night, when Maureen had deliberately spiked my rum and Coke with a triple helping of rum and I got everyone dancing to Ariana Grande's 'Dangerous Woman'.

No responses to the advert yet.

I'm midway through a coffee and walnut cake bake. Ever since I bought this glass dome cake stand from Sainsbury's, I feel that I've got to make something to go in it. When I come in from work and there's a home-made something under that dome, it's as if I've got my priorities right in life (cake being very near the top).

Right this moment I'm having fun, singing along to Abba, smashing walnuts into pieces in a plastic bag with my rolling pin to the beat of 'Money, Money, Money' when Maureen floats in. She's on the phone, and Harvey the cat is so entranced by the train on her rainbow lace dress that he sticks his claws into it and ends up being dragged along behind her until she comes to a halt at the fridge. She turns down the music and shoos off Harvey.

'You've got a booking for Friday through till Sunday.' She hands me the phone.

'Eh? What? Who?' I listen to it. There's no one there.

'Through HebWeb,' she tells me. 'You were too busy cavorting to Abba to hear your phone. It's a bloke called Nick and his partner Fergus. They're walking the Calderdale Way and need accommodation for two nights. They'll arrive at four.'

'I... oh. When?'

'Friday through till Sunday. Nick and Fergus. Arriving at four. OK? I've said you'll text them. Last number dialled. All right, Little Miss Landlady?'

'Yes, fantastic.'

'It seems that your "Money, Money, Money" incantation brought speedy dividends.'

'Incantation?'

'You were bellowing to the universe, Janet, it heard you.'

I've been in text communication with Nick, and we've agreed a round sum of £70 a night instead of £74, and he'll BACS the money the day they arrive. I prep the cottage but, this time, try not to go overboard. I can't decide whether to make up one bed – the double – or supply bedding for two. Would it seem rude or lazy to only make up one bed? What if they sleep apart? Some couples do. In the end, I make up both the double bed and one of the new single beds in the same bedroom. If they don't like it, they can always tell me and I'll make up the sofa bed for one of them.

I buy a nice loaf, a block of butter and some milk, make sure there's coffee and teabags and sugar, snip a few jolly daisies out of the garden and stick them in a jug on the kitchen table, then spray a bit of polish into the air – an old cleaning lady trick – and we're done.

At 4.05 p.m. Nick and Fergus pull up in an old Saab and park on the road. *Ping!* There's a notification on my phone – I've just been paid £140. The chaps wander down the drive with a couple of bags. I pop my head out of the door.

'Hello, and welcome to Lavander Cottage. The door is unlocked, ready for you, and the key is just inside on the little table.'

'Lovely, thank you.'

They go into the cottage, and it's not until a quarter to eleven on Sunday morning that I see them again when one of them puts a bin bag outside. Ten minutes later, they head down the drive with their bags in tow. Out I pop.

'Everything been OK?'

'Lovely, thank you.'

As soon as the Saab pulls away I'm in, not sure what to expect. The milk is half used, the bread and butter unopened. An empty bottle of red wine, a cardboard collection of soup cartons and an M&S ginger cake box stand on the table. Some washing-up rests on the draining board. Towels are left in the shower. Everywhere else is immaculate. I find a woolly grey sock and a tube of heel balm under the sofa, decide they've both seen better days and that I'll throw them away rather than stick them in the post. Upstairs, both beds are rumpled.

Nervously, I open the guest book.

Lovely stay, thank you. Nick & Fergus. Plus a little doodle of two footprints and countryside.

I've stripped the beds, got my first wash on and am enjoying a slice of toast from the artisan loaf and it's only 11.45 a.m. My bank account is £140 better off, and I'm browsing cruise brochures by midday. This B&B lark is the best decision I've ever made ever. Hurrah!

• •

TIPS FOR RUNNING A B&B

How do you let people know your B&B exists? Website? Cards? Ads? All of the above?

You think B&B, but you might be happier letting the place 'self-catering'.

Always check under beds for leftovers. *There will be something.*

Try to establish sleeping arrangements in advance – save on the washing.

Give yourself a pat on the back. You did it!

CHAPTER 5

Booking No. 3: The Croatians

THE CROATIANS ARE COMING!
Today, out of the blue, an email from someone called Hans.

Can you accommodate three Croatian workers for three weeks?
Working locally. Start Thursday. How much would this cost?

I email him straight back. *Yes, I can. I'll work something out re cost and be back in touch.*

I'm on reception at work and am so keyed up that I mix up Isabelle Young and Alan Bishop's next appointments. I have to ring them both back and apologise after I realise I've booked Isabelle in for root canal treatment with Miles when she's had dentures for over ten years.

I text Chloë for advice. *What shall I say?*

She's back like lightning, I hope it was in her break time.

£37 pp x 3 = £111 per night x 21 nights = £2,331. Discount £231 for long bking? Suggest £2,100 total in advance.

I email with just that, and Hans is back in half an hour over email to confirm the booking.

You should arrive after two, I respond. Then I remember: *It's not a B&B*, I add quickly.

OK.

I write back. *I look forward to meeting you, Hans.*

He responds, *No, I'm not coming. I live in Croatia.*

OK. Who is coming?

Three guys. Good guys.

I write back, *Thank you.*

I daren't send him anything else. It might feel like harassment. And then, moments later, I get a notice from PayPal. I've just been paid £2,100! It's too good to be true. Now I'm really nervous. I email him again. *No pets.*

He emails back. *No pets. No worries.*

Three Croatian men are now living in the garage. They turn up in a taxi, all carrying large sports holdalls. I do a bit of showing round, they look at me through their eyebrows, and only one of them seems to speak a little English. The nonspeaking other two throw themselves down on the sofa and switch on the TV, so it doesn't feel appropriate to run through the leaflets of things to do in Hebden.

I've bought them an artisan loaf, some carnations, a pot of apricot jam, some milk and butter. I'd topped up the tea, coffee and sugar and done them one of my fruit cakes and a biscuit barrel of English classics: the bourbon, the fig roll, the Jammie Dodger and the custard cream. I am showing these to Diain, at least that's what I think he is called, when I hear the *tish* of a can being opened and glance over to see that both the big other one and the little other one are gulping from cans of foreign lager and starting to roll cigarettes. CIGARETTES! Inside the cottage! My insides curdle. What did the advert say? THEY CAN'T SMOKE IN THE COTTAGE! But I never actually put it in the ad. It's my fault, I'll have to live with it.

'No smoking in cottage.'

I blurt it out, and they all turn and stare at me like they understand English all of a sudden. A very fast conversation breaks out between them all, and I can tell it is not very jolly.

'Thank you. If you need anything,' I gabble, 'let me know, I'm just next door.'

I get out of there, run back to the house and hide in the living room. I'm sucking up big breaths of adrenalin from the sheer fear of what has happened. After a minute or two, I realise that Maureen is perched in the corner staring out into the garden.

I am shaking as I tell her, 'They're here.'

'Are they good-looking?'

'They're scary.'

'Ooh – I like a challenge.'

'Maureen.'

'*Mitzi.*'

'Guess what? I've told them off for smoking.' I gulp just thinking about it.

'Good for you.'

I can tell she is feeling mischievous, as she wanders over to lean against the mantelpiece so she can stare at me. I know these moods. I need to quickly deflect her on to her favourite subject: herself.

'Why are you interested anyway? I thought you were making another go of it with Peter?'

'We've drifted apart. He's far too dull, we've nothing in common. He's actually much more your type.'

'Thank you and no, thank you.'

'He actually prefers the name *Maureen*,' she says with a hiss.

I recognise that this is a serious 'thou-shalt-not-pass' moment for my sister. She wheels around to me and really starts paying attention, which is not good. I am already weak from the confrontation with the Croatians, and I think she can sense it, so she is taking her moment to go in for the kill.

'It's not natural,' she lets rip. 'How long has it been since you had sex? Your joints will seize up. If you're gay, you can just say so. I certainly wouldn't be surprised, and you'll get plenty of love in Hebden. I'd turn myself, if I could. Life would be so much easier if I didn't love cock so much.'

'Maureen, do you mind! I'm trying to relax in here. Where's the paper? Honestly, I don't want to hear about your sex life.'

I've just about had enough for today. I go into the kitchen and pull the *Mail* out of the bread bin. Too bad if she sees me reading it. She can groan all she wants. It's my home: I should be able to read and enjoy whatever I want. I pay to keep the roof over all our heads. I return to the living room, put my feet on the pouffe and settle down to try and concentrate on an article about Selina Scott's date night with Trump. But there's no escape.

'It's clinically proven that regular sex helps keep you supple.'

'Thank you. I find cod liver oil works very well indeed.'

'I've not told Peter yet. I've nothing else going on, you know. It keeps me busy whilst I decide my next move.'

I know she is tormenting me now with her moral laxity. It's something she has always done, and it's never failed to touch a nerve. I can't decide if I am jealous or repulsed. Maureen has always provoked these responses in me, and I can't hold back like I might in company. This is sibling stuff, and it just comes out.

'Poor Peter,' I murmur to myself.

'What? *Poor Peter!* I'm not twisting his arm, Janet. Nice dinner, wine, come round to mine. We're both grown-ups. What's the issue?'

'You don't love him?'

'No.'

'In your head, you've split up with him?'

'More or less, yes.'

'And you can still go ahead, and...?'

'Sleep with him, Janet? Yes. We're not in the 1950s, love, I'm not a virgin and I do have needs. In fact, I'm going to drop by Lavander Cottage to borrow some milk and check out the Latvians.'

'Croatians.'

'Yes. Dirty, brutish East Europeans, sexually deprived, strong and gagging-for-it physical labourers. Just my type.'

'This week,' I say.

I don't know where it comes from, but it pops out and it surprises us both. She was hoping to shock me. Instead, for once, I have shocked her. It makes us both laugh. In fact, we are howling around the room. We end up hanging off each other with laughter.

Maureen drives me absolutely mad. But I love my crazy big sister. I really do.

It's on the news that the government are going to get tough on big business for not paying tax. I think about the £80 cash I made out of the Turners and the £140 from Nick and Fergus, and my stomach turns. I've just had £2,100 go into my account: how will I pay tax on it? I decide to put half of it away, just in case, for when the tax man comes. Then they say Amazon got a £1.3 billion tax rebate last year. I cannot remember ever getting a tax rebate. There was that one time when I got a cheque from HMRC for £0.03 and Franklin pinned it up above the calendar for a joke. One. three billion seems like an awful lot of money to me. It's a lot of bunion operations.

The Croatians have been in the cottage all day today. They don't work at weekends, so they are smoking out of the windows and mooching at the door, puffing away angrily. It's not been very good weather either, so their collars are up, and I've even seen them in hats. If I am in the kitchen when I hear the cottage door open, I have to sneak away into another room. It's not much of a head turn for them to be able to stare straight into the kitchen if they look from the cottage door and, I have to be honest, they're an intimidating group. They are impervious to pleasantries, sullen-looking and they never smile. I keep trying.

'Good morning. This rain!' I gesture at the skies. 'It's meant to clear up a bit this afternoon.'

I say this to the small one. He barely acknowledges me, and the cigarette butt drops involuntarily from his mouth to the ground, where he eliminates it with a twist of his heel before he slopes back into the B&B. Honestly. Do they hate life? Are they suffering from war trauma? Is their job horrible? Or is it personal to me? Why does so much sex traffic come from Eastern Europe? Why don't their mothers bring them up to smile? Rude. Arrogant. Beastly.

The whole thing gives me food for thought. I have so many nice men I say hello to, but sex doesn't come into it. Maybe that's me: I'm not sexy stuff. I'm solid stuff. I'm a steady size 12 and often have to buy a 14 because I'm top-heavy. I once had my colours done by a friend of Maureen's called Leanne Buttle. She was swathed in a lilac shawl in the middle of summer. The colour might have suited her normally, but she was so red in the face, it being one of the hottest days of the year, and a bit worse for wear on Prosecco, that lilac didn't do it for her that day.

'You're a classic ingénue,' she told me, 'on the yellow end of caramel, olives, creams. All the neutrals.'

'Bland... that just about sums it up.' Maureen was watching us from the sofa with a mojito on the go.

'Thank you, Maureen, there's nothing bland about olive,' I countered. My sister had been in one of her moods that day from the off.

'There's nothing exciting about it either.'

'I work in a dentist's surgery, remember, and the patients aren't looking for thrills. They want a calm, pleasant receptionist with some nice neutral...'

'Just dull. Do me, Leanne, and even if you think neutral, please don't say it. I'm a fuchsia-pink and lime-green kind of spirit, so forget colouring, think personality. I've actually got one.'

And I don't? Just so you know, I have grey-green eyes and quite long lashes of which I'm proud. I'm forty-four and I don't feel old. Apart from a bit of knee squeaking when I squat down to weed in the garden and an ankle that rattles like a bag of marbles on a long ramble, I'm doing OK. I still colour my hair a soft caramel brown (Leanne would approve of the caramel, since according to her it's one of my colours), and I will continue with that, I've decided, as long as I've hair to colour.

There are a lot of go-greyers in Hebden; it's a pretty widespread movement. I once made the mistake of booking into Terrafunda, the hairdressers, when Justin at Curl Up 'n' Dye was booked solid for two weeks because of a rash of divorce parties. Well, the Terrafunda experience was initially very nice, with tea in china cups and some lovely magazines. Then I noticed quite a lot of youngish-looking female stylists there who had let their hair go grey. And they looked terrific – being tall, skinny model types. As they scrabbled around to find my colour then gently, then quite persistently, went on to tell me about the power of silver and the poison that infiltrates the brain every time a dye is applied, it dawned on me that I was, well, in a cult of grey. Talk about fifty shades, I noticed three: salt and pepper – suits no one; growing out – suits no one; then those stunning model types with silver hair so platinum it was blonde – really, who were they kidding? Guess what, they were gorgeous, and it suited them. I was the only person in there with dyed brown hair.

It gave me a flashback to when I took Chloë to a baby yoga class in Hebden. We were all laughing and getting on great with our cute little babies in their cute Babygros, then we popped them out and laid them in front of us, and silence dropped like a stone. Chloë was the only baby there in a disposable nappy. Worse, a Jessie-from-*Toy-Story* nappy. The rest of them were wearing huge terry towelling things, the type my mum used to have to wash by hand in the 1970s. All those poor, right-on little babies with nappy rash so sore and red they looked like burn victims, and Chloë gurgling away with a bottom as soft and smooth as two rosy apples. Well, those right-on mums hated me, because they were desperate to run and buy a 48-pack of disposables and sleep well again, but peer pressure and the tyranny of the fascist left, well, it runs deep round here. When the break came, I was out of there. The semicircle of ladies and the rush to get the boobs out was horribly intimidating; the cloud of

43

disapproval from the nappy would be nothing compared to the hate that would come my way at the sight of my contented, chubby baby guzzling on a bottle of formula, as they wrestled with tiny, underweight, hangry babies.

And here at Curl Up 'n' Dye, I'd done it again. I'd stumbled on a Hebden let's-go-back-to-the-old-ways cult. Not necessarily the good ways, just the old ways, as if the old ways hold special virtue. I couldn't wait to get out of there, even when they suggested that they left my hair curly.

'You have a great, natural curl. Let's leave it to do its own thing, shall we?'

That was when I turned around to my stylist and said, 'Thanks, Prudence, but if I'm paying fifty-three quid I want it caramel brown and straightened until it's burnt to a crisp, please.'

I remember how she laughed very nervously and went off to chat to her salt-and-pepper crew-mates before returning with a dusty pair of straighteners.

If I open a window in the kitchen these days, I can literally hear the Croatians light up, and then I have to rush over and close the window to avoid their smoke drifting in. Closing a window and dropping a blind every time they open the door feels so unwelcoming. I've taken to microwaving half cups of tea, as it's faster than making a new one, and we're all snacking rather than cooking. It's not good. I must make an effort to cook a meal this week. I'm also, come dusk, surreptitiously wandering onto the drive and collecting the scatterings of home-made cigarette butts they have discarded with bitter flicks. Well, that's what I imagine they are doing. I think maybe they wouldn't have come here, had they known they couldn't smoke inside Lavander Cottage. I feel bad about that. Especially as I listen to the forecast tonight and apparently we're due squally wind and rain for the week.

It's a pretty dull Saturday night, and I'm feeling a bit down. Chloë is out, Maureen is out, and I wonder why I am all by myself with no plans. I need to do something about it. Time passes. Eventually I go upstairs to bed, and Chloë doesn't return home until after 2 a.m. I go downstairs and check that the door is locked after I hear her come in. I assume that my sister is spending the night at Peter's. It's tiring being the boring security guard, so if she's forgotten her key, it's tough.

Sunday is a whirl of washing and cleaning. Looking after the cottage has taken up a lot of time recently, and I've neglected our home. I can tell by the build-up of limescale in the bathroom and the dust on the bedside table. Eventually I feel that I've done enough to justify a rest. I relax in front of *Countryfile* with my feet in the Scholl vibrating footbath, determined to use up some out-of-date lemon verbena essential oil, on the principle that use-by dates are just a ruse to make us buy more. In this case I'm not completely sure, given that the smell coming from the footbath is quite a pungent pong, but I have been battling a verruca.

I notice, for the first time, that John Craven is looking older these days. Maybe all that fresh air has weathered him and he's actually younger than he looks? He has been around for ever. He was a grown-up when my mum was alive and still cooking tea for us. I suppose I've known him that long he's like an old friend. I've seen him more often than many of my extended family and, truth be told, he seems a lot nicer than most of them.

I drift through the 'Museum Collection' brochure online and ask myself if I can justify treating myself to a wool shawl inspired by a tapestry design from 1927 by Gunta Stölzl, the German textile designer and first female master of the Bauhaus School. It is £75, which isn't cheap, and if I splash out on that I'll also need to buy the *How to Tie a Scarf* book at £7.99.

All in all, I'm enjoying a rare moment of pure, uninterrupted pleasure when Chloë creeps in and whispers in a warning fashion: 'Mum, *LAURA's* here, she wants *a WORD*.'

Laura Watson is the glamazon from down the road; she owns the biggest new-build house in the area and throws huge parties with her extreme extrovert, barrister husband Oliver. She's a tall, perfectly toned blonde, always immaculately groomed, perfect kids tucked away at private school, and specialises in how to wear pastel pashminas. Let's put it this way: she's got every edition of the *How to Tie a Scarf* book. We don't generally pass the time of day, Laura and me. Over the years, she's discovered I never have any gossip about anyone she considers of interest. As polite as I always try to be, I realised early on that she's one of those people who *appear* very friendly but, in reality, are very judgmental. If we lived in a Russian KGB state, she's the kind of person who'd be ratting on you as fast as you could say 'sauerkraut'. What makes her dangerous is that she knows, by your refusal to engage in her gossiping ways, that *you* judge *her*. And she simply hates that. So, I have always felt with Laura: *approach with caution*.

Anyway, I take my feet out of the footbath and, as I've forgotten to bring a towel downstairs, I have to wipe them on the rug. So now the rug will smell of lemon verbena and I'll catch a verruca every time I step on it. I struggle into my flip-flops and lurch to the front door.

'Hi, Laura. Everything OK?' I enquire, fake smile plastered to my face.

'I'm good, thank you, Janet. I need to talk to you about something.'

By her face, I know this isn't chit-chat. She sniffs like a bloodhound and there isn't even an attempt at a smile.

'Do come in.' I open the door wider.

I'm flailing. What is she after? I don't want her in the living room where the evidence of a crumpled packet of Jammie Dodgers is there for all to see. I haven't cleared up after Sunday dinner, so the kitchen isn't the best either.

'Come through, I'm just tidying up.'

'Who is it?' Maureen leans over the banister. '*Oh, hello, Laura. Happy New Year.*'

Laura cranes to look up and, on spotting Maureen, her manner takes on an inescapable air of chilliness.

'It's May.'

'I don't let time dictate my chance to spread happiness, Laura.'

'Of course *you* don't. Thank you.' She says the words through barely gritted teeth and struggles to maintain her snidey charm. I feel quite worried. Has Maureen done something to offend Laura? It's a terrible conclusion to jump to, but Laura wouldn't be the first married woman we've had turn up on the doorstep looking for blood.

I usher her out of the hall, away from Maureen, who is hanging over the banister making the sort of face a baboon would be proud of. Having taken Laura into the kitchen, I pull out a chair and point it at the garden to avoid her having to stare at the half-eaten shepherd's pie on the table. I begin to collect plates and attempt to be as graceful and noiseless as possible. Unfortunately, I manage to drop a fork full of mash on the floor that splodges very close to Laura's suede camel Footglove shoe.

'Sorry. How can I help, Laura?'

'It's been my intention to come and speak to you, Janet, for a few days now. I've been keeping my eyes on things and reviewing the situation and, having done a little bit of research, I thought it appropriate to draw your attention to the fact you've no planning permission.'

'Sorry, you what?'

I am crouched, fork in hand. I carefully scoop up the mash and, balancing precariously, I struggle to get myself up and place it on the plate on the table. I swear I can hear my own heartbeat even over the creaks of my knees.

'What was that, Laura?' I repeat breathlessly.

Laura is gloating, like Queen Boudicca sat in her kitchen chair chariot, and I can tell she is ready to move in for the kill.

'I have seen not one, Janet, but *two* white van men parked on the street for the last two weeks. You've made no endeavours to intervene, and I have been faced with insolent, unresponsive behaviour from the people driving these vehicles. I don't know where they come from, or whether they can even read, but I've left three notes on their windscreen asking them to explain why they are parking there. No response. Nothing. I watched and, at first, I assumed they must be friends of "Mitzi's", she gives a tinkling laugh, 'but there's two of them together, and even your sister...' She leaves a long pause. Read into that what you will, but the long and the short of it is: Maureen's a tart but not *that* much of a tart. The hackles on the back of my neck are rising, the cheeky cowbag.

'Anyway, I watch them, Janet, and they are not coming into your house but heading down to your garage.'

The Croatians. Lavander Cottage. It is dawning on me.

'And they are clearly staying there.' Her face is turning red. 'There are lights on and they come and go in working hours, and they're clearly staying there and, well...'

'Yes?'

'And having done some research, I can see on the Calderdale planning portal that you haven't applied for planning permission for your B&B business, Janet. It's just not appropriate to simply set up a business in a residential area without thinking about other residents and the impact on this area with parking facilities and the types of people you might attract alongside the type of people who actually pay their taxes to live here.'

I don't have words. Not good ones. This is where Maureen would come in handy.

'They're going soon,' I pathetically counter, but she is in full flow.

'I didn't want to complain formally before I'd given you a chance to explain. I certainly wasn't worried about telling you to your face. Anyway, there you have it. I'm contacting the council tomorrow. And if you can ask them to stop expectorating into the drain? Many thanks. I'll leave you to your cleaning up, Janet.'

She stands up, glances around with disdain, and brushes her hands across her immaculate, dove-grey trousers to dismiss any invisible crumbs before readjusting her camel pashmina to be even more effortlessly organised around her neck.

'I'll see myself out.'

She needs to. I can't stand up. Round one: Janet Jackson out for the count. Laura Watson wins.

'The nosy bitch!'

I can always rely on Maureen to cut to the nub of things, especially when she's on her sixth glass of Prosecco.

'I'll give her uptight arse a kicking that will see her into next year, never mind tomorrow, the interfering cow.'

Maureen is miming to the laundry basket the kicking she is going to give to Laura. I spend a moment contemplating the picture. Something is niggling at me and I have to say it.

'Maureen?'

'What?'

'You haven't slept with Oliver, have you?'

She stops kicking the basket and hovers on one leg for a moment before stamping her foot down and putting her free hand on her hip. She tips the last of her glass down her neck and adopts a suitably outraged pose.

'What? Oliver?'

'Yes.'

'Oliver Watson? Me?'

'Yes.'

(High voice) 'No!'

'R...iiight...'

Maureen makes a slow and deliberate reach for the opened bottle in the fridge, shaking her head thoughtfully all the while. Without looking, she tips it into the tilted glass, wasting a drop.

'What makes you ask that?' she says casually.

What made me ask is that I have a strong suspicion that something else is going on with Laura. That was a full-frontal attack, not her usual sneaky, insinuating style. Something's not right.

'She was so mad, it felt a bit more than just a complaint about the Croatians parking on the street.'

'Well, look, I don't *think* I've slept with Oliver.' Maureen is staring into the air, almost counting out loud on her fingers, and I knew with the word '*think*' and the body language that she probably has slept with him and that this is Laura's chance for revenge.

'Right. Because, well, she was really very determined and seemed... very bitter.'

I sit down with my big cup of tea, the cup with the watercolour painting of the glorious Victorian railway house with the dream cottage garden. I can't help but give a big sigh. Maureen dances on the spot for a moment before pulling up a chair opposite.

'Is she really going to be able to cause you problems?'

'I'm not sure.'

As she speaks, Chloë powers into the room in her unicorn onesie, her eyes only visible through a luminous green face pack. She is holding her laptop.

'Right,' she announces to us. 'We've like got this.'

'Yes!' Maureen leaps up off her chair, feels giddy and sits down again. She pokes a middle finger in the air, saying, 'Swivel on that, *bi-yatch*.'

'Go on,' I say. I'm not quite as optimistic as Maureen.

'It says you don't like need planning permission to have someone like stay in an annexe. The cottage is merely like an annexe to the main house, isn't it? It doesn't like have separate electric or anything, does it?'

'No.'

'So, exactly, it's not like a separate dwelling. And these are like only your second or third, in fact, just say they're like your first guests, and get onto the council like first thing and see what they say. She can't do anything if it's like an annexe.'

'Right. Thanks, love.' I give her a kiss.

'You're a genius, Chloë, love,' Maureen says loudly. 'Screw you, Laura chuffin' uptight arsehole. Who does she think she is, snooty arsey bitch? I remember her when she was sucking Bobby Phelan off round the back of the Old Crown.'

'Lovely. That's lovely, Maureen,' I interrupt quickly. 'Enough of a trip down memory lane for one night.'

Chloë grins at me and mimes glass to mouth. I wonder if growing up with a verging-on-the-alcoholic auntie will scare her off booze for life or provide her with useful don't-do-this experience. Oh God, please don't let me have broken the law.

I spend ten minutes slowly demolishing a loaf of bread, turning it into hot, buttered toast, convincing myself I'm just having a bit of supper. After a Sunday dinner? With a crumble to finish? I'm in full panic-eat mode.

Approaching bedtime, Maureen wanders in dressed for bed in a silky, full-length, grey dressing gown and matching silk nightie. She watches me, as I chew my way, inch by inch, through the loaf.

'Christmas party, couple of years ago.'

'What?' I nearly choke.

'Thinking about it. Like I said, it was two or three years ago now. We were both drunk...'

I feel my stomach clench. This is the confession. I hate stories that Maureen begins with 'We were both drunk...'

'Did she catch you at it?'

'Oh no.' Maureen cackles. 'It was over way too fast. Just a Christmas quickie in the conservatory, against the steamed-up windows, me in my naughty elf outfit and him in his Secret Santa. It was romantic, the Christmas lights reflecting off the ceiling and lovely choral music playing.'

'Yes, that would have been the kids from the primary school in the other room. It was a fundraiser for Liberian orphanages.'

'Yes, that's right.' The morality of shagging the host's husband whilst a children's choir belt out 'Little Donkey' is entirely lost on my sister.

'Well, she's obviously found out or had her suspicions.'

'How? He wouldn't say; he doesn't want to be found out. You know he's texted and asked me three times since to meet up with him, and I've always refused, *because he's married.*'

'Well done, Maureen.'

'Yes, I think so. I'm not just a quick shag. I'm after something much more meaningful.'

'I know you are.'

'OK. I'm off to bed if the interrogation is over. Goodnight, Janet.'

'Yep,' I say. 'Night night.'

'Janet?'

'Yes, Maureen?'

'I think Peter does actually really like you.'

'I'm not interested.'

'I know you're not. But he talks about you a lot. If you happened to go into the library and he did, say, ask you out, I wouldn't be bothered. At all. In fact, I'm seeing a bloke from the Bull at the moment and, to be honest, it would help me out 'cos Peter's the type... he doesn't know how to be cruel to be kind, you know what I mean? He can't say "I don't want to be with you" 'cos he's scared of hurting my feelings, and, well, I'm not hurt. I'm relieved, 'cos he's not my type at all, as you know. And, well, he's really your type.'

'OK. Right. Thanks. I'll bear it in mind.'

Classic Maureen. She causes me inescapable amounts of aggro and somehow transforms a confession that's caused me this aggro into a situation where she is actually doing me a favour. So, out of the generosity of her heart, she'll organise something for me that I don't even want, which is actually, on reflection, getting me to clean up some other mess she's got herself involved with.

My sister is wasted as a lazy hippy. She should be a member of some diplomatic team or a political whip or a spin doctor or something, because she is one skilful operator.

What a day. I'm totally unravelled and spend ten minutes staring into space trying to unpack my thoughts. I've been a B&B

owner for exactly six weeks. Now it's probably going to be over. Three years working up to it, three bookings, six weeks and we're done. I still owe £24,860. I'm going to be working, flogging my guts out, until I'm eighty.

After I've done all the washing-up and put the footbath away and dragged myself up to bed, I lie there in the dark and the quiet. Unaccountably, the worries and many reasons to be anxious vanish, and the person I see when I close my eyes is... Peter.

. . . .

TIPS FOR RUNNING A B&B

Assuming you don't want smokers, put NO SMOKING in any advertising.

You won't get on with every guest. Tell yourself that's OK.

Crikey, who knew? Planning permission *is a thing*. You might have to check if you need some.

Are you on good terms with your neighbours? It might help if you are.

CHAPTER 6

Maureen is up very early for Maureen and has positioned herself behind the curtain in the living room so she can stare at the road without being spotted.

'They've gone. I'm going in.'

She is wearing head-to-toe black; a jersey catsuit with matching gloves and soft-soled trainers. She comes back minutes later, speaking with a throaty rasp and sounding like a cross between Humphrey Bogart and a Siberian husky.

'You better get in here, sweetheart.'

It feels so wrong sneaking in, even though it's technically my garage/cottage. To make it feel more appropriate, we take three clean bath towels and a change of bedding. I've decided that once is enough to change their sheets, halfway during the three-week period, but I will change their towels more often. I have supplied two huge towels per huge Croatian so far. If Laura is calling in the full force of the law, we need to make sure the cottage is respectable. And, oh my, respectable it's not. There are large Tupperware tubs everywhere, full to the brim with tobacco. They don't need to smoke it, they're farming the ruddy stuff. A tobacco factory in Hebbleroyd! The headlines don't bear thinking about. 'Suburban Ciggie Scandal', 'Janet the Joint', 'Life at Jackson High-ts.'

I feel sick imagining Laura Watson's smug face, as I'm handcuffed, hands behind my back, and pushed out into the street, head down into the back of a police van. I wander around the place contemplating the scandal and the clean-up; the place stinks of Old Holborn, ham and stale sweat. Just contemplating the state of the place makes me break out into a sweat. I go to the biscuit barrel, hoping for a sympathy fig roll. Empty. But I notice my fruit cake is untouched.

Maureen is pacing around amongst the debris. She says, 'No sign of any class A drugs.'

She is in full detective mode. I've no idea what she is on about, as she heads up the stairs, brandishing a rolling pin.

'CHECK THIS OUT!' she bawls.

I don't want to. I follow her nervously up the stairs into the bedroom. The smell coming from the room is intense and it isn't wafting from my rose bowl of potpourri, which I notice is kicked under the single bed. I wonder if these three big men take turns at sleeping in the double bed? Instead, on the chest of drawers, is a machine that resembles something out of a medieval torture museum. On further inspection, it becomes clear that it is a giant cigarette-rolling machine. Piled up around it on the floor are boxes and boxes and boxes of expertly rolled cigarettes, boxes of packed ones, and what looks like a dozen pairs of dirty boxers. The room resembles, for all intents and purposes, the stock cupboard of a 1980s Best's Stationary store. I know because I worked in one. Briefly.

I was thirteen and technically shouldn't have been there. As it was, I looked older and nodded enthusiastically when the manager Darren asked me if I was seventeen. *We needed the money.* There had been a rash of concerts in Huddersfield, the latest being a Soup Dragons gig that we were desperate to get to – well, Maureen was desperate to get to and I quite fancied it. I lasted five weeks at Best's before Jerry, the area manager, turned up and appeared to have a mini stroke when he saw me behind the counter serving the bus station alcoholic, Curly, with twenty Benson & Hedges.

'How old is she, Darren?'

I looked up and saw a large, sweaty man, holding his chest, leaning against the stack of the *Daily Mirror*.

Beside me, I felt Darren shrug. He was leaning over and filling up the boxes of chocolate bars at the front of the counter.

'Er, hi Jerry. I dunno exactly. Janet, how old are you, love?'

'Thirteen.'

'THIRTEEN!' Jerry now holds his chest, as Marathon chocolate bars topple out of their box.

'How was I supposed to know?' Darren says, looking shocked.

'Because she's wearing a motherfucking school uniform!' Jerry explodes, his face puce.

Curly the tramp jumps into the conversation at this point. 'Excuse me, but can you mind your language, please, young man.

This young lady *is only thirteen.'*

Jerry looks mortified, as does Darren, who's trying to recover himself.

'I j-just thought she'd made the effort to look smart,' he stutters.

'She does look smart,' Curly nods. 'In fact, she's the smartest one in here.'

Jerry is now raging. 'Well, yes, she will do, 'cos *SHE'S GOT A BLOODY PREFECT BADGE ON!*'

'No surprise there,' Curly says sagely. 'She actually has the best customer service skills. She's polite and accurate with the change. I've been coming into this store every day for the last three years, and she's by far the most pleasant and competent member of staff I've had dealings with.'

Darren, on Jerry the area manager's insistence, accompanies Curly the tramp out of the shop. They then bundle me off with £10 extra pay and make me promise never to tell anyone what I'd been doing. I was fine with that. The money was enough to get us to the concert, and Maureen got an autograph and a kiss from Sean Dickson. I liked the Best's Stationery & News job. You met a lot of interesting people. Maureen was always trying to persuade me to steal her some Silk Cut, but I was having none of that. Nowadays, I dare say I'd be something you'd share on social media: the school kid, serving the homeless man cigarettes. You could get away with so much more in those days.

'What do we do?'

This from Maureen who always has an opinion on everything so, coming from her, this indecision is unusual. Even she is looking taken aback by the scale of the factory premises we are housing. She picks up a box of the cigarettes, as if she is going to spirit it into her pocket, then has second thoughts and puts it back.

'I don't know,' I tell her, realising we can't very well change the beds now. The Croatians mustn't know we've been in here.

'I know – refer to the handbook.'

'Maureen, there isn't a handbook for dealing with a Croatian cigarette factory.'

'OK. We leave now. They won't know we've been here. They've no reason to suspect we know anything.'

We're both a little rattled and nervous and bickering about

whether we've left any traces of our presence. I spot that Maureen has left a long hair on one of the pillowcases and, both panicking a bit, we lock up at speed and creep back home.

Though we don't let on, we are both of us loitering, hiding together in the living room, waiting for something to happen. Nothing happens. Except Maureen finds a bottle of wine behind the sofa. There's no post and no phone calls. We are still lurking in the living room when Chloë comes home from school. She walks into the living room accompanied by a tall, good-looking lad who has the start of a moustache growing on his lip. Maureen smiles brightly at him, and Chloë positions herself in front of him so Maureen can no longer make direct eye contact. I try to appear relaxed on the sofa, feeling conspicuous with nothing on the TV and six empty packets of Seabrook crinkle cut, cheese and onion lying between us.

'Hello, love, good day at school? Who's your friend?'

'OK. Greg. What's up? What are you doing?' Her eyes have narrowed.

'Nothing. We've been doing nothing. We've just been talking and things.'

'Oh, right. Did you speak to the planning office?'

'No, not today, it's been hectic round here.'

The bottle rolls out from under the sofa.

Maureen and I exchange looks. Maureen bursts out laughing. Chloë shakes her head and pushes the young man out of the room. I'm tempted to get up and follow her, but I stand up and feel a bit wobbly, so I sit down again.

Chloë puts her head back round the door and hisses, 'Thanks, Mum, for embarrassing me in front of Greg.'

'I didn't know Greg was coming.'

She hard stares at me, as she leaves the room. Moments later she shouts through the door, 'I suppose that is all the cheese and onion gone?'

My nerves are jangling. I feel very shamefaced. Maureen picks up two empty packets and dances around as if she's wielding handkerchiefs in a Morris dance.

'Cheese and onion, cheese and onion, ten bags full and now they're empty, cheese and onion. Come on! Saddleworth playing field, 1984.'

I grab a couple of packets, and we perform a little reel that we did oh so long ago. Midway through, I realise that Chloë has stuck her head round the door and is not looking impressed. I sit back down immediately.

'Sorry, love,' I say breathlessly.

But she's gone.

We are still camped in the living room and nervously eating our way through the entire contents of the biscuit tin when the Croatians arrive back from work. We sneak our way into the kitchen and loiter out of sight of their front door. Would they know we've been in? Would they be out in five minutes knocking down our door? It would be OK as long as we were together. I could face them down with Maureen next to me. We decide that if we have to challenge them, and it does get nasty, Maureen, who was a women's self-defence teacher at one point, will elbow them in the face while I shove Vim in their eyes.

Nothing happens. They don't come back out. By 8.30 p.m. I am exhausted by the effort of doing nothing. It must be how Maureen feels most of the time. The wine doesn't help. It really knocks it out of you.

Greg leaves at 8.45 p.m. I don't introduce myself and hope Chloë will forgive me. I am in bed for ten past nine, browsing websites for illegal tobacco farms. I find a June Crawford from Craven in Wharfedale, aged forty-nine. In 1992, she got nine years suspended sentence for intent to supply. I'm not anticipating sweet dreams tonight.

The next morning, I wake up early and strip the bed, and have the washing hanging out to dry by the time I leave. I walk into work today along the canal. The Canada goose population has got bigger every year and it's a crush pushing past them all, plus there are a few nasty hisses as they get territorial around the dot-to-dot of nests perched precariously on the canal bank. The higgledy-piggledy canal barges and boats moored up along the route, lots of them puffing out woodsmoke from the chimneys, is very picturesque, and even with all the worry of Laura and the Croatians, I can't help but feel a glimmer of satisfaction about living in such a beautiful place. It will all be OK. I could sell everything if the lawsuit gets expensive and probably afford two barges, one for me and Chloë, and one for Maureen. It might need to be three; Chloë is getting to that age. Look at the size of Greg, he's a young man.

Work is a doddle, for a change. There is one cancellation and a no-show before lunch. I am looking at a two-hour window, which is lovely, because I can now obsess over the webpage Chloë has built for Lavander Cottage. I'm glued to it, and mid-morning we have an email through the website requesting accommodation for spring bank holiday. I um and ah but say no, as they want to bring a supposedly 'very well-behaved terrier'. No pets!

I read an article in *Good Health*. It's a definite advantage to working there – free access to up-to-date magazine subscriptions. Anyway: mindset. Success or failure in life is all about mindset. So, I muster up my courage and, after a lot of internal pep talk, I call the planning office at Calderdale Council. By the time I've endured three puts on hold, eight minutes of Wagner's *Ring Cycle* and a surprise exchange with a lovely man, Clive, who supervises truss design, I am a broken woman.

'Hello, you're through to the planning office. Shannon speaking, how can I help?'

'Oh hello, Sharon.'

'It's Shannon.'

'Sorry, Shannon.'

'It's fine, go ahead. Can I ask who's calling?'

'Yes. Janet. I'm Janet.'

'OK, Janet.'

I'm a receptionist. I know myself what a nightmare it is on the phone. I've had so many occasions when the client is so softly spoken, or the phone line so bad, you're shouting at them to speak up. So why I have to turn into a moron at this point I do not know. Then I remember: *positive mindset.*

'Hello, Shannon, I'm Janet. There's outline planning permission on my garage.'

'OK. Can I stop you there? What's the postcode, Janet? Do you have a surname?'

'Yes, I have a surname.'

'Great. What is it? It will help with the search.'

'OK. Of course. Sorry. Jackson.'

'Great. Jackson. Janet Jackson. Oh, ha! I can see why you didn't want to tell me now. "I'm Janet from the Block". I bet you get that all the time.'

I can't risk offending her. It's *not* a Janet Jackson song. Over the years, for obvious reasons, I have become fully acquainted with every song in Ms Jackson's catalogue, and 'Jenny from the Block' (not Janet) is not one of them.

'Ha, yes. Of course.'

'And your postcode?'

'HX6 5TN.'

'OK. I'm taking a look through our portal. Do you have access to a computer, Janet Jackson? I love that. "Janet Jackson on the phone, everybody!" Yes, she makes me want to scream. Not really, Janet, don't get worried. What's the issue?'

'Er...' *Positive mindset, positive mindset...* 'I bought the house a long time ago.'

'Can you speak up, Janet? It's not a great line. I'm struggling to hear you.'

'Yes, OK. Well, the house had a garage – a big garage – and it had outline planning permission to turn the garage into a granny flat. It's *definitely* an annexe, because it shares the same electricity and, well, I've made it into a granny flat now so is there anything else I need to do?'

'Mmm... let me have a look. Mmm... No, you've never had any permissions granted for a building of any sort.'

My stomach flip-flops.

'But when I bought it thirteen years ago it said on the estate agent's details that there was outline planning permission for a granny flat.'

'That's estate agent blurb. It's not here.'

'Oh.' Gulp. 'What do I do now?'

I think of the hundreds of hours of sitting on reception at Valley Dental, the thousands of pounds outlay on doing it up, the night after night spent painting, the endless conversations persuading Barry the builder to turn up and Ted the plumber to repair the boiler pump, twice. The millions of cups of tea, the weeks of surfing for cheap Velux blinds and door handles, are spinning in front of my eyes. I'm dizzy with it all. I put my head down on the reception desk and feel my cheek on the cool, melamine worktop. I'm OK. It's all going to be OK.

'Hi, Janet, you OK?'

'No.'

'What can I do to help?'

I sit up bolt upright. This isn't a conversation that is happening in my head. Standing in front of me is Peter. He is crouched down with his head cocked and a clump of hair falling across the bridge of his nose and his big, brown eyes are looking concerned, but he has a smile playing at the corner of his mouth.

'Er...'

'Hmmm. Right. OK, Janet. If you can prove it's over ten years old, you might be able to apply under retrospective development in which case you don't need approvals.'

I smile at Peter and gesture so he knows I'm on the phone. He smiles back, he points at a seat in the empty reception. I give him a thumbs up. He picks up a copy of *Men's Health*. It's a good read, that September issue. I snap out of whatever dream I am in when I realise the phone is blaring.

'Hello? Are you there, Janet? Did you get all that? You need to prove the annexe is over ten years old.'

'It's definitely over ten years old, because I've lived here thirteen years.'

'Can you prove that though?'

'Prove what?'

'That the building is over ten years old?'

'It was here when I bought the house.'

'But can you prove it?'

'I don't know. What would be proof?'

'Pictures?'

'I might have.'

'Good luck. Apply for retrospective permission through the portal.'

The phone clicks off far away. I put my phone down and smile over at Peter.

'Hello. Sorry about that. It was the council. About my garage – *cottage*. I might be in trouble.'

'Oh. I wanted to see if you fancied a cup of tea in Delish? They're doing an offer thing with two teas and a piece of cake for the price of one, and I thought, I can't drink two teas, I wonder if Janet's working today.'

'I *am* on my lunch.'

'It sounds like you need a break.'

'Yes. I'm having trouble with the council. And my neighbour. And the Croatians.'

'Sounds like you've got a lot on.'

'I have, I suppose.'

I attempt to slip my shoes on as discreetly as I can, but my feet have swollen in the heat and are resisting; it's as if I have one toe too many. I wish, wish, wish, I'd taken more notice of what I'd put on this morning. I was probably a bit hung-over, thinking about it, and had blindly reached for whatever I could find closest to hand – a white blouse and my old black cotton, knee-length skirt that's got far too many in the way of bobbles. God, I even think I have a navy bra on. *Under a white blouse.* Our grandma, who was a stickler for propriety, not being from farming stock but shopkeeping stock, well, she knew all the rules of etiquette, and a coloured bra under a white blouse is an absolute no-no.

Still, Peter doesn't seem to be bothered. He gives me a huge smile, as he opens the door for me. Though he has a crooked set of teeth at the bottom, he also has dimples when he smiles, which are, well, cute.

We share a large slice of lemon and elderflower cake and a pot of Earl Grey. His name is Peter Crouch. Like the footballer. I wouldn't have known who Peter Crouch was if it wasn't for Abbey Clancy on *Strictly*. We bond over sharing a famous surname. You have to have a strong sense of self, we agree, to not feel intimidated by the popularity of your namesake. Janet Jackson being American and a black woman helps with me, I think. There's not much in the way of comparison. I can't play or sing a note of music. I enjoy music, but unlike some people, I don't need it on all the time as a background to my life. I prefer quiet. Or birdsong. Peter is unlikely to get mistaken for Peter Crouch. He doesn't like football much. He's also a sensible size i.e. he's not too tall. His legs are not noteworthily long. He's slightly smaller than me. Shortish. He's a lovely size.

Though I make a mental note that I can't wear my wedges.

That evening, I get home and think, *What a day*. I have lunch with Peter Crouch, and I find out I might have to knock down the cottage. I don't want to demolish the garage. Please God it doesn't come to that. I feel like sending a dog poo sandwich through the door to bloody Laura Watson. Maureen is floating around at teatime looking bored. I feel guilty, and know I should tell her about Peter, but resist the urge when she opens a second bottle of Shiraz under the pretext of wanting something liquid to go with her Spanish omelette.

I have a good surreptitious stare at the cottage. Surely the Croatians will leave soon and take their dodgy tobacco with them? As for Lavander Cottage, of course it's over ten years old! It's twenty, probably thirty years old. Bits of it, such as the front bit, are probably nearer eighty years old. This is going to be easy, you can tell just by looking at it. I'll get Shannon to come and inspect it. I'm so proud of my cottage. It's lovely. Laura Watson is not going to crush my B&B dream. No one is. Not without a fight.

. . . .

TIPS FOR RUNNING A B&B

If you need to enter the property whilst guests are in, take clean towels – good cover.

Hold your nerves, wannabe B&B-ers. Remember, nothing comes easy.

CHAPTER 7

Today is Wednesday 16 May. It's Janet Jackson's birthday. I wonder if Mother was inspired to call me Janet for that reason? No, can't be. Janet wasn't in the Jackson 5, imagine that – Maureen's rage if I'd deliberately been given a pop star name. I sometimes wonder if Maureen is angry I was born. She was there enjoying all the attention and out comes Janet to steal away the glory. Not that I got much of a look-in for glory with Maureen around. She saw to that.

I seem to recall being trapped under a washing basket for quite a while, but have no specific memory of Maureen having a go at me until I was about three and a half, when she stole my Eccles cake off me. It must have been a birthday or something similar, as we didn't get Eccles cakes willy-nilly. Mother was not in the farmhouse-cook type of mould. She didn't do cake or birthdays or presents much. She couldn't get to the shops, I suppose. We were out of the way. Everything was so much effort. Shopping. Cooking. Washing. Heating. Getting us to school. Father was always so remote, busy doing something. And we were utterly and completely broke, I remember.

Look on the bright side, Janet, I tell myself. Compared to the other Janet's dad, ours was a dream. I'd rather not see my father at all than have one who beats you up until you dance well.

Maybe Maureen was pleased to have me around. At last she had a captive audience: someone to complain to, someone to pay attention to her, someone she could dress up for and show off to, an ally to plot an escape with, all from the moment I opened my eyes in the morning until we went to bed. With regard to our escape plan, we knew where we were going, and when; we simply needed to work out how we were going to get there. It was pretty blooming hard to escape from where we lived. Marsden is the last bit of Yorkshire, the very top of Huddersfield before you topple over into Lancashire. There were not a lot of buses near our farm, not a lot of anything but relentless wind, sideways rain, ice, sleet and mud made from a mixture of silage, manure and animal droppings. No wonder school wasn't the popularity contest Maureen hoped for. We stunk. It's fair to say that our parents were better with animals. They were set up for them. Looking back, I reckon we two girls were quite an inconvenience. We got in the way.

Thinking of Janet Jackson, I hope she's OK. She's gone quiet since she exposed her nipple with help from Justin Timberlake at the Super Bowl. I was working at Morrisons at the time and had to put up with a lot of sniggers.

Supervisor Adrian (nineteen) started it by approaching me very seriously in the locker room, making sure there were plenty of people around who could hear, before he loudly asked me, 'Janet, it's a family show, how could you?' followed up with, 'Janet, it's the biggest advert break on American television. What were you thinking?'

I laughed along – once I knew what they were talking about. One of the warehouse lads showed me on his phone. What did add to the tension that day, though, was that I was wearing a size 12 old C&A blouse that had two buttons straining around my chest area. After a particularly enthusiastic bit of restocking on the cereal aisle, I was a button down. I spent the rest of the week in polo necks.

But let's get back to today. I'm so glad to reach my day off. After answering two emails asking if the cottage is free for spring bank holiday, I spend all afternoon searching for proof that the garage I have walked past for thirteen years has been there ten years or more. I don't have any. I got all minimalist after the split with Franklin and threw everything away. Including the pictures of him standing in the garage next to his Ducati bike, holding his 'I just passed my bike licence' certificate with its all-important date on, there for all to see. The unfortunate fact is I have no evidence. Not a shred. The garage is not on the deeds because it's a later addition. So, it does not exist in the past, only in my everyday reality. It's as if I'm watching an episode of *Doctor Who*, where nothing makes sense, even when the plot is explained at the end. It makes me think anything could suddenly not exist if you put it through the planning test.

I pluck up courage and ring Shannon in planning.

'Hello, Shannon? It's Janet... Janet Jackson.'

'Janet, *hello*.'

She says the 'hello' in a Lionel Richie *Hellooo* way. I'm not going to point out the absurdity to her; people have strange song associations. Janet had a lot of hits in the 1980s. Plus Shannon is being friendly.

Having an infamous name, I remind myself often, is annoying but can also be very useful. There are definite positives at times like this. They help to make up for the annoying times, such as when Jim the postman starts gyrating in my face like he did this morning, singing Janet's 'What Have You Done for Me Lately?' and doing a series of 'slut drops'. I find the term pretty revolting. Chloë explained it to me when Maureen was showing off her slut drop after a jolly night out with the Hebbleroyd Women's Institute.

I don't encourage Jim, but I do let him finish the whole chorus before closing the door. It happens to be one of my favourite songs of Janet's, and one I found myself humming a lot for the last five years of my marriage.

'Hi, Shannon. Er... I'm not sure I can prove the garage, um... *cottage* has been there over ten years, except I know it has, of course, because I live next to it.'

'Apply for retrospective planning, Janet. Like I told you. Remember? Download the form from the portal. We'll send someone out to visit.'

'That's it?'

'That's it.'

'OK. Thank you very much, Shannon.'

'Coolio. And Janet...?'

'Yes?'

'Hold back on the Airbnb maybe until we get this sorted. Don't want any more complaints, eh?'

My head feels like it has just been pushed into a bucket of cold water. *Any more complaints?*

'Er... right. No. Yes. Quite so. You're right.'

'OK, thanks. I'll keep an eye out for the form.'

And so, like that, *I know* Laura bloody Watson has complained. That's the last home-made Christmas cake and card she's getting off me. Period.

Period. I have no idea why I'm using that word. Chloë has made me subscribe to Netflix and we're binge watching *Jane the*

Virgin. It's obviously having an impact, and not a good one. *Jane the Virgin*, period and slut drops. I'm not sure the world is getting better really. Where will it all end? Social media is coarsening our culture. I heard that today when I accidentally slipped on to Radio 4. Yes, I can definitely say, 'Radio 4. *It's happening.*'

I've managed to send in the form to planning. Chloë helped me upload it. It wasn't that hard, and there wasn't that much to say on it. The garage building was built when? I guessed it was put up in the 1980s. It was newer than the house but not born yesterday. We just made it up in the end and chose 1985, year of Live Aid.

'Why year of Live Aid, Mum?'

'I don't know, I just love Freddie Mercury.'

While we are doing it, Peter texts asking if I'd like to go to Midgley Open Gardens on Sunday. Chloë sees his name come up on my phone.

'Peter?'

'Er... yes. Peter.'

'Who's Peter?'

There is a mixture of suspicion, incredulity, protectiveness and resentment in her voice. It is difficult to know what to do.

'Peter – you know.'

'No, I don't. Which Peter are you talking about?'

'Oh dear. It's the Peter who was seeing Auntie Maureen. YOU'RE COPPING OFF WITH AUNTIE MAUREEN'S BLOKE?'

'No, no, no. Not at all. Please leave it. *Drop it.* I'll say no. Stop that thought right there.'

'Drop it? Dream on... this is too good! Does she know?'

'Yes. No. She doesn't know but she's not bothered. They're friends. They're not even friends. She isn't interested in him, she asked me to take him off her hands.'

'TAKE HIM OFF HER HANDS? What is this – a boyfriend swap? Is this the sort of thing sisters do? Wow. I always wanted a sister. This is exactly why. That is *sooo* cool. Why didn't you have more kids after me? Why, why, why? I want to take my sister's boyfriends off her hands. *That is so unfair.* Why make me a miserable only child? You know I'll have to bury you alone? Wow, I'd love a sister. Why didn't you have more kids? That's just evil. I want a sister I can cheat on. I WANT ONE!'

I am exhausted. I blurt it all out.

'I'm very sorry, love, but I had three miscarriages trying for another baby and then your dad had an affair.'

'Oh.' She's shocked into silence.

'I didn't want you to be alone. I didn't, then I couldn't, then I didn't want more babies with your father. Plus, I had the one I wanted. *You*. Thank you for helping me upload this, by the way.' I take a breath. 'Peter's nice. We've only had a cup of tea. We have a lot in common. We'll probably be friends. I don't know. Do you mind?'

Chloë is staring at me, open-mouthed. Then a shrug and: 'Whatev.'

'Thank you. I'm going to put the kettle on. Do you want a cup of tea?'

'Yes, please.'

Well, at least that's got *that* over with.

A last-minute email request has come, enquiring about booking accommodation this week. I am tempted to write a long reply to that person explaining that this is the fifth request for accommodation over spring bank holiday, and maybe they need to think about planning ahead? But I resist. It's easy to be ridiculously busy when you have young children and you're working. There were times when Chloë was little, and Franklin wasn't pulling his weight around the house or around work or around anything. I was running between shifts at Morrisons to come home, clean, cook, do the laundry, watch the baby and run back out again. I felt as if I was losing my marbles.

I can remember the moment I finally accepted that something was wrong in my marriage and I needed to make a change. I'd crawled in from a late shift. I was exhausted, having been up most of the night before with Chloë's colic. I got into the house, and there was nothing to eat. No butter, no cereal. I checked upstairs and found Chloë sleeping on a towel, no sheet, in her cot. So, I trudged back downstairs and was eating what was left of a packet of dry cream crackers, heaving a basket full of dirty laundry, when I stepped in a Harvey deposit. Having cleaned that up, and filled the washing machine, I then got on with rinsing out the baby's bottles and putting on the steriliser. I was in front of the washing machine, pushing a second load of dirty clothes into it, while piling clean clothes from the dryer into the basket, when I fell asleep – on my knees, at the open washing machine door.

When I woke up, it was three in the morning and I could hear Chloë crying. I made her a bottle and went upstairs. When I peered into our bedroom, I saw that Franklin was no longer in bed. He must have come down, seen me, taken the car and gone out. It was an epiphany. Franklin would probably let me die of exhaustion before he'd step in to help. Properly help. I don't know why I wasn't tougher. How did I let him get away with it all for so long? Because I was so bloody exhausted. So, I won't be mean with late-minute bookers. Not ever.

Peter asking me out has made me feel strange. Out of nowhere, my sex drive has made an appearance. I've not thought about sex for such a long time. It's a part of you that can die with divorce, as if all the hormones that stimulate that part of you wither away with the decree absolute. The clear evidence of the withering is in my underwear drawer; I look at it properly for the first time in years. It is a tangle of wrinkled looking elastic and grey and frayed edges. So, I sit down and do a click and collect on an ivory lingerie set from Marks & Spencer. I get a little overexcited staring at the gorgeous women online in all their stockings and suspenders. Not that I've gone lesbian. And not that there's anything wrong with that. I live in Hebden Bridge, after all – the capital of lesbianism in the UK.

I always remember the magician who came to perform at Chloë's sixth birthday party, and how he had explained to me afterwards what a relief it had been – how easy her party had been for him. He had gone to one the day before in the centre of Hebden where he had shouted out to a young boy: 'Hello, young man, do you want to bring your dad up?'

The boy replied, 'I don't have a dad, I have a mum and a mum.'

'OK, son, no problem, bring one of your mums up.' Then, 'What about you, young lady, do you want to bring your dad up?'

'I don't have a dad, I have two mums.'

'OK, great, get one of your mums up here as well. Now you,

young feller over there, do you want to bring your dad or your mum up?'

'I prefer guardian, and we call her Frank.'

The poor man was broken.

So, for the first time in ages, I am thinking about sex. I hope I'm not going to regret this. Once those hormones start whirring back to life, who knows what will happen? I'll probably start throwing out pheromones and not be able to control myself, and before I know it, I'll end up kissing a stranger and getting shouted at by his angry wife. Then we'll all end up having sex.

I sneak out of the house and meet Peter in the Co-op car park. His car is an oldish Nissan Micra. It's green. The car is immaculate inside, and he's brought a flask. I swear when I see the flask my heart skips a beat. We chat away about favourite gardens and favourite plants. He's a fan of delphiniums, I prefer a hydrangea. We then spend a heavenly three hours stomping our way through other people's green spaces. Some are wildly over-optimistic, putting themselves forward for an open garden: under-planted, poor plant examples, and I didn't point it out to Peter but there was definitely a cat poo corner in one of them.

I wear the new underwear. I know nothing is going to happen. There is no way Peter is going to be seeing it. But it felt nice to know that, if I had an accident on a slippery paving slab or something, and for some reason I had to be taken to hospital and they had to cut away my clothes, I was wearing nice, matching underwear, just in case Peter happened to catch a glimpse in the ambulance or something.

We buy a home-made Bakewell tart from one of the houses; the pastry is frankly a lot tougher than I expected, although they have a fabulous wisteria, which always makes me think these people know what they're doing in life. Clearly not when it comes to pastry. However, once Peter gets the flask out of the car and we find a nice bench with a view over the valley, even with the slight drizzle and the chewy pastry, it's still lovely.

When I arrive home, Chloë is cooking sausages and mash, and Maureen is hanging up washing on the airer. They both have an air of martyrdom about them.

Maureen says, 'This is the third load I've had out of here today, the *third*.'

Chloë says, 'I hope you're hungry? We need to get a new masher, the handle is about to drop off this one with the number of potatoes I've peeled and mashed today.'

I secretly enjoy these signs of their domesticity. It's reassuring that they might have picked up something from me along the way. Yes, I think, I might have to leave them to it a bit more often. The evening floats past me, as I bask in a perfect day.

. . . .

TIP ON MIDLIFE ROMANCE

Take it slow.

Everyone around you will be shocked you're getting up to something.

. . . .

TIP ON LIFE

Flasks are brilliant.

CHAPTER 8

Work hits like a sledgehammer; it's hectic, lots of complaints and the coffee machine breaks down so Tony is furious.

'It's top of the range!' he fumes.

I don't want to say 'from ten years ago.'

Anyway, thank goodness Miles sees sense and orders a replacement, so calm should be restored tomorrow. I know I shouldn't, but I find myself once again thanking God for Amazon Prime.

I see a missed call on my mobile but don't get a chance to listen to the message until I'm on my lunch break, queuing for a sandwich in Cheese Please. I know that I should get up earlier and cobble some lunch together from home, but this is my one treat of the day. While waiting in the queue, I check the message: it's Shannon from planning telling me she can come over this week to view the cottage. The stress of it has me ordering a foot-long Cheddar cheese torpedo with everything in it, plus a Diet Coke and a chocolate-covered flapjack.

Back outside the surgery, I call Maureen in a panic. 'Planning are coming! Planning are coming!' I bleat.

'When, what?' She sounds half asleep. 'What are you on about?'

'To view the cottage. They're coming.'

'Oh, right.'

'We've got to get them out of there.'

'Right. Who?'

'The Benson & Hedges factory, of course! The one we're running next door!'

'Yes, yes, I get you. What do you want to do?'

'I want you to tell them to go.'

'OK, but I'm not even dressed. They're not here, I can see, there's no vans outside.'

'Maureen, please, just go and clean it up.'

'Janet... Janet, calm down. We can't just pile in there and clear it up. And on my own? It'd take me days. When are they due to leave?'

I am in total panic mode. I can't remember. They've been there forever. Then it comes to me.

'They came on the tenth for three weeks.'

We both flail around saying numbers out loud.

'Thirty-first. Thirty-first.' Maureen gets there first.

'Right, when is that? When is that!'

We are both mumbling on the line to each other. I'm desperately scanning my mind for the last date I can remember. I'm a blooming receptionist for a dental surgery, for heaven's sake – my whole life is dates. The thirty-first... it rings a bell.

'It's today, I think,' Maureen yawns.

I nearly faint with relief. 'Have they gone?'

'Well, I don't know, do I? I was asleep until fifteen minutes ago. I told you, I can't see any vans.'

'Maureen, report back.'

An agonising forty minutes later, my sister texts me.

Found key, get your arse over here – FAGAGEDDON.

That's it, I decide. Drastic action is needed. I feign a coughing fit. It's quite good, and in full view of a busy reception. I target it to happen when I know Fiona and Judy are due down to collect patients. Before I know it, the cough really has got a hold of me. I am off the chair, on my knees, and eighty-year-old Mr Earnshaw is giving me a Heimlich manoeuvre (which feels more like a minor sexual assault). Judy and Fiona wrestle him off me, and I am sitting there on the floor, panting, eyes streaming. Judy goes for some water, and Fiona readjusts my skirt. My phone beeps; a message pops up from Maureen:

Are you coming?

I don't know if Fiona sees it; her eyes flick towards it, but she doesn't let on. When I say I want to go home, she agrees straight away. I don't risk asking Tony, who would have my skeleton propped up on that front desk issuing TePe sticks to miserable zombie patients, gums quivering.

I am halfway home, stuck in the line of queuing traffic that is the consequence of the eighteen-month flood alleviation works at Hebbleroyd – £20 million, it cost; how do they justify it? – when

Peter rings asking if I'd like to go on a midnight walk on Saturday, organised by the local hospice. I say, 'Yes, sounds lovely,' so I can seem like a nice, enthusiastic person who says yes to things. I am desperate to get off the phone, as I am horribly worried about the cottage and Shannon, and the effort of being calm, nice and enthusiastic is exhausting. As soon as I say yes to Peter, I regret it. A midnight walk? I like to be in bed for 10.30 p.m. at the latest.

Whilst I am contemplating the horrors of my upcoming weekend, I switch on the radio to hear the news announcer mention that it's Tuesday, 29 May. The Croatians don't leave for another two days. I can't go in and tidy up even if I want to. I call planning and leave a message for Shannon asking can she please come Thursday or Friday afternoon, as these are the only times I can be around to let her in. I am firm. It should give me enough time.

When I get in, Maureen has a glass in her hand, and she and Chloë are in high spirits as *Love Island* is starting tonight. Maureen attempts to reassure me that although she was wading through tobacco when she looked in, with her help, I should be able to turn the cottage around in a couple of hours. I try to peer through our blinds, but they're rammed tight to the windowsill and the Croatians are due back at any moment, so I daren't risk opening the door.

Maureen and Chloë try to pull me into their plans for *Love Island* – cocktails and bikinis seem to sum it up. I watch five minutes, but that's enough. I'm still going through *Jane the Virgin*. Chloë cannot understand what's taking me so long. She tells me that she has binge-watched, twice, *The Crown* and *Stranger Things* and is currently enjoying the new season of *Grace and Frankie*. Apparently, I will like *Grace and Frankie*, because it's about crazy old people behaving badly. Jane Fonda is in it. I'm forty-four, Jane Fonda is eighty. I don't think there's anything more depressing than an eighty-year-old who is more glamorous and attractive than I'll ever be.

I'm off TV. I'm too busy on YouTube. Chloë introduced me to the joys of its instructional videos, and I have to say they're my favourite things on the internet. I have discovered a fabulous way to restore old silver (grit), and a novel way to clean the dishwasher if it's not cleaning to its optimum (salt).

I am about to go upstairs for a bath, when I notice that the lights are on in Lavander Cottage. Bravely, I decide to tackle the Croatians. I knock on their door, and the small, less grumpy one comes out pulling the door closed tight behind him so I can't see inside.

I tell him: 'I need to get in early Thursday to clean for next people?'

For some unknown reason, I deliver this with an accent. He nods. I try to get a peek inside, but he is a genius at obscuring everything and then abruptly closes the door in my face.

I go to bed with the sound of Chloë and Maureen 'phwoar-ing' and squealing every two minutes. I've put a mix of herbs in a plastic bag under my pillow, a tip from a good sleep guru on YouTube. *We shall see.* My chances of getting a good night's sleep are usually curtailed by Maureen and Chloë's bedtime routine. They insist on running up and down the stairs a number of times for endless food and water supplies. This requires every light in the house to be switched on and off a number of times before they finally, finally slam their doors for the tenth time, which means it's bedtime, but they leave the light on so I have to get up, go downstairs and turn it off, check all the doors and windows and then begin the tussle with Harvey to go into the kitchen. He prefers the top of the stairs, but this is a no-no, as he could trip one of us up and we'd break our neck, plus he always manages to open my bedroom door and then attempts to suffocate me by leaping onto my head in the very early hours.

I'm not anticipating a great night. My tummy is growling. I have been constipated since Shannon's call.

Thursday eventually arrives, and I am up ridiculously early. I drag the mop and metal bucket along the drive at 6.30 a.m. and plant it outside the cottage. Safe to say, it is noisy. I then go back inside for the hoover, which I scrape with a little more care, and then, with real purpose, drop my metal housekeeper's box outside the door. I go back home and make myself a piece of toast and a cup of tea and then, steeling myself, knock on the door of Lavander Cottage at 7 a.m. The blinds on the front window immediately shoot up and, in a double surprise, the big one opens the front door *with a smile*! He has three gigantic, wrapped holdalls balancing from him and an enormous wheelie suitcase big enough to hold the cigarette machine *and* the stock room of WHSmith.

'Hello,' I say.

He wanders past me, followed by the two others, who look tired and dejected and give half-hearted grimaces of acknowledgement to me as they pass.

'Hello.'

'Gud bye.'

The small one seems the most miserable, as he drags two suitcases and a sports shop's worth of holdalls down the drive, all the while yawning as if he is sucking in a black hole. The big one then steps around me to go back into the cottage. He returns with three black bin bags and stacks them neatly next to the wheelie bin. He turns as he does it, gives me a shallow nod and, without any more acknowledgement, they pile into the vans and away they go.

'Goodbye, the Croatians.'

I step inside the cottage door with a mixture of nervousness and dread. What a lovely surprise it is to discover a tidyish room. Not immaculate, not 'mother-in-law's-visiting' clean, but way, *way* better than I was expecting. All the bed linen is in a pile in the living room with the towels, ready to be collected. The washing-up has been done, the fridge is empty and the bathroom is acceptable. There are no cigarettes anywhere: true, I find little threads of tobacco in the corners as I hoover, but no loose cigarette papers, no empty or torn boxes. *They must've been cleaning for hours.* The only real giveaway of the factory we'd been housing was the overwhelming and undeniable stink of tobacco.

I carry every jar of potpourri, every lavender bag, every diffuser stick and oils, every plug-in air freshener I own out of the house and into the cottage. *And I have a lot of them.* Every room has a minimum of three in it. I use four cans of Febreze walking round the place and open every window wide. Even with a slight drizzle, I think it's worth it, plus doesn't drizzle damp down smells? I've read that somewhere. Maybe YouTube?

They've even managed to fix the dodgy non-Velux blind, and left a message in the guest book.

Good House. And they've drawn a smiley face.

God bless the Croatians. Not that I ever want them back. I don't know if I even want to continue running a B&B after this.

By eleven thirty, having turned Lavander Cottage around within an inch of its life, I am famished and bedraggled. I am running between houses, carrying smelly stuff away and bringing in clean sheets, cleaning stuff, nicer cushions. Every time I re-enter, I'm not sure if it smells worse or better than the time before, my sense of smell being impacted by the persistent thin rain that has gradually soaked me to the skin. I hope I don't get a cold. I've decided I might be going a bit deaf and they're all interconnected: ear, nose, throat. I know because I stumbled on a YouTube doctor doing a talk about spotting nose cancer. I didn't stick with it to the end. There's only so much staring up nostrils with a small torch I'm prepared to look at, never mind do.

As I carry a giant porcelain washbowl full of glass pebbles over to the cottage (I had to roll an old Sure deodorant rollerball over them, as I'm running short of suitable smells), a car suddenly pulls up and a woman jumps out. Short. Bouncy. Enthusiastic. In a full-length, yellow raincoat and matching flowery wellington boots, she bears a strong resemblance to how I imagine Mrs Birdseye might look.

'Janet?'

I put the bowl down on the drive and go to shake her hand.

'You'll freeze in that outfit, love,' she says briskly. 'Precipitation due in the next half hour from the north – an Arctic blast to get us all ready for winter.'

'Shannon? Thanks for the advice. Hello, come in. I'll get a cardy, make you a cup of tea.'

I guide her into the house and away from the cottage, praying that the tobacco smell will vanish by the time we get there.

'Very nice, Janet. How long have you lived here?'

' 'Thirteen.'

'Lovely, right.'

'Are you local, Shannon? Do you take milk and sugar?'

'Strong, no sugar, little bit of milk. Yes, I'm from Mixenden, the rough end. Escaped at twenty-two once I'd got my degree. Live in a massive house up Pellon now. Built my own. Why not? I married a builder and know a lot about planning! Ha!'

'Ha!' I laugh heartily with Shannon; she's such a jolly, confident character. Lovely, open, honest, no side to her at all. *I am dying to go to the loo.*

I fling the biscuit jar at her, make an incoherent excuse and rush to the bathroom. Shannon's arrival has brought the constipation to a swift conclusion.

When I return downstairs, in a cardigan, as a reason for my delay, I am relieved to see Shannon reading the *Mail* I'd hidden in the veg rack.

'Sorry about that.'

'No problem. Shall we have a look at this there castle, then?'

'Yes, please.'

I try to sound enthusiastic, but I'm feeling fragile. I pull on my garden raincoat. We wander outside, and Janet splashes energetically around the perimeter of the building, humming and hawing.

'How long do you say it's been here?'

'As long as we've lived here.'

She takes lots of photographs on her phone.

'Let's get them footings. You can see it's been built on something else at some point. Greenhouse, I reckon. When was the main house constructed?'

'1912.'

'Early example, I would've put it around 1925. It's a very nice house, Janet, nice detail in the brick course.'

'Yes, I do like it myself.'

'And I can tell you like to garden.'

'I do. I love gardening.'

'Well, you can see the cottage isn't anywhere near as old as the house. Different gauge of engineering brick.'

'Yes. Right. I'm sure you're right.'

'I am. OK, I think I've got enough.'

She puts her phone away. We are at the front door of the cottage. Here we go.

'So, you're running a little Airbnb from here?'

Gulp. I'm ready for the loo all over again. I hold it together. Just.

'Well. I've only done a B&B once, actually. I didn't like all the cooking. It's an annexe, you know, it's got no separate electricity or anything.'

'Perfect, that's what I needed to hear. Annexe. Not a problem, Janet.'

I open the door to the cottage, take a deep breath. I don't know what I am thinking: that I might do a large exhale as I walk in and somehow send clean, non-tobacco-smelling air that I could waft behind me as Shannon walks into it. I think again when I remember I had mackerel on toast for my breakfast. I step inside and she follows me, but as soon as her head pokes around the door she stops, coughs and wafts her hand in front of her face.

'Bit sensitive to perfume smells; brings my asthma on... Wow, that's strong. All looks lovely, Janet. I'll be in touch in the next few days.'

And she hands me her cup, waves and is gone.

I am in shock. Thank God it's over. I race back home to the bathroom where I am parked intermittently for the next hour. Thank heavens the Croatians were long gone by the time she arrived.

I wonder what will happen to the cottage now?

. . . .

TIPS FOR RUNNING A B&B

When thinking about opening a B&B, ask yourself these questions:

Can you cope with stress?

Can you deal with strangers?

If it's a 'no' to either of the above, maybe it's not for you. Just a thought.

CHAPTER 9

There's a slime incident in Valley Dental reception. Home-made slime is all the rage with the kids, apparently, and someone has put browny-purply-glittery stuff across the newly upholstered reception seating. Tony blows his top when I tell him and kicks the leaflet stand.

'Bastard little shits, we've just had that seat done.'

I'm glad there's no one in reception. He hates kids. Both his kids are locked away in boarding school. *Probably for the best.*

The slime rage (not Tony's) reminds me of when Chloë really got into those lollipop-type confections that childless people probably never have to encounter: they're called 'cake pops' and consist of cake crumbs mixed with chocolate or icing, formed into balls or cubes and attached to a lolly stick. Pure sugar. My daughter did her first and only backward flip after consuming ten different varieties of hundreds and thousands.

Anyway, I get on YouTube for the last hour and a half of the day, searching 'slime removal'. I find a video of a guy removing chewing gum from a car seat with black industrial tape. I fly round to Dobby's Hardware and catch them just before they close at 4 p.m. Seriously, how much money is there in hardware? They're never open. I then painstakingly, on my knees for an hour, pull and pull at the slime using sections of gaffer tape. I go through almost the entire roll, and after an hour it is definitely looking better.

So much so that when Miles comes out to leave at half past five, he says, 'Where's the slime? I can't see it. You're a marvel. Thank you, Janet.'

I swear he has a glisten of a tear in his eye. Men. *Soft buggers.*

When Judy, his dental assistant, wanders down, I tell her Miles was looking a bit emotional.

'He's on a trial separation with his wife,' she explains, 'so now he's worrying about what the divorce might cost. His tax return has just come in, and he reckons he's going to struggle to afford the yacht in the Maldives over Xmas.'

Right. Puts my tin of Quality Street bonus into context.

Greg is at ours again when I get home. He and Chloë are laughing in her bedroom. The door is closed. I'm not sure if this is appropriate and am tempted to call Victoria for advice, but it doesn't seem very trusting of me. I make some tea for myself, then think again and take some cordial with a few chocolate chip cookies on a plate upstairs and knock gently on the door. Chloë opens it. They are both fully dressed. She sits casually on the bed and picks up a games console thing.

'Greg brought his Xbox over,' she says. 'He's teaching me how to play *Grand Theft Auto*.'

I watch it for two minutes. It is grotesquely violent and adrenalin driven, like ogling at close quarters some obscene car crash involving members of a boy band.

'Fantastic.'

'Yes, Mum, it's great. We're gonna be at it all night.'

Greg gives a little hiccup at this and then Chloë bursts out laughing.

'What I mean is, we're going to be playing this all night.' She fake hits Greg. 'Is it OK if Greg kips here tonight? I'll use the spare mattress. We'll keep the noise down.'

Greg smiles over at me. I attempt to remain upright and friendly and smiley and easy-going, though inside it feels as if I am being repeatedly bashed like a giant punchbag.

'OK, then. Let's see.'

This is the extent of my wordage. It means nothing. It's just holding material to get me the hell out of there. How did I ever fall for this? What is she saying? Is he her boyfriend? They are so relaxed about asking me. Is this how they are now, the millennials? 'Hi, Mum, I'm losing my virginity tonight with Greg, here. OK if we do it at yours with a backdrop of extreme violence and casual car crash?'

I have no idea what to do. I try calling Maureen, but her phone rings out. She's being a bit mysterious lately. There's bound to be a man involved. I make myself a nice Earl Grey and sit down with the *Mail* to try and pull my equilibrium steady. This is a futile exercise, as they are doing a favourite TV crushes and Martin Compston is there, shirt off, from *Line of Duty*. He looks full of vigour, and, well, he's just sex on legs.

Chloë appears as I am poring over the headlines. 'Ay up, Mum, fancy getting interrogated by CID do you?'

I immediately put the paper down. '*No, I do not.* I'm worried about tariffs on UK fisheries, if you must know.'

'Oh, right. *Sorry.* Fish what?'

'Yes.'

'Right. What does that mean?'

'More expense, that's what. *More expense.*'

'Right. What d'you mean?'

'Everything fish. Everything fish-related going up in price, *again.*'

'Right. I didn't know we bought a lot of fish.'

I'm angry, and I don't even know why. She definitely doesn't know why, and it's not remotely fair of me. Still, I can't resist how I'm feeling.

'You OK, Mum? You seem a bit tense.' She takes some KitKats out of the biscuit box and a packet of Cheesestrings and two yoghurts out of the fridge, picks up two spoons then shoves a bag of bread rolls and a bottle of Coke under her arm.

'No, no, I'm fine,' I lie, offering a tray and two plates.

'Right.' She gives me an eye-roll and a big, laboured sigh. 'You don't seem fine.'

And then the words pour out of me, unstoppably. 'Are you planning to sleep with Greg? Because I'm not comfortable with him sleeping here when I've not met his mother – and are you using contraception? Are you on the pill already, without telling me what's going on? Chloë, you're only sixteen you know. It's not legal! You've got your whole life ahead of you, plenty of time yet to find out about sex. I'm not an idiot. I know you know, but *you don't know everything.* Sex should be a precious thing with two people who love each other and then it's a nice memory. Not a "wham-bam-thank-you-ma'am now let's play Garbage". Is Greg nice? Does he treat his mother well? Because that's an important way to judge what a person is like.' I come to a breathless halt.

'*Whoa, whoa!* Steady there. Bloody hell, Mum! Pack it in. Reel it back in. Greg's my mate. There is no sex going on. Blimey, I'm not stupid. Don't you trust me? I'm not that much of an idiot. I'd hardly invite him to stay, plan to lose my virginity and tell *you* about it.'

'Right. Right. OK. I suppose.'

'There's no "suppose" about it. Give me some credit. Deffo no sex. We're friends only. *Got it?*' She starts to load her supplies onto the tray and takes a couple of glasses down for the Coke.

'OK, good. Yes, if you say so.'

'I do. So, can Greg stay the night in my room?'

'Yes, I suppose so, if his mother is OK with it.'

'She's chill, honestly. It's cool.'

'OK, great. As long as she's *chill.*' I imagine some laid-back hippy mother, recumbent on a floor cushion, covered in drug ash and transgender lovers.

'He'll check in with her once she's finished work at the court.'

'Court?' I make a supreme effort not to sound too interested.

'Yes, she's a solicitor. Barrister, I think. I'll make sure he asks her. Now, have we got any microwave popcorn?'

I then imagine some tall, overbearing, steely-eyed harridan chastising Chloë for being eight months' pregnant with a court order in her hand telling her to 'stay away from my Greg or I'll take you down for aggravated assault.'

'There's a packet of salted ones behind the old Raisin Wheats,' I say feebly.

'Oh well, better than nothing. If you're going to the shops at all...?'

'I wasn't.'

'OK. Just if you were...'

Longish pause to allow the guilt to kick in.

'Why, what are you wanting?'

'Just some samosas, or some noodles? A takeout would be great from Hammad's. Pizza? Or a Chinese?'

An hour or so later, I end up ordering in three large pizzas – margherita, hot veggie supreme and a pepperoni – and get them delivered. We are enjoying them from the boxes in the living room in front of a very dramatic episode of *Coronation Street*. We are midway into the commercial break when Greg smiles over at me.

'This will do, Mrs J, eh?'

I smile back at him. 'It'll do me, Greg.'

I am as friendly and laid-back as I can humanly be. I keep a steady watch on where his eyes are going, and there's a lot of glancing at Chloë's legs. She's oblivious, but she's definitely happy. In some quiet way, I think this is a gentle introduction to what being a boyfriend and girlfriend might be for both of them. Having calmed down and eaten a very nice pizza with a glass of Prosecco, I am awash with gratitude that I am here to witness it. Franklin misses out on so much. Our little girl, ready or not, is growing up.

I spend the night on tenterhooks, wondering if they are having sex. I curse my dodgy hearing. At half eleven, convinced I am going deaf as I can't hear anything, I dig out the Hopi candle Maureen bought me for my birthday/Christmas and nervously light it, painfully spilling six beeswax globules on my face. I stick it into my worst performing ear. It is a painful fifteen minutes, but when I feel I can take no more, I lift the candle out and there is a pool of wax dribbling from my ear and a definite change in my hearing. Now it sounds as if I am in the engine room of a large ship, with a weird added 'whoosh' as if I am constantly near the sea. I manage five minutes in the other ear before I am so tired, I give up. I creep up and listen at Chloë's door, feeling weirdly disorientated and guilty. I decide that even if they are at it like rabbits in there, I'm not going to be able to hear them, or do anything about it.

I collapse into a weird, troubled sleep, where I am carving ears out of slime whilst on a yacht near Cornwall. Peter is steering with no top on, Miles is playing a harmonica whilst sitting up in the rigging, and Chloë is on the gangplank ready to get pushed off by an unknown, steely-eyed pirate.

I'm actually pleased to be woken up at 5 a.m. by Harvey sitting on my head.

· ·

TIPS ON TEENAGE DAUGHTERS

Prepare the bank balance – they and their friends will eat you out of house and home.

Trust them. They're more clued-up than we ever were.

CHAPTER 10

It's the midnight walk. Why did I say I'd do this? I attempt a snooze in the afternoon, but I'm exhausted at 8 p.m. and asleep on the sofa at 10 p.m. when Peter comes to pick me up. We are traipsing round at reasonable speed and reach the halfway point by the hospice where there are drinks and loos and there is a nice atmosphere. I'm loitering in the tea queue when I bump into Laura Watson. She is immaculate in a head torch, jazzy matching rainbow leggings, with a trendy water jug welded around her hand.

'Hi, Janet.'

I am grateful to be on my own and that Peter is in the loo. The last thing I want is to have to introduce him to her at this tentative stage.

'Laura.'

I remain friendly but a little more aloof than normal. I'm not a hypocrite, I'm not about to fake chumminess when I'm still very annoyed with her. Then I remember that I need to keep her onside, as I've got the Lamberts, a booking through the website, coming to stay in the cottage next weekend. I do not want her complaining to Shannon in planning again, not whilst we're waiting on the retrospective planning decision. So, it is a struggle, but I fake chumminess.

'Enjoying the walk, Laura? It'll be nothing to you with all that fitness you do.'

She's so easily flattered I could see her beam in the flood of her head torch.

'It's a fun night out, Janet, what can I say? And for such a good cause. And who is this?'

Peter arrives, far too friendly.

'This is Peter. Peter, this is Laura, my neighbour from down the road. You might remember me mentioning her.' Her eyes narrow, and I let the moment linger before adding, 'She's our most glamorous neighbour.'

'Oh, gosh, I wouldn't say that, honestly, Janet. What is it that you do, Peter?'

'D'you know, we'd love to chat, Laura, but we're trying to get back as quickly as possible. I'm up horribly early for a thing.'

'Of course, lovely to see you, enjoy the rest of the walk. Halfway there! It's very noble of you to do it in fancy dress too. You must be boiling in there!'

And off she trots. I am boiling. Absolutely sweating cobs, but fancy dress? I was convinced I was going to be cold so I was wearing a huge outdoorsy, red Rab coat that had belonged to Franklin during his biking era. Chloë had tried to dissuade me, *a number of times,* but I'd ignored her. It's so huge and puffy, it feels as if I am walking the route with a heavy winter duvet. I'd matched it with a red bobble hat, gloves and black boots, so I suppose there is a touch of the Mrs Christmas about the outfit. Peter is so polite, he never said a word.

'She's my neighbour nemesis, Peter.'

'I thought so.'

'I am very hot in this coat.'

'Let me carry it for you.'

By mile six, around 2.30 in the morning, Peter is looking very red in the face and the conversation has dwindled away to:

'Not long now.'

'Nearly there.'

I must have said, 'I could do with a cup of tea,' about twenty times. I am tired, hot and cranky. My boots are rubbing my feet, I am starving and thirsty, and this is not my idea of a good time. I am exuding resentment.

'Sorry I'm not very chatty, Peter. I'm usually in bed for ten thirty, so I'm feeling a bit tired and hungry, and my boots are hurting, so it's making me a little bit cranky.'

'Oh God, you don't have to explain, I'm just thinking myself this was a stupid idea. Whatever was I thinking? I've just always fancied doing it and never really had anyone to do it with. I'm sorry, it's a disastrous idea. I can only apologise.'

'Don't worry.'

'Not long now.'

Peter drives me home, and I am almost asleep in the front seat when he pulls up on the drive. I go to open the door and turn to say goodnight when he kisses me with such passion, such *unexpected passion*, that I am blown away. It is a kiss of such intention. I am awake. I am more awake than I have been in years. The adrenalin courses through me, and we are kissing madly in the car.

I don't offer, there is no discussion beyond a mumbled, 'Oh, yes, please,' and a 'Watch out for the cat – he scratches.'

We stumble into the house, his arms are wrapped around me, and before I know it, we are making love in the living room. It's safe to say we are both surprised. We lie on the sofa afterwards, giggling.

'I suppose what I should've said is, "Would you like a cuppa?" '

'Oh, would I!'

We pick through our clothes, trying to decide what is respectable. I go into the kitchen, see the eggs and decide I'm hungry.

'Fancy a pancake?' I look in the fridge. 'With chocolate, cream and raspberries?'

'Are you kidding? Wow.'

It has to be one of my all-time favourite middle-of-the-night meals.

We eat three each, which I justify by virtue of the fact we have just walked seven miles. The pancakes are delicious, and before I know it we are kissing again, and this time we head upstairs to the bedroom. Yes, yes, yes, *yes*! Janet Jackson has got her mojo back.

• •

TIP ON NEW BOYFRIENDS IN YOUR 40S

You've still got it. Enjoy it while you can.

CHAPTER 11

'Franklin's at the door.'

'*What*?'

Maureen pokes her head around the door of the bedroom, already dressed, looking glamorous, and hands me a cup of tea. Peter looks horrified, as if this is the worst thing that has ever happened to him. *Stunned in the headlights* does not do justice to the look of alarm on his face. Maureen is, however, as cool as a cucumber, as I knew she would be, and doesn't bat an eyelid. I think it's safe to say she enjoys – but doesn't exploit – how uncomfortable he is feeling.

'Morning, Pete,' she says blithely, then to me: 'Are you expecting him?'

'No.'

'Well, he's here, and he's looking very smart.'

'Oh.'

Franklin only ever looks smart when he's in trouble or after something. I can't compute it. I have had two men in my life in the last fifteen years. What are they doing in my house at the same time on the same day? After five hours' sleep?

'Tell Chloë he's here,' I say. 'He must be here to see Chloë.'

'He's brought flowers.'

Maureen and I look at each other, gauging the moment.

'Chloë likes flowers,' I say.

Maureen's left eyebrow creeps upwards, like a question mark, and she says, 'I'll put the kettle on.'

She leaves the room, and Peter, who is for all intents and purposes catatonic, silently mouths at me, 'Franklin?'

'My ex-husband.'

'Your ex-husband, right.' His voice is high and rasping.

If fear were a thing that is available to buy, Peter, at this moment, is selling a maxi-pack.

'*Peter*.'

He rotates his head towards me like an arthritic shop

mannequin.

'I don't know why he's here. I haven't seen him in months. Please don't worry.'

I have to properly force myself to hold his gaze, so he can see I am being truthful. I watch the terror leak away from him a little, as we share a tentative smile between us.

'And Mitzi?' he whispers.

'Oh, Maureen's fine with our being together. *Totally fine*. She knows all about it. In fact, she encouraged it.'

I can't help but giggle to myself when I say that, thinking of how Chloë has reacted, and wondering what on earth kind of women Peter will think we are. I have to be honest and say I am almost enjoying the fact that sometimes, yes, Janet Jackson can surprise everyone, even herself, with her laid-back, laissez-faire, bohemian carry-on.

'Really?'

'Absolutely.'

His shoulders slump.

'I'll bring you a cup of tea and the paper,' I say soothingly. 'Please *relax*.'

'I... er... yes. OK. Great. If you think so. OK.'

I pat him reassuringly and then pelt out of the bedroom. There is absolutely no way this is all entirely OK, and there is no way I am getting changed in front of Peter, *no way*. I streak across that room like Mrs Usain Bolt grabbing whatever clothes I can scoop up, as I dash past. I douse myself with the showerhead and throw a lot of make-up at my face. Peter has already had enough shocks for one day, and a 3 a.m. bedtime, despite the best efforts of Bobbi Brown concealer, is showing on the old face. Plus, Franklin is here. I can't help but want to look, at the very least, reasonable. For some reason, it's always important that when Franklin sees me, I'm looking goodish, so he can regret at leisure the mistakes he made by cheating on me and know that his not being in my life has not in any way broken me.

When I dart back into the bedroom, wearing what can only be described as an embarrassing patchwork of the formal and the informal – a FatFace Cuba T-shirt with an office pencil skirt – Peter is dressed, sitting bolt upright on the edge of the now made bed. He smiles at me and reaches out his hand, which leaves me at a bit of a loss as to what to do. It seems so familiar and intimate, which is ridiculous given we'd been *really* intimate. I decide the polite thing to do is take a seat next to him, which is what I do, whereupon he firmly takes my hand in his and stares into my eyes.

'Thank you, Janet. *Thank you.* Thank you for a wonderful night. You're a wonderful woman, Janet. I'm a little bit in love with you.'

At this, I confess, I instinctively pull away. He, in turn, immediately writhes in his seat.

'I mean... Sorry, *way too much.* I mean, *I really like you.* I'm a little bit *ready* to fall in love with you. Ugh. Oh. That sounds ridiculous. What am I thinking? Too much. I'm so sorry.'

I am up on my feet and head for the door.

'Ha. Thank you, yourself. Look at me, I'm all flustered. I'm going. Downstairs. Can I get you a cup of tea, yes?'

I don't wait for an answer. I smile at him, as I close the bedroom door. *In love with me?* I didn't know where to put myself. I'll have to talk to Maureen about this. Is this what he always does? He couldn't mean it, could he? I know he likes my pancakes, but it's way too much for a first sex thing, isn't it? Jane the Virgin would find this unbelievably weird.

I can't help but wonder what all these men are doing in the house. What *are* they doing here? Is it like a magnetic thing: when one appears it attracts another? I am a bit rattled, which I put down to being tired, and barge into the kitchen unprepared for the sight of Franklin, who I haven't seen in eight months. He is slumped at the table in a dark charcoal suit and white shirt, an overlarge knot in his black tie. He always seems taller than his surroundings – nothing ever quite fits his overlarge frame and today is no different; the room shrinks with him in it. He is five years older than me, Franklin, and today he looks it. His parents were both West Indian, so he has a rich, brown skin, though he looks mottled and very marked under the eyes, and there is a grizzle of grey clinging around his chin, which makes him look older and more statesmanlike. His hair is shorter than I remember.

'Nine thirty on a Sunday morning?' I say. 'Suit and tie? Are you off to church?'

'A funeral. My girlfriend Ruby's.'

Maureen and I share a serious exchange of looks. I absolutely was not prepared for *that* one, and drop into the seat next to him.

'I'm sorry, I didn't know you had a girlfriend. I don't ask Chloë...'

'It's OK. It's been eighteen months. We were very happy. She'd not been feeling well for about six months and then it came in... terminal lung cancer. At forty-six. She died ten days ago.'

He stifles a sob, and I dive into the big drawer for tissues. I give him a packet that he squeezes in his hand. I am patting him on the shoulder, and Maureen puts two fresh teas down beside us.

'Is everything OK... upstairs?' she whispers, surreptitiously indicating with her head to me, as if I didn't understand what 'upstairs' means.

I am attempting to convey, 'No, everything is not fine – Peter has just said he's in love with me and now Franklin is here with a dead girlfriend' with just my eyes, whilst Franklin unwraps the tissues and gives his nose a big blow.

'It's been the worst three months of my life,' he says hoarsely, and with that bombshell, he collapses onto my shoulder in a heap and weeps.

Being such a big man, he is a weight, and I'm doing my best to support him, though his head is dropping perilously close to my chest. I can't help but feel a tiny bit piqued, irrational as it is, that breaking up with his wife and the mother of his child might be up there with the worst experiences of his life, but I push the silly thought away. He's always lived in the now, Franklin. His girlfriend has just died; of course this must feel like the end of the world. I am contemplating all this when Peter puts his head around the kitchen door. There is no escaping the fact that Franklin, at this point, is heaving heavily into my bosom.

Peter says in a whisper, 'I'm going to get off now.'

I manage to extract myself from Franklin's grip. I don't want to be cynical, but he seems to be making it especially difficult for me. I hurry out to catch up with Peter and close the front door behind me so we won't be overheard.

'Thanks for a lovely time, Peter.'

'Yes, yes. Me, too.'

There is an awkward pause, until Peter clears his throat and speaks.

'I'm really very embarrassed about what I said upstairs, Janet. I wasn't thinking straight. It's all been a bit of a whirlwind and, well, you're lovely, really lovely. That's all I meant to say.'

I desperately want to take him at his word and to let it go. It's OK, I decide, he didn't mean it. We all get it wrong sometimes. He hadn't said anything horrible. It was actually very nice. It was probably, just like he said, the surprise whirlwind unexpectedness of it all. A spur-of-the-moment thing. Maureen had just barged in on us, after all, and then Franklin had turned up. Oh gosh, standing there I feel so sorry for Peter, and know that I have to at least try to explain what's going on.

'Franklin, I mean my ex-husband in there – well, he's just lost his girlfriend.'

This doesn't register on Peter's face in any way, so I decide further explanation is needed.

'Lost *as in died.*'

'*Oh.* Oh, I'm sorry.'

We are centimetres apart, yet it's so hard to know what the etiquette should be. I want to hug him, but can't. I feel incapable of making the first move and remain welded to the spot whilst Peter looks equally at a loss.

'Great geraniums, such a brilliant plant for ground cover,' he finally manages.

'Yes, I love them. I mulch them very heavily in winter to try and keep hold of them,' I reply faintly.

'I'd like to see you again.'

'Yes, please.'

Peter then reaches round me and gives my back a squeeze and kisses me on the cheek. A soft kiss and a warm hand. The thrill of being touched by a stranger who had and could bring me pleasure is very real and exotic, even when he jumps in his little green car, stalls it, crunches his reverse gear horribly and bucks away with what looks like toilet roll hanging from the driver's-side door.

I am left feeling a hum of happiness, a warm shower of possibility and excitement washing over me. He is nice – really nice, Peter. Having sex again has been, well, fantastic. I'd been very free and liberated, I decide. That's what a very late bedtime and seven miles of charity walk exercise pheromones can do for you.

Very much like riding a bike, it all came back to me. The years of abstinence are over. Even if I never make love with Peter again, I'm on a new chapter. It is such a relief to lose my post-divorce virginity. Feelings of new possibilities unfurl like multicoloured streamers, free at last to dance in the breeze.

'Janet, get your arse back in here, he's asked for more tea.' It's Maureen, as always, on hand to bring me back to earth. When I go back in, Franklin is munching through toast and has my *Mail* open on the problem pages. He is pouring from the teapot and gives me a quizzical, what's-going-on head wobble, which I refuse to acknowledge.

'He looks nice?'

I ignore him, saying, 'I'll have a cup, if there is one.' I am determined not to discuss my tiny seedling of a romance with Franklin and make a huge effort to stop my feelings from showing on my face. 'What time's the funeral?' I ask.

'Soon. I should go, beat the traffic. Thanks for the tea. I might pop back later and see Chloë, if I'm not interrupting anything,' he says meaningfully.

'Fine, of course, anytime.'

He is taking an age to slurp down the dregs of his cup and heaves himself out of the chair with all the energy of an exhausted sloth. He even manages to make the closing of the paper feel as if we are watching a man operating at slow motion. I feel for him, the sheer weight of sadness that hangs from him. I walk with him to the door and we share a look – a look borne out of years of familiarity. We were together 23 years, married for ten of those and all that time hovers between us.

'I'm sorry about Ruby. I hope it goes OK.'

'Thank you.'

I repeat silently in my mind. *It's OK if I am pleased to see you, Franklin, it doesn't mean I want you back.*

'You're a good woman, Janet.'

Yes, of course, I'm kind, but you should know, Franklin, I'm not the pushover I once was.

'Take care, hope it goes as well as it can.'

He lunges towards me, as if for a kiss, and I delicately turn my cheek. I've had another man's lips on mine for the first time in a very long time, and I want to hold on to that feeling. I don't want Franklin's stamp on me.

He pauses at the door of the car and looks at the flowers in the passenger car seat, then glances over at me.

'She liked gaudy bloomers. That's what she called them.'

'Sounds like a lady with a sense of humour.'

'Yes. Yes, my Ruby had a great sense of humour.' He throws the bouquet into the back seat and drives away without a wave.

'Well, that's the start of fuckin' trouble.'

It's Maureen, a glass of something on the go. She raises her eyebrows in a knowing way before leaving the kitchen and heading up the stairs. I don't want to engage.

I don't know what I think. He's gone. They are all gone. The sun suddenly appears from behind the beech tree and throws a long, glorious ray all over the garden. I take in the hydrangea, sprouting a multitude of flower heads, the low-growing nasturtium gathering pace and even the lupins, which are always a worry, making themselves known and resisting the blackfly. I'm aware that a heavy bag of boulders I've been dragging around for the last five years has melted away; I didn't even know it was there. I manage a bit of deadheading before the pull for a huge pot of tea drags me into the kitchen and I immediately feel starving. And then I spot them – just past their sell-by date, of course.

What else? Crumpets.

. . . .

TIP ON EX-HUSBANDS

Remember you divorced them for good reason.

. . . .

TIP ON GARDENS

Nasturtiums give excellent ground cover.

CHAPTER 12

I don't hear from Peter today. I walk past the library on my way to the post office and think about popping in, but resist. Not ladylike. Even the word sounds old-fashioned. I can't escape its clutches though. I give myself a talking-to after I catch myself doodling his name on the reception pad. *No more thinking about Peter today.*

Once back home, I'm stuck into chores again, the endless cycle of emptying the dishwasher and filling it up with the pile of dirty crockery on the side. Where does it all come from? I wash my own plate up after every meal.

Maureen is very jolly and insists on a kitchen disco. She grabs me between dances and glasses, yelling, 'I'm not bothered at all about Peter, don't you worry, Janet. I am enjoying carnal relations with a mystery man at the moment.'

He's married. *Obviously.* Though it is good news, in the sense that I genuinely don't have to worry about her being upset about Peter. I keep checking my phone to see if I have a message from him. Suddenly, I have an insight into what keeps Chloë and Maureen glued to their phones. *Hope.* I think I might be too old for romance.

It's just after seven o'clock the next morning, and I am getting ready for work when there is a knock on the door. I am expecting a parcel, having succumbed to the charms of another M&S lingerie set. Thinking it a bit early for post but, who knows, new shifts et cetera, I open the door and fully expect to find Jim performing a little Jackson medley. Instead, it's Franklin, in the same suit, only he is looking a lot the worse for wear.

'Morning, Janet, is Chloë about?'

'Dad!' Chloë bounds down the stairs and throws her arms around him. 'You OK, Daddy? I'm so sorry about Ruby.'

'It's not been good, sweetheart.'

She drags him inside, and I can't help but look at my watch. She needs to set off to school in the next thirty minutes, and I need to get to work.

'Did it go OK, Franklin?'

'It was brutal, brutal.'

'You poor thing, Dad. Do you want a cup of tea?'

He does, of course, and an egg butty and some mushrooms – *that would be lovely* – and a tiny sliver of bacon, *only if you have some.*

He doesn't pause for breath between choked-up splutters and long anecdotes.

'A wonderful woman has met her maker... her time here on earth cruelly cut short. We were friends and lovers for the last two years. She gave me great comfort at a difficult time, and I hope, in return, as I nursed her through a terminal diagnosis over the last six months, I have done her memory and our affection for one another justice.'

'It must have been awful.'

'It's been tragic, Janet, just tragic.'

I give him his second cup of tea and realise he not only looks a bit rough around the edges, he also smells it; a mixture of alcohol and body odour. I insist that Chloë and I need to get a move on, and literally push Chloë towards the door.

As we all leave together, I pat Franklin on the shoulder. 'You take care, eh?'

'You don't need to worry about me.'

Chloë gives him a huge hug. He kisses the top of her head a number of times. I close the door behind me and lock it.

Chloë is already in the car, pulling on her seat belt, when Franklin sidles up next to me and whispers: 'Any chance I can have a shower?'

Franklin is now living in his car in front of the house. *Temporarily.* We have cottage guests, the Lamberts, arriving on Friday, and he's promised to move the car while they're here. I see Laura Watson in Hebden; she's heading into the expensive deli. She's bound to complain if he's parked on the road and, as I'm still waiting on a planning decision, I don't want her ruining my chances. I have a minor panic attack thinking about what Shannon said about laying off paying guests. It's only a short booking. This is not the Croatians moving in for weeks. I'm allowed people staying over in my own home, aren't I? I'll put all the money in a savings account and not touch it for when I'm sued for being a guest house racketeer. Gulp.

The weather is gloriously sunny. Maureen is currently obsessed with football. There's a championship rival thing going on, so she is eating every meal in front of the TV.

'I can't talk. I don't want to, they're warming up.'

She's favouring someone on one team for their beard, someone else for their muscle and someone else for their kit. It seems odd when Franklin joins her and Chloë on the sofa for the match. I don't stay to watch. I'm not very interested in football, and the Franklin thing feels too weird.

Instead, I search through the local listings for holiday lets, just to see what's going on. There aren't many, a couple of really expensive ones up on the tops here that have hot tubs and moorland views. Well, I can't compete with that and the cost per night is eye-watering. I've taken the decision to reduce the welcome basket, mainly because I don't have one any more, so I've decided I'm supplying bread, milk and butter. That's all. I've ordered a multipack of the little individual portions of butter, which seems more economical. I just need to decide how many portions per party. Two per person? Three per person? I'll give the Lamberts two each. They are definitely coming and, so far, the emails have been straightforward and undemanding. I feel a bit unnerved, wondering what's to come. They arrive tomorrow after 4 p.m. and plan to leave on Sunday at 11 a.m. They have a four-year-old child and don't need anything. They'll arrive by taxi and plan to visit friends in the area. I'm charging £148 for the two nights. They're paying by cash. Surely it can't be this simple?

As I walk through Lavander Cottage doing some final checks on Thursday morning, Chloë comes in and hangs around beside me. I'm waiting for her to ask me for some money.

'It looks great.' She sniffs. 'It smells like... *deodorant*.'

'Thank you. Let's hope they like it.'

'Mum, have you thought any more about maybe Dad staying here?'

The question hits me with the force of a kick in the stomach.

'Chloë, love, we don't really know his circumstances,' I manage.

'His circumstances are that he's homeless, Mum. *Homeless.*'

'He's mid-accommodation, love, that's all. He'll sort himself out, and we have people coming to stay, *paying people*, in here, tomorrow.'

I should have paid more attention last night. I'd half listened, half pretended to be too busy to listen, when Maureen was pouring drinks and interrogating Franklin who had no problem outpouring. I'd heard:

'So, where are you living, Franklin?'

'Ah, good question, Mitzi, good question. I was living with Ruby up until the recent unfortunate circumstances but, now, it seems I'm not considered a sitting tenant as my name is not on the official paperwork. As from next Tuesday, I will officially be on the homeless register. Yes, that's right!' He smiled, pleased with the drama of it all, oblivious to the horror on Chloë's face.

I had anticipated what was coming next and deliberately avoided catching anyone's eye. I drifted away, duster in hand, into the kitchen. Maureen, of course, was straight on it and followed, glaring at me, as I emptied the dishwasher.

'You have to tell him he can't move in here, Janet.'

I was so relieved. 'Exactly. No, please, God.'

Chloë then rushed into the kitchen with a couple of dirty cups and flicked on the kettle, looking terribly serious.

'Can't he move into the cottage, Mum?'

'Absolutely no way,' scoffed Maureen. 'If I'm not allowed, bloody Franklin isn't.'

'But he's got nowhere to go – you heard him. Mum, he can't be homeless.'

I felt, at the time, like creeping into the dishwasher and closing its door behind me. Instead I sighed and said, 'I'll make us another cup of tea.'

Let's think positively at this point. I have had, for all intents and purposes, a decent bash at life. At forty-four, I have learned some things: I'm a size 12 in M&S; careful brushing is the key to keeping all your own teeth, and I've survived being six years single. Survived. That says it all. People *survive* earthquakes and car crashes. It's like I'm trying to convince myself I'm doing OK.

I've plenty of reasons to be cheerful. I've got my health. I'm at an age where I know it's 10,000 steps a day now, or two decades of isolation and *Bargain Hunt* repeats. No, thank you. I haven't deviated from my childhood plan to reach a healthy century. I want to be able to open the telegram *and know what it is*. I'm not sure which royal will be signing it, or whether the post office will still exist, but all being well, it'll be King William signing it off and a golden post office drone dropping the telegram on my head, as I snooze in a deckchair in my beautiful garden with *The Archers* omnibus in the background and a robot vacuum cleaner presenting me with a decaf Earl Grey.

I'm looking forward to retiring at sixty-five – sooner, if I possibly can. Early retirement. *The dream.* I feel as if I've worked for ever. The one and only chance I have to realise my dream lies in the cottage and my B&B business. *My only chance.* I have spent years working, supporting Franklin through a dozen careers whilst he enjoyed the fruits of my labours, followed by those of Debbie Bullough. *Don't be a fool, Janet Jackson,* I tell myself, *just for once, see the future, think of yourself and don't be a fool.*

'He's not moving into the cottage,' I say, calm but tight-lipped.

'Oh, Mum.'

'No, love, that's not happening. He's a grown man, and he needs to sort himself out, and I'm not taking responsibility for that. I supported your father for decades, and he didn't *appreciate it.* So the answer is no.'

'Well, that's that, then. He'll have to be homeless, *my own dad.*'

Chloë has two cups of tea in her hand, both of them wobbling with her frustration. I look at her noble, sweet, loyal face and I'm proud of her.

'We'll help him though, if we can,' I promise.

CHAPTER 13

Booking No. 4: The Lamberts

I received a call from Peter first thing in the morning asking me out for dinner tonight and apologising profusely for not having been in touch. His mum hasn't been well, and he'd had to take time off work to go and visit her in North Yorkshire. She's got six dogs, all of which he hates, so he was hectic, in a blur of sorting social services and social care queries for his mum, finding dog sanctuaries for the dogs and A & E for him. He has had two separate nasty bites from the terrier and the labradoodle. His mum doesn't know he's put the dogs into care yet, but he and the doctors are convinced she's got early-onset Alzheimer's, so there's a good chance she'll never realise they're missing.

Franklin, keeping to his promise, drives his house-car away for the weekend, reassuring Chloë that he will be back on Monday. Our daughter is home for a brief hiatus to get changed from school before rushing out to meet her pal Macey. They are hanging at her house tonight.

'I'll be back tomorrow at some point, is that OK? Thanks. *Love you.* Have you got a little bit of money? Say eight quid for bus fares so I can get into Halifax first thing from school and pick up a lipstick I'm desperate for? A tenner, amazing, thank you. *Love you.'*

Maureen is spending a rare night away with the mystery man. She explains: 'He's told his wife he needs to go and see a dance troupe in Cumbria who he's thinking about putting on at the arts festival.'

So, clues are emerging as to who the lucky chap might be. Maureen seems extremely happy.

'He encourages me, Janet, *to be me.* He likes me. He finds me funny and intelligent and interesting. It's as if he truly gets me. He could be The One.'

'He's somebody else's *One,* Maureen.'

'They're very unhappy though.'

I want to shake her, but her eyes are full of 'don't ruin this, I'm happy.'

'Have a good time,' I say instead.

I peer out of the kitchen window, as 'The One' picks her up at 4.30 p.m. in a black Jeep. My sister is wearing a flowing, purple, floral gown that is slit to the thigh, and has her hair pinned up with a small top hat with a peacock feather on it perched on her head at a curious, gravity-defying angle. I know who the man is – I recognise him immediately. He's scared of seeing me so sits looking straight ahead so he's only visible in profile. It's Harry Latham, who runs the arts festival. I know him from Valley Dental: he had all four wisdom teeth removed in one go and replaced six mercury fillings with white cosmetic veneers.

I snort quietly to myself. He's picked the wrong person if he's hoping to go anywhere incognito. Maureen does not do shame, guilt or sorry.

While I'm snorting, the Lamberts appear, a textbook happy family who ooh and aah around the cottage and seem genuinely delighted with it. They coo over the tiny butters, and the little girl, Rowan, claps when she sees the basket of toys I've pulled together from Chloë's old toy collection. It's exactly the reaction I'd hoped for when I thought about doing the cottage, all those years ago. It feels wonderful to have everything so appreciated. I show them around at 4 p.m. At 4.10 p.m. I hand over the keys and I am out of there, all duties and responsibilities relinquished.

I go back inside to the quiet of the house, then feel lost in the sudden silence of it all. I do a bit of wiping round and shuffle the papers for recycling, and then walk into Hebden to go and meet Peter. It's nice to have something to do with someone.

We have a tasty lamb curry and pakoras at Hammad's, and then Peter walks me home. He agrees to come in only after I reassure him for the tenth time that, really, no one is home.

What can I say about our night together? It's relaxed, romantic and I make more pancakes!

Chloë arrives back the next day as we are eating lunch at 1.30-ish. She doesn't even seem to notice us, as she rushes upstairs, head down and red-eyed. I follow her up to ask if she is OK and does she want something to eat? She gips at the idea of food and says she is just really tired and pulls her duvet over her head. I wonder why she's so upset, then Peter suggests she might be hung-over. When she doesn't get up for the rest of the day and texts me asking for two bacon sandwiches at teatime, I think he might be onto something. Peter has organised to meet friends in Hebden for a drink at 7 p.m. and asks if I want to go?

'Sorry, I've arranged to do something too,' I tell him (like have a bath and read the paper), 'but thank you.'

Then I'm sorry when he's gone, but meeting friends feels far too soon.

I get a lovely goodbye from the Lamberts.

'We've loved it here; it's like the place is brand new.'

I explain it is, and how they were only the fourth guests to use it.

'You should get it on Airbnb,' they urge me. 'Everyone uses Airbnb.'

I love the Lamberts. The cottage is as tidy as when they arrived. They leave the cash tied with a ribbon and a lovely message in the guest book:

Weekend of 9 June

The cottage is beautiful, well equipped, and the hosts are fantastic. A lovely, quiet stay, we can't wait to visit again. Our little daughter Rowan loved the toys and the flowers. Three big kisses, please say we can come again. Aiofe, Tom and Rowan Lambert. X

I officially love being a B&B hostess! I know it's not really B&B. It's self-catering, but S&C doesn't have quite the same *je ne sais quoi* as B&B.

I take my time turning the cottage around, discover another odd sock under the bed and notice we've run out of teabags. There's something *so* satisfying about finishing off the rooms one by one. It's less of a joy to wander back into my own house with basketfuls of B&B washing and realise it looks like a tip. I'm only two washes in and there's damp sheets hanging all over the shop. I ask Chloë five times to bring her rubbish out of her room. She eventually wanders down carrying some manky tea-stained mugs in one hand and a packed wastepaper bin containing the usual number of biscuit wrappers and six empty Sprite bottles in the other. I don't understand: when we're constantly being told we've ruined the planet for the next generation, why they leave us to do all the recycling? I for one have never seen a teenager at a shoe bin, have you?

The house is in reasonable shape, and I'm munching my way through my second home-made cheese and onion pasty when Maureen turns up. She opens the patio door and does a pirouette.

'Hello, sister, where's the mister? How can he resist her? Turn up the transistor.'

Apparently, she and the not-so-mystery man ended up at an impromptu 'spoken word' event in Harrogate. Maureen found herself moved to deliver a few lines she'd jotted down on a beer mat. According to her, it went down very well, and she now needs to dedicate herself to the muse. This muse mainly seems to involve her throwing towels around the bathroom floor, piling a mountain of clothes into the wash basket and eating her way through a box of thirty Jaffa Cakes.

At 9.30 p.m., whilst I'm lying in bed, reading a savoury filo pastry recipe from an old *Good Housekeeping*, Chloë pops her head around the door to say she needs her entire uniform washing. It's been at the bottom of her school bag all weekend.

Aaarrrggghhh!

. . . .

TIPS FOR RUNNING A B&B

Some more questions to ask yourself before you set up a B&B:

Do you like cleaning? There's a lot of it.

Do you enjoy washing? Ditto a lot.

Can you bear having a tidy B&B and an untidy home? Prepare yourself!

And most importantly, enjoy it when it all goes right!

CHAPTER 14

A dinner date with Peter. We agree to try the new Greek place. I'm not a fan of stuffed vine leaves or baklava, but I don't want to be miserable as it's nice to be asked (*praying for lamb kebabs*). Chloë is staying in, with a plan to play all-night *Fortnite* with Greg, who is coming over shortly. Maureen wants to cook for Harry Latham. Maureen doesn't eat, never mind cook, so it's been bizarre watching her flick manically through recipe books. When I offer to defrost one of my home-made steak and ale pies she near collapses in gratitude. In return, I ask her to keep a sex watch on Chloë and Greg. She reassures me she'll make at least two surprise interruptions to check what's going on. Franklin is brooding in his house/car. He's said he'll move the car this weekend 'at some point', which doesn't bode well. He's looking quite miserable and visibly slumps when I walked past in my low-to-moderate heels and burgundy satin top to meet Peter.

Later, when Peter offers to walk me home, I explain it's a bit awkward at mine at the moment as Maureen is 'entertaining'. He looks confused and then pleased and then worried as he – reluctantly, to my mind – suggests we go back to his. When we arrive at his door, he asks for five minutes before I come in, as he needs to do 'a quick pant check'.

'Oh.'

'In case I've left any lying around,' he explains hurriedly.

'Yours or somebody else's?'

He giggles nervously and runs inside. I've been standing outside now for a whole nine minutes, during which time I've said hello to three clients – teeth whitening, brace and front caps – before Peter finally lets me in.

His home is a small flat above the kebab house on Bridge Street. It's pleasant enough, lots of pattern: Liberty print; William Morris. If I had to make a guess, I'd say he's got a lot of his soft furnishings from his mother. He apologises for the smell, though it is more the hot fat coming up from below and stinging my eyes that gets to me. After ten minutes of attempted pleasant chit-chat over the racket of a woman screaming for her money back, Peter offers again to walk me back to mine. He asks if I would mind going back via his allotment, as he'd like to show me his plot. I make a joke about that.

After a bit of a struggle over the locked gate, and a stumble through the darkness, we bash our way through a series of raised beds and wheelbarrows, negotiate round abandoned tools, loose rock, weed piles and compost bins toward the far end of the site, where he proudly introduces me to his plot. From what I can see, in the torch of an old iPhone, it's full to the brim with flowers and climbers and even a couple of trees. Peter picks me some flowers, what look to be dahlias, some roses, daisies and a couple of sprays of gypsophila. I contemplate the silence, the sound of lovely tinkling bells in the evening breeze and those harmonic wooden clatter things, and then a vicious angry voice bellows across the site.

'What the fuck d'you think you're doing in here! Fuck off before I call the police. This is a fucking allotment, not the fucking Co-op. Buy some flowers if you want some.'

'Hi, Gerald, it's me, Peter.'

'Oh, Peter, right. What the fuck are you doing here?'

'Hi. Yes, sorry, Gerald, I just wanted to show Janet my plot.'

'Aye, right. I bet you did.' There's a hideous snigger. 'OK. Well, I'm locking up again now, so are you ready to come out?'

'Yes, yes. Sorry to get you out, Gerald.'

We hurry towards where we think he is, tripping on a fork and bashing into at least two wheelbarrows. I accidentally break the stem of a large sunflower, and Peter grabs onto a wicker sweet pea climbing frame, as he stumbles on a loose rock and brings it crunching down. Gerald is in his sixties, I'd say, one hand holding onto the waistline of his pyjamas, a *shotgun* balanced in the crook of his other arm.

'Blimey. Shotgun, Gerald?'

'How else do you think I keep the bastards off? You're lucky I didn't blow your knackers off.'

'Yes, very. Sorry to disturb you, Gerald.'

'It was the light. I can see the whole site from my bedroom window, so any light and I'm out.'

'Right, well, I'll let you know next time.'

'There won't be a next time. The site's closed at nine p.m. for a reason. So I can get some sleep. S'cuse me, miss.'

He yanks the gate behind us, cursing under his breath, as he puts the lock and chain on and we creep away like naughty kids.

I whisper to Peter, 'You're lucky you didn't get your knackers blown off there, Peter.'

'Aren't I just?'

We both laugh, and Peter pulls me under the canal bridge and we have a smoochy, quite hot-and-bothered kiss.

'You're a great kisser, Janet Jackson.'

'You're not bad yourself, Peter Crouch.'

I am praying that Franklin has gone, though the hope shrivels away the closer we get to home. I can actually hear him as we approach the drive. Anyone with ears can hear him.

'Is that snoring?' says Peter.

'Not sure.' (*Liar.*)

'It does sound like someone's snoring.'

'Yes, it does a bit.' (*A bit!*)

As we walk past Franklin's car, it all becomes apparent.

'It's your ex-husband, Janet.'

'Is it?'

'In his car.'

'Oh. Yes, so it is.'

'Do you want me to wake him up?'

'No, no, leave him be. He's horrible if he doesn't get his sleep.'

'Did you know...?'

'He's been homeless since his girlfriend died.'

'Oh. He's living here, then?'

'Not exactly. He's staying in his car, on the drive. But not on a weekend. That's the rule.'

'It's the weekend now.'

'Yes, something's gone awry.'

It is at this point that we hear a scream from inside the house. I'm not sure what it is, but it sounded like Maureen.

'Excuse me.' I unlock the front door and, no question, Maureen is having loud, unadulterated, screamy sex. I pull the door to behind me. Peter has obviously heard it too.

'Maybe it's best if I...'

We are interrupted by Chloë piling down the stairs at high speed.

'Can you tell her to shut up, Mum? We're trying to concentrate in a four-way shoot-out, and she's panting and screaming like she's on bloody S*ex Factor.*'

Cue another loud yelp from Maureen. Peter looks horribly flustered.

'It's probably best if I get on home,' he says.

'I don't know,' my daughter says snidely, 'you could come in, stop over and let's see if Mum can get any louder than Maureen.'

I plaster on my best '*ha, ha, ha,* aren't-teenagers-great' smile.

'It's very quiet at ours usually, during the week,' I suggest, in some vain attempt to deflect from the hideous, embarrassing circumstances.

Peter kisses me chastely on the cheek and leaves. He glares at Franklin in his car as he passes by. As soon as he has left the drive, I go to close the front door. Franklin sits up in the car, waves, winks and smiles before settling himself down again. I don't smile back. In fact, I throw daggers at him, as I slam the door loudly three times in the vain hope Maureen will hear me.

I can't help feeling like the baggage of my life is seriously cramping any chances of a romantic future.

· ·

TIP ON FAMILY LIFE

Avoid ex-husbands living on your drive if at all possible.

CHAPTER 15

Booking No. 5: The House-Hunters

There's a totally unexpected heatwave and now I have run out of sun cream and summery clothes. A retired dentist, Mr Horton, who I worked with when I was first starting out as a dental receptionist comes into the practice today. He stops to say hello and reminds me of the times when Mr Bacon, who used to be Mr Horton's client, came into the surgery, and the laughs we had asking him to 'lean back'. My former boss also recalls the time we gave the wrong dentures to the wrong client and how we had to drive to their house and organise a swap on the ruse of a 'mobile check-up'. I was carrying the right dentures in a handkerchief, as Mr Horton persuaded Mr Clegg to pop the wrong set out of his mouth on the doorstep so he could have 'a quick quality service check' and swap them with the others without him realising.

'I've done a little tweak,' Mr Horton said smoothly. 'Now, are they feeling any better?'

'Uh...' *chomp, chomp, click* '...actually, yes, they definitely seem to be sitting better.'

'Wonderful news. Thanks, Mr Clegg.'

One soak and scrub later in a bath of sterilised water and gift boxed up in a plastic case, the dentures were received with delight by Mr Neville, who was of course unaware they'd been chomping on Mr Clegg's breakfast thirty minutes earlier. Ah, those were the days.

Peter and I are going out to dinner again. I approached him this time. I'm determined not to let all my family responsibilities get in the way of my love life. We agree to try the bistro in Hebbleroyd. The food at the Greek restaurant we tried last week was greasy and overpriced, and the portions were very small, even though we were having a supposed 'early-bird' deal. Tonight, I have nobbled everyone to please go out. Franklin has moved out to see his mate at the local Texaco garage; Chloë is off to Greg's for a sleepover at his mum's (I'm assuming that will be very well supervised); Maureen was not able to guarantee her whereabouts but promised to keep well out of the way.

All goes well until Harvey scratches Peter. Given Peter's just got over the dog bites sustained at his mother's, he's understandably a bit off animals. Within five minutes, the welt is bright red and pulsing. I give him a Piriton, which he has never taken before, and within ten minutes, probably because he has drunk a couple of beers and a glass of red wine, he is asleep on the sofa. Antihistamines can affect people weirdly; I do know this. I was once in St Pancras station in London and I'd recently started suffering with hay fever. Having spoken to the Boots pharmacist, I bought very expensive antihistamine eye drops to try and stem the streaming, relentless, irritable symptoms in both eyes. I dropped two drops in one eye and was hit by a wave of chronic pain that sent me reeling backwards into a pillar then sinking to the floor concussed.

Presumably, this is what has happened to Peter. Anyway, he's asleep on the sofa and I've put a thin duvet over him. I make myself a peppermint tea and settle down in front of some rubbish TV, consoling myself with the fact I've had my dinner paid for. So much for my attempts at a love life. I hope the other Janet Jackson has better luck in that department.

The next day, as I wave a fully revived Peter off, I get a last-minute request for a couple to stay at the cottage tonight! They sound nice enough on the phone, if a bit desperate, and given the cottage is all set up, why not? Half an hour later, a red-faced, sweaty, bickering lesbian couple turn up. Apparently, they are in town looking at houses to buy. They want to get a dog, so they are in search of house with a garden.

'The valley widens at Hebble, so your chances of getting a garden will increase tenfold,' I explain.

One of them says immediately, 'I told you this. The valley widens, so if we buy on the outskirts of a popular area there's a guarantee of incremental return.'

'Oh, give it a rest, Phil Spencer,' snaps the other woman, and she turns to me with a sigh, saying, 'Can you tell me where the nearest off-licence is please?'

As I explain how to get to the Co-op, 'Phil' gives me £70 cash in a brown envelope.

The couple leave the front door open, for some reason, well after 9 p.m. – possibly as it's still so hot – and I can still hear them bickering about 'incremental return bullshit' at bedtime.

Cash is lovely, I think, fondling the notes. When Chloë asks for a bit of money to go and buy some snacks, it's a great feeling to dip into the cash rather than go through the usual palaver of a bank transfer. *I love my B&B.* I find myself praying to the universe to please let planning be OK. I know I'm being a bit devil-may-care. I've had two bookings since Shannon came, but I keep telling myself they are little, tiny stays, and I can't turn people down. I can't resist the buzz of guests and the nice comments and the feeling I'm not just a dental receptionist any more, I'm a B&B owner, I'm my own boss, I've got cash and all together it makes me feel so good.

The positive feelings linger all afternoon, even when I'm cleaning up from the house-hunters, it's not a drama they've barely touched anything. Though I did notice, both beds were used!

Peter pops into work today carrying another bunch of flowers for me from his allotment. He looks impressed as I am on a phone call on my headphones, as well as responding to a patient in reception, and printing off an appointment at the same time. We end up shaking hands quite formally as he leaves, which is strange, but a public kiss seems too much for both of us. The flowers sit in a bucket under my desk most of the day. They smell wonderful. I am feeling blessed. The cottage seems to be working. I'm five bookings in now. Chloë seems happy, and I've got someone bringing me flowers. The only downside is I have a sandal tan line that is not shifting. Flip-flops tomorrow.

When I get home, there's a letter from planning: the Lavander Cottage HAS PASSED! We've got retrospective planning! *In your face, Laura Watson.* I feel like doing a dance and wiggling my bottom in her general direction. I restrain from either doing this or mentioning this plan to Maureen who would, in an instant, put it into action and force me to go along with her. I spend the last of the cash from the house-hunters on buying a bottle of Prosecco and insist that we all go into Lavander Cottage and have a glass in celebration. Maureen has drunk hers within seconds. I ignore her hints to refill her glass. Chloë tells me she prefers Prosecco cocktails, and I am left wondering when has my daughter had cocktails? Even Franklin is jolly after a glass of bubbly.

'Well done, Jan,' he says. 'I did like the garage as a garage, but it's a house thing now. Good on you.'

I'm ever so chuffed. I hang around all evening in the cottage fluffing cushions and rearranging the crockery.

Peter rings and offers to bring round a bottle of Prosecco to celebrate the planning decision. I suggest we get together at the weekend, and offer to cook. Peter has insisted on paying for the last two weeks of meals out, and I just think it's a lot for a librarian; he can't be earning a huge wage. Peter doesn't let on, but I can tell he's delighted or relieved, one or the other. Especially so once I have confirmed and reassured him that the house will be ours alone. Though this, of course, requires a lot of manoeuvring of people without them really understanding what's going on. I don't want to breed resentment or make everyone feel pushed about for a second time, but needs must.

I know Chloë is desperate to stop over at her mate Nisha's, as they've been planning a Harry Potter marathon for ages, so I encourage her to do it and give her cash for goodies. I explain to Maureen that I need some alone time with Peter and persuade her out with a twenty-pound note. Franklin – I just insist he parks up elsewhere for the night. He looks depressed but, let's be honest, I can't tell the difference between a depressed day and a not-depressed day with him at the moment.

Anyway, Saturday can't arrive fast enough. My mojo is definitely back on and working. Not having sex in six years is easier, it turns out, than not having sex in two weeks for some reason – after you've had sex again for the first time in six years. Well, I definitely want a lot more of it.

So much so that, even given the fantastic menu, if I do say so myself...

Home-made steak and ale pudding
Minted crushed peas

Baby roast potatoes
Onion gravy

Ginger cheesecake
Amaretto ice cream

...we have barely got the first glass of Prosecco down before we bounce up the stair carpet on our way to the bedroom. Janet Jackson is a sex goddess, and not a bad cook either! We are soon rushing back down for dinner. It's a food, sex, food, sex spectacular. Sunday, Peter is up and off early for an outing with a rambling group. He tries to persuade me to go along: they're doing a 10K up to Lumb Falls, but I'm more interested in doing the garden. I need to tie up some roses that are flopping all over the place and divide some rudbeckia that is looking very congested. Also, I feel a bit guilty about not spending enough time with Chloë recently – not that she seems bothered. These days, she runs upstairs as soon as she comes in with barely a hello.

I decide to try and tempt her down with a big Sunday dinner: a roast chicken – her favourite –lots of veg and a great pile of roast potatoes and Yorkshire puds. One by one, Chloë, Franklin and Maureen appear around the table, tempted in by the smell, and they demolish everything. It should be a bit strange having Franklin there, but Chloë is so happy and I'm in the afterglow of a wonderful night. It's great to have my food so appreciated – I love cooking for everyone. Let's be frank, I love everything at the moment.

Maureen gives us a blow-by-blow account of her evening, which she spent doing some impromptu spoken word at the White Lion after a fight had broken out: she decided what was needed to restore the atmosphere was a dirty limerick or two. I persuade her that one dirty limerick is enough for Sunday dinner. Chloë says she and Nisha had got so scared after one of the later Harry Potters that they had watched the last one downstairs with Nisha's mum. Franklin stays quiet about his evening and picks at the remains of his chicken. He only manages a smile when Chloë insists on him playing 'snap the wishbone' and she wins. I don't know how I'm left with the washing-up, but Franklin offers to dry and, after a few words, we both go quiet listening to the birdsong that drifts in through the open window.

'Beautiful,' he says.

'Yes. Wonderful.'

'Fancy a glass outside?'

I know Franklin well enough to understand that he is not in a good place. And as much as I want to be oblivious and not get drawn into his problems, I still care for this man and want him to be OK... mainly for Chloë's sake. She needs her dad. We sit together in the garden absorbing the quiet. It's a perfect evening. He pours two large glasses of red wine, but there's no way I'm getting through all that.

'That's enough for me. You all right, Franklin? You seem a bit... down.'

'What's it all about, eh, Janet? I can't see the point at the moment.' He drains his glass and refills it to the brim.

'You're grieving, Franklin. Life always feels dark for a while. You'll bounce back.'

'Will I?' He goes with gusto at the glass.

'Of course you will. Please go steady on the wine.' I grab the bottle from the table. 'Sorry to be judge-y, but it's a depressant. You know this. It's not going to help. Maybe try weekends only?'

'It's Sunday today.'

'Sundays don't count, it's work tomorrow.'

'Oh, yes.'

He slumps. I get up, stand behind him and give him a hug and plant a kiss on the top of his head.

'Come on, let's get you set up with a bed in the back room. A good night's sleep can do wonders, and is it just me, or is it...' (I make a point of sniffing loudly) '...shower time?'

I nudge a smile out of him and go inside to dig out some bedding. I wrestle the two fold-down beds out of the cottage from the Turner stay and put them next to each other in the downstairs back room. It used to be a dining room but, as we now eat in the kitchen or in front of the TV, nobody much goes in there and it's a bit of dumping ground. I make a bodged attempt to wrap a double sheet across them both and stick a duvet and a couple of pillows on there. I also set up a side table and a little lamp. It will do. Franklin wanders in wrapped in a towel. He's a big, handsome guy, and I make an effort not to feel anything. I hurry out.

'Thank you, Janet, thank you,' I hear him say, as I dash upstairs. I don't reply and go straight to bed.

It's a busy day at Valley Dental and having made the decision to cycle in to try to get some exercise today, I regret it at my leisure when rain starts pouring down just as I'm heading home. I'm a drowned rat, as I wander around the house collecting dirty crockery to stick in the dishwasher. I'm towelling my hair when I head into the living room and find Franklin sitting in front of *Pointless*, surrounded by used tissues, and although he attempts to pulls himself together, he's obviously struggling. I make a cup of tea for us both and go and sit with him.

'I'm OK,' he says gruffly.

'I know you are.'

'I'll get back on my feet.'

'I know you will.'

We watch *Antiques Road Trip* together. It's something we used to discuss doing ourselves at one time.

'I've lost my job,' he tells me.

'Ah. OK.'

'My car has stopped working.'

'Right.'

'I was using it as a taxi.'

'I see. Have you checked the battery?'

'I've had it on charge for the last three days.'

'Right.'

I make cauliflower cheese for tea. It has always been Franklin's favourite.

I catch sight of him later slumped in the driver's seat. I insist Chloë takes him a hot chocolate and encourages him inside to watch something with her. I tell him he can carry on sleeping in the dining room for the moment. The car is just too sad.

He's mooching around the house for the next three days, and I can think of little else but what to do about Franklin. He's taking over the house. I find his socks in the bathroom, there's barely any milk for a cup of tea this morning, his shirts are in the wash basket and he's so blooming big and noisy with his sneezing and his coughing and blowing his nose. It's like I'm going back in time. He makes a rare outing to visit someone in Hebden, so I hijack a nice curry meal – chicken tikka masala and home-made flatbreads – to drill Chloë and Maureen.

'I think we need to find Franklin a shelter of some sort,' I announce suddenly.

Chloë nearly leaps out of her seat. 'WHAT! A shelter? What kind of shelter? A homeless shelter? For Dad? No. It'd kill him. He can stay here. What's wrong with here?'

'Chloë, I'm no longer comfortable with having your dad here. We divorced over six years ago now.'

'He's desperate, Mum.'

Maureen pipes up: 'We all get lonely and down on our luck sometimes. He's in need of shelter and compassion. Surely, as fellow humans, we can offer him that?'

'The only person subsidising all this compassion is me,' I say hotly. 'I'm the only person out working to support us all, and I don't want to – and can't afford to – support Franklin too. He's a grown man.'

'Mum, please, it's not for ever.'

I give up with that 'please'. I make myself a cup of tea and a toasted fruit teacake and flick through an old *Good Housekeeping*. Franklin turns up half an hour or so later with some eggs. I nod my appreciation but don't get up. I can hear Maureen and Chloë chatting with him.

Chloë comes in looking for a drink and asks, 'When do the next people arrive in the cottage, Mum?'

'Oh, a few people have made enquiries. I need to get in and get it sorted tomorrow.' I have had no enquiries, but I wanted to divert the 'why can't Dad move in' query again.

I don't like lying to Chloë, but this is what having Franklin around does for our relationship. I am in bed for 8.30 p.m. I feel quite down listening to the laughter drifting up the stairs. I occupy myself with fantasy menus for the next two weeks based on a limitless budget and time, and once I get past the lobster bisque and the chocolate fondant on day three, I'm soon at spag bol and shepherd's pie. Imagination was never my strong suit. I might need to get creative though, if I'm to keep Chloë and Franklin at bay.

Some new guests need to book themselves in – and soon.

I spend every spare minute between clients glued to the HebWeb booking portal trying to work out if there is a way to book the cottage myself, but not from my log-in. We currently have bookings in for spring bank, and that's it. I am about to hit a six-week block booking from the Valley Dental computer when I realise quite how stupid I'm being, as the fantasy guests won't actually turn up, and maybe I need to employ actors? I decide I am losing the plot and might need to do an Alzheimer's test at some point. It's at this moment, Peter pops his head in. Do I fancy some lunch?

Hebden is full of cafés. You trip over one as you come out of another. It's about getting to know who does what well and when. There's platters and toasties, traditional big Yorkshire meals with sausages and gravy, egg and chips, all-day breakfasts, fish and chips and the street food curry stall, Greek mezze, vegan mezze, Sri Lankan mezze, Brazilian taco and refried beans, four different pizza places and even a sushi shop. Peter is dilly-dallying around the toastie queue, but I spot that the Watermill is doing a cheese and onion pie with peas special and their scones are to die for, so I bundle him into there.

Once we get settled, Peter is away. I can't get a word in. His mum is not well again, and he's got to go over to Grassington again tomorrow to give her some support. I offer to bake him a cake to take with him. This cheers him up. He tells me that coffee and walnut is his favourite. He opens up about his work and how the manager of the library has stopped washing, so his personal body odour has to be smelled to be believed. He knows Jojo Moyes and Marian Keyes are the most popular authors and *The Greatest Showman* is still the most in-demand DVD. He tells me his favourite book is *Germinal* by Zola. I don't think he is very impressed when I say the last book I'd read was Steve Davis's autobiography, only because it was left in the reception at work. I do crack a little joke though, saying that it wasn't very 'interesting'. I explain I am more into cookbooks and gardening books, more factual stuff, which he seems to appreciate.

'I'll try to get you the new Nigella when it comes back in.'

'Thank you. I'll do your cake for you tonight. Come round and collect it before you go.'

We have a steamy five minutes at his, before I rush back to work. His flat really does stink of hot fat. I don't think I could stomach a full night of it.

I use Chloë as an excuse: 'She's not expecting me to be out tonight... plus I want to get back and do this cake.' He's miserable. I try to cheer him up with a cuddle and a kiss, but he's holding on tight and I know he's gutted about his mum and the smelly man at work and his stinky flat. I'm feeling a bit down too, but I can't really explain my ex-partner-living-with-me woes. It's not right somehow. I want to invite Peter round to the house, but when I think about Franklin being there it feels impossible. Something has to be done.

When I get in and Chloë suggests takeout Friday, I don't join in the conversation but defrost a minestrone soup and go to bed early. Not that anyone notices. Tracks from the *Sounds of the 70s* 1977 CD blasts up the stairs from 8 p.m. till 1 a.m., when I decide I have had enough. I stamp downstairs and turn the sound right down just as 'Yes Sir, I Can Boogie' comes on for the third time.

Peter is round early and I'm up and at it, already busy decorating his cake. I'm a bit behind, as I'd had to gut the kitchen before I could start baking, as it was a tip and Franklin had just deposited a pile of dirty crockery from the living room onto the pristine side.

I was in a right old sulk, and it must have been obvious because Peter asks the question, 'Everything OK? You seem a bit tense.'

Well, now it's my time to sort of explode. Not in an angry, shouty way, which I never do – well, maybe once every three years or so – but in heated whispers. Having ensured all the doors are closed, I pour out all my ex-husband problems: the impossible dilemma of trying to be a nice person whilst feeling that no one around you gives a monkey's about how you might feel; being forced to be the only hard face around here and the only one who is shouldering all the responsibility for keeping everyone and everything going.

Franklin walks in amid one of these rages, but Peter and I expertly switch tack onto his mother's dog, before returning to the whispery rage. Peter, it turns out, is a brilliant listener. It is *sooo* good to get it off my chest. He doesn't interrupt, he doesn't judge, and he sympathises, nodding in all the right places. I can't stop. Why is everyone looking at the cottage as a solution when it represents my only chance to save for an early retirement? How, how, *how* am I going to throw my ex-husband out without my daughter hating me? Without my sister going all forlorn and depressed? What if leaving here does send Franklin over the edge and he turns into an alcoholic? Then he's on the streets and sleeping in doorways. What if he dies? Chloë will never forgive me. I'll never forgive myself.

I barely take a breath for twenty minutes; the cake is abandoned half-decorated and I have a serious sweat on.

Peter walks over and puts his arm around me, says: 'Shall we maybe make a list and see if we can work out a solution for each thing, one by one?'

'Don't you have to get to your mum's?'

'Yes, but if I'm there a bit later, it's fine.'

I'm so happy. I love a list.

Cottage
Action
Agree to get the cottage onto as many sites as possible.
Theory
It's far too occupied for anyone to live in it. Or rent out permanently.
Other action
Get Maureen to help (ahem)?

Franklin
Action
Ask Maureen to help. Explain having ex-husband around is causing me real angst. Can she help him find a job? (I want to laugh when Peter suggests this, however, I conclude she is good at finding jobs, just not sticking at them. We shall see.)
Suggest to Franklin, out of earshot of Chloë or Maureen, that he start looking for a job and alternative accommodation.

Chloë
Action
Take out for shopping trip and explain (and this was Peter's genius suggestion) that this will be the last one for a while unless I get help soon, as I'm running out of money, and can

she persuade her dad to begin looking for a job.
Theory
If Franklin finds a job, it won't be long before he wants to get out and about, sees a nice woman and starts to get romantic. Obviously, that cannot happen here. It's a great plan.
I also suggest that, if he can bear it, having Peter around a bit more often during the week will make the house seem more mine than anyone else's. And having him at my side for support will make me feel less like I'm being pushed around.

It's another great element to the plan, and Peter beams. It's my way of saying 'thank you, I like you.' He seems very, very happy, and we even sneak off into the utility and have a very smoochy kiss before Chloë interrupts us while she is searching for cookie dough ice cream.

We wander around the garden together, our hands touching, and he helps me deadhead the geranium and stake up the blousy hydrangea. I'm so sad when he leaves. It's the first time I've really felt that pang of longing when I'm waving him off. Like twines round the heart, pulling tight. I occupy myself with the garden. It's in full miracle, with the roses stalking up the trellis and the heady lavender perfume, the scarlet geums reaching into everything and the neon cosmos plants all wound in with the sweet peas. The world feels full of joy and optimism. Come on, Janet, I tell myself. It's all going to be OK.

· ·

TIP FOR RUNNING A B&B

Never take sides in an argument that your guests are having. You don't want to be named in the divorce.

· ·

TIP ON LIFE

Sometimes helping other people is not being kind to yourself.

CHAPTER 16

Maureen is distraught. She was up on time, but the train was cancelled so she missed a meeting with the Job Centre. Her benefits have now been suspended. We don't know how long for, but six weeks is average, apparently, according to some mates of hers at the White Swan. She's moping around the house trying to offer me help with things like the washing-up. I want to say, 'Yes, you can help', but it would feel so pointed today, as if the dynamic has changed with her new jobless, penniless status. It would feel as if I now expect her to help me as a penance, making her a sort of Cinderella and me the heartless stepmother, when, if I'm being brutally honest, it feels like the other way round usually, what with her swanning about in her long, grand dresses and me in my rubber gloves.

After forty minutes of her mooching around, I tell her she's fine and to go and watch telly. With Franklin on my homeless register and now Maureen off benefits, I feel grateful to have a job with a permanent contract and a roof over my head.

To add to our woes, Harvey seems to have gone missing. He doesn't like the Felix casserole sachets I bought in bulk from the big store called The Range. I blame myself for penny-pinching.

I reluctantly agree to go food shopping at Lidl with Maureen and Chloë after work. I know it's never a good idea to shop when hungry, but I've no choice. There has been a volley of complaints over the last month about the quality of snacks in the house, and with Harvey missing I can't bear the thought of driving Chloë out too, with the awful food. I don't have the heart to say Franklin is eating us out of house and home. This shopping trip, we all know, is a consequence of his appetite. He lives in the kitchen cupboard, but no one wants to acknowledge the impact his being around is having. So, by the time we're done, the trolley is absolutely heaving and comes to £137.00. This is a *weekly* shop.

I realise that the way things are going, shopping for Chloë, Maureen *and Franklin* now, I am going to be financially up the creek unless I do something about it soon. I make the decision I'm going to put the cottage on Airbnb. When I tell them this in the car on the way home, and say that I'm going to need some help, there is general moaning. So I point out to Chloë that her three types of smoothie, Ben and Jerry's cookie dough ice cream, hot chilli Doritos and salt and vinegar Pringle tubes do not grow on trees and, similarly, Maureen's forty-eight small bottles of Polish Zywiec lager, kilo of salted peanuts and three bottles of Merlot have to be paid for somehow, it shuts them both up. The wittering begins again in the endless traffic chaos of flood roadworks.

My sister and daughter both disappear with their snacks once the shopping has been put away, and something about having a house full of food means I'm no longer hungry. I make beans on toast and Franklin joins me. We sit together and discuss the weather, the garden looking nice, his car battery playing up, what happened to his motorbike badge collection – nothing really important, nothing that I should have said – but it was nice, it was relaxed, and he even scraped his plate and put it in the dishwasher.

Two days later, Harvey is still missing. I feel very sad using the sticky roller on my blue chinos to clean off cat hair from when he sat on the washing. I'm contemplating creating *Have you seen this cat?* posters and get engrossed in looking through old photographs trying to find one of him. The bulk of the photos are from when Franklin was around. Looking through them stirs up all the old emotions, good and bad; the silly face-pulling, hand in hand on the beach, watching him watching Chloë on a donkey, whitewashed buildings, blue skies, cool sunglasses and him, posed astride a motorbike.

It's as if the past is a glue. I could stare at this stuff forever, when what I want to do is move on, take more pictures and add to the pile. I get ruthless and spirit away a third of those that feature Franklin. I daren't put them in the main bin in case anyone spots them, so I stick them in an old cat food box at the bottom of the recycling. No one ever does the recycling bar me, so I know I'm safe. I don't find one photo of the cat.

As per the plan, Peter comes to stay overnight. It's a bit strange when he and Franklin say hello to each other in the kitchen. We go to bed early, but it's not the most relaxing of stopovers. The bathroom never stops being used and the endless palaver of the lights being switched on and off wakes Peter, who looks horribly disorientated and complains of eye cramp. I didn't know that was a thing, so I am not very sympathetic. He has set the alarm for just after 6.30 a.m., as he has an author's visit to arrange and will need to organise furniture for the event at the library.

I make him an egg and mushroom bap to take with him then plod around in my dressing gown clearing the dishwasher. Fifteen minutes later, there's a knock at the door. It's Peter, looking wretched and carrying a muddy bin liner. He explains that he has just collected the squashed remains of Harvey from the side of the road and they are now in the bag.

I start to sniffle, at the exact moment that Chloë comes down for her regular giant mug of posh, wake-me-up coffee. She immediately comforts me, with an accusatory stare at Peter. Once I tell her what has happened, she fills up. Unbelievably for this time in the morning, sensing drama at any distance, Maureen swishes in, and once we explain she goes into full wailing, mourning mode.

'It's my fault he's gone!' she grieves. 'He'd pulled a pom-pom off my Aztec dressing gown when I passed him on the stairs, so I'd kicked him.'

We're all getting very weepy and the tissues are flying, and poor Peter is standing there with the bin bag, when I completely automatically open the patio door to let Harvey in, who is pawing at the door.

Jubilation as we realise Harvey is alive! Harvey is back from the dead! Cuddles, cream and a tin of tuna for Harvey. Poor Peter doesn't have time for a cup of tea now though. He is late and has to dispose of unknown animal remains on his way to work.

We try very hard not to laugh, as we wave him off, but the truth is we are hysterical and hanging off each other. Franklin, looking very grizzled, comes to the door to see what the noise is about at the precise moment Laura Watson jogs past in a revealing lime-green Lycra onesie and matching bumbag. Between the pair of them, they put us even further on the floor. When we go back inside it is nine thirty in the morning, and I am emotionally and physically worn out. Harvey seems to appreciate all the love and affection for the first hour, then he's had enough and lashes out at Chloë, giving her a scratch on the face which she can't cover up even with Maureen's performance artist panstick.

After all the excitement of the morning, I am grateful it's a day off and happy that the weather is dry enough to get in a few hours in the garden. That night, I manage to cook a shepherd's pie for us all, and we enjoy all being together in a kind of dysfunctional family way.

Peter texts me in the morning to enquire how the plan is progressing. I think he's somewhat put out I didn't invite him over last night, but I was just too tired. I suppose, from his point of view, I'm at home with my ex-husband. It can't be comfortable thinking about that from a smelly flat. I determine to crack on with the plan and spend the day on Airbnb setting up a profile for the cottage. It's pretty easy because we've done all the hard work before, with the leaflets and everything. Chloë approves it, when she eventually gets up at 2.30 p.m. That's the school holidays for you! I take a deep breath and send it up to the internet universe at half past three, with prayers and good wishes.

Just three hours later, I get a request for a stopover for Monday night from a woman called Ellen who is visiting her mum in hospital. I press 'accept' and gulp. That was so quick! I spend a couple of hours cleaning the cottage with Dettol antibacterial just to be on the safe side. I don't want our visitor taking germs into her mum if she's in hospital. Our first Airbnb. A new chapter.

CHAPTER 17

Booking Nos. 6 and 7: Ellen & Donalda

I shall still be at work when Ellen arrives at 3 p.m., so Maureen agrees to be there to let her into Lavander Cottage. Everything goes well. *So* well, in fact, that Ellen and Maureen are drinking wine when I get home at six o'clock. Apparently, they have a mutual love of *The Chase*.

Ellen is going to stay another night, as it turns out that her mum is seriously ill with suspected pneumonia in Calderdale General Hospital. When she comes across to the house to ask if she can extend her stay, Ellen ends up stopping with us for quite a while. That first night, she spends telling us about her lovely mum who's worked herself to the bone over the years fostering multiple children, and how her sister, who's in Australia (and very selfish), refuses to come back, even though she's loaded with money from her job working for Sydney Opera boat tours. We hear how Ellen is the only one who gets up here to visit her mum. The sisters do have a brother, but he fell out with his dad after a fight over some vintage Lego set one Christmas Day many years ago. The father and son hadn't spoken for fifteen years and, even when the dad died, the son didn't come to the funeral and even to this day remains estranged from their mother.

Ellen herself is struggling to keep a roof over her head, she tells us. She's a bookkeeper for a charity and suffers with psoriasis. She's been ten years single and doesn't think she'll ever find anyone, and she's quite lonely and had to give up her cat last year as it was aggravating her skin condition.

I am exhausted by the time I drag myself to bed. Fortunately, Maureen is available to continue the listening and drinking well into the night. I check my emails last thing and have another request through Airbnb for Thursday through till Sunday. I am so exhausted, I just clicked 'accept', thinking, I'll sort it out in the morning.

The next day is the hottest day of the year, apparently, in the UK. Not in Hebden Bridge; we've had cloud cover for three days and everyone is complaining. That's how spoilt we are. Cloud cover and we're up in arms. I remember past Julys when we were actually flooded. Once, when we'd planned a barbecue, it rained so much that Franklin brought the barbecue (one of those tin trays) into the house. We had to open all the windows because of the smoke, which brought on a mild asthma attack for Sharon, one of our neighbours. We were all so cold, we were standing around indoors in our anoraks, the fire on full blast, chewing on corn on the cobs that weren't cooked properly. *That's* July.

Neither Maureen nor Ellen are up when I leave for work today. I put a note through the cottage door explaining to Ellen that I have new people coming to stay from Thursday over the weekend and 'hope that is OK'.

On the Thursday morning, I'm poised from 7 a.m. with my cleaning kit to get into the cottage in preparation for the exit of Ellen and the arrival of Donalda Stokes, her seventeen-year-old daughter Dash and her husband Frederick at 4 p.m.

At ten past nine, Ellen comes rushing out of the cottage in her pyjamas, her face tear-streaked with mascara. She rushes to the patio door, bangs on it and falls into my arms, wailing, 'Mum's died!'

I shout for Maureen who's good at these emotional moments. She flies down the stairs, traipsing red silk satin like a mascot for the Chinese state circus. She weeps with Ellen like an expert. After about half an hour of mutual moaning, Maureen seems to get bored and goes off on one, explaining to Ellen about how *our* dead mother preferred chickens to children and how she should count herself lucky. At the same time, I try to remind Ellen, in as gentle a way as possible, that the cottage is booked from Thursday to Sunday. Maureen shakes her head and rubs her finger and thumb together behind Ellen's back, as if I'm a money-grabbing monster. I'm feeling horribly compromised, but can't and won't now refuse the booking; it is a whole weekend – three nights' income, after all. So in a desperate attempt to make things OK, I suggest that maybe Ellen can stay in our house whilst things get sorted out? Ellen immediately stops crying and agrees.

I clean the cottage thoroughly, *I have to*. Ellen is quite a messy cook, eater and washer, so it seems; there is sauce all over the cooker, the table and the floor. We carry her stuff (there's lots of it) over to the main house, and I don't know how I agree to it, but anyway, she's got all her bags in my bedroom.

Meanwhile, Donalda has rung me six times on her way from Hunstanton to check the location of the cottage and how to get there.

Whilst I nip out to get some milk and bread, I ask Maureen to be ready to welcome Donalda, but she somehow forgets to keep a lookout. So, on my return from the Co-op, I find Donalda – who is a very large, intimidating woman – sitting in her huge black Land Rover Discovery, glaring at me when I approach the car window with the bag of shopping for the welcome basket.

I tap on the window. 'Hello, is it Donalda?'

She imperiously lets the window go right down before speaking to me.

'We've been waiting over eight minutes.'

'I do apologise. I wanted to get you some fresh bread. Would you like to come in?'

I end up dragging two enormous suitcases down the drive, just as Laura Watson pulls up down the street and does an exaggeratedly slow reverse (she never reverses) into her drive. If I'd had a spare hand I would have pointedly waved. As it was, I was pushed to wiggle an eyebrow.

I need to think about talking to the council. Is this Airbnb all legal? You can bet if it's not, Laura will be on it.

I show the newcomers around the cottage. Donalda, it turns out, is difficult to please. She picks up the tea towel and sniffs it. She goes into the bedroom, sits on the bed, then bounces on it and loudly harrumphs. After she has rearranged all four pillows at least five times each, I'm ready to throttle her. She punches the cushions on the sofa, and they're M&S Designers Guild so I *know* there's nothing wrong with them. When she rubs the hand towel in the bathroom on her chin and scowls, I decide I really need to get out of there before I say something I might regret. I fake interest in my phone, pretend to text someone and make my excuses. I leave Dash and Frederick, who seem happy enough, making tea and tucking into the cookie jar. No sooner have I left the cottage than I get a call from Donalda asking about the Wi-Fi code. I return and show them the code in the welcome pack and follow it by picking up the router and showing them the same code on the back of that.

I am anxious all night expecting a knock on the door or another call from Donalda. It comes at ten past eleven when I am almost asleep on the camp bed in Chloë's room, so I don't answer. I let the call go and then receive a text moments later.

What time do we need to leave on Sunday?

I respond, *11 a.m.*

We may need to leave a little later. Can we store our luggage until we come back?

I am so tired I write, *Discuss tomorrow. Goodnight.*

I can feel the vibration of a return text, but I hide it under the bed and force myself to turn the light off and get some sleep.

I read Donalda's text early the next morning after a restless and uncomfortable night. It says, *We are attending a morning service at Halifax Minster and visiting an Open Gardens event in Cragg Vale Sunday. We shall be out most of the day. Are we at liberty to leave our luggage until we leave later that day?*

I respond at 7 a.m. *As long as you have everything packed up you can leave the luggage in the main house.*

She responds at 7.01 a.m. *Thank you. I detected a smoky smell in the kitchen cupboard and have found two cigarette butts in the far corner. I have put them in the bin.*

Hosting Donalda is like having *The Hotel Inspector* come to visit, only with less charm and humour, and without the curly, attractive hair of Alex Polizzi.

When Peter comes round for tea tonight, as per our plan, he can't understand why Ellen is camped out in my bedroom. I try to explain, but he doesn't seem very convinced or understanding. I don't know what to say or do and open a bottle of Pinot Grigio I have been saving for a while and concentrate on making a nice chicken pie.

Franklin overhears Peter asking me how long Ellen is staying, and immediately chips in with: 'She's a big eater, that woman. She's demolished the whole jar of Nutella.'

I respond with, 'Her mother's just died.'

'Has she?' Franklin looks sceptical.

'What do you mean?'

'She doesn't seem very upset for someone who's just lost her mother.'

'Of course she's upset. People respond to grief in different ways.'

'I've sat in on way too many conversations now,' he tells me, 'and at no point has she talked about arrangements or contacting the rest of the family or even visiting the hospital. I don't even believe she's here visiting her mother. Mark my words, there's something fishy about her.'

I can't understand what he's on about.

'Don't be unkind,' I say.

Franklin tuts at me and then wanders out of the kitchen with two bottles of Polish lager and a tub of chilli Doritos. Peter avoids catching my eye, until eventually he does, and I know there's a pointedness about it.

'What?' I snap.

'It might be worth phoning the hospital.'

'Don't be ridiculous.'

He goes outside into the garden with his glass of wine and shakes his head to himself a number of times when he thinks I'm not able to see him.

Meanwhile, Ellen and Maureen appear in the kitchen both looking incredibly glamorous and already very merry, as they disappear off into Halifax in a taxi.

I uncork a second bottle of Pinot Grigio that I have definitely been saving for a special occasion and share my vague concerns about Ellen to Chloë, as I'm loading the dishwasher. Within twenty-five minutes, Chloë has established that Ellen does not have a mother in Calderdale General and that there have been no female deaths this week, though one older lady called Joyce did have a nasty turn, but thankfully she's pulled through. We decide to act. Chloë helps me pack up all of Ellen's belongings from my bedroom, where they are strewn across the floor. She takes two of my best scarves, a mascara and my bottle of Thierry Mugler out of Ellen's many bags, and we pile everything by the front door.

I send a text to Maureen: *Ellen not what she seems, think you should probably come home.*

I don't get a reply for the next five minutes, after which Chloë gets on the phone and leaves a message.

'Maureen, she's a lying cowbag who's nicked some of my mum's stuff. Get your arse home now and bring her with you, we're kicking her out. She doesn't even have a mother in hospital.'

I am exhausted and agitated waiting for them to come back in. I am probably also quite merry. Peter asks politely if I would mind if he went upstairs to read? I tell him to help himself whilst I do some cleaning downstairs in my pyjamas. I am bleaching the sink when Donalda comes over to complain about the smell of cooking. I apologise and then, as she stamps away, I immediately regret it. THAT IS IT! A switch flicks. I am sick and tired and disappointed in myself for feeling like a complete pushover from all these horrible people who think nothing about taking advantage of me. When I hear the taxi pulling up on the drive, I pick up all of Ellen's bags, six of them between my fingers, go out, open the boot of the taxi, as Ellen and Maureen stagger out of it, and say, 'Please wait,' to the taxi driver.

'Ellen, your bags are packed and they're in the boot of the car. I want you out of my house. You have been lying to us about your situation, and I don't want to hear any more of your lies, thank you. Please ask this gentleman to take you wherever you plan to go. Goodbye.'

Ellen begins to giggle and bluster at the same time, saying, 'I've paid my way.'

'Yes, for two nights only so it's time to go.'

Maureen looks absolutely furious. Thankfully, Franklin and Chloë appear and steer my sister inside. Ellen can't decide what to do with her face, too intoxicated to think straight, but with it enough to comprehend what is going on. She lurches into the back of the taxi and closes the door.

She winds the window down and, almost enjoying the ridiculous spectacle, says loudly, 'Doncaster, driver, and put your foot down. Bye, Maureen love, I'll text you.' She sticks two fingers up at me. 'Bitch!'

'Yes, you are,' I respond, as fast as lightning, and off Ellen the Liar goes into the night.

I don't know how they manage it, but Maureen is hushed and out of sight when I go back in. Franklin is locking the patio doors and turning off the lights. We are both standing there in the dark and, I don't know why but, surfing my assertive, confident self, I know I can say anything.

'Thank you, Franklin – oh, and could you please try and sort yourself out. I don't want you to be sad and I don't want to have to ask you to leave but, well, you need to get a job. I'm broke, I can't support everyone. You're not helping yourself or me, and you need to get a grip.'

'Understood, Janet.'

'Thank you.'

I leave him there in the dark. I am feeling like Rocky Balboa walking to the top of the steps, only I am slightly too drunk to make it up in one go.

Chloë gives me a hug when I stagger out of the bathroom.

'Well done, Mum.'

I don't know what it's for, but positives and hugs from Chloë are too rare to argue with.

When I go into the bedroom, Peter is asleep. My *Which Guide to Everything* is in his hand. I make a little bit of noise cleaning my teeth and getting changed. He stirs and asks me if I'm OK, do I need anything? I tell him I need a good, solid hug and he interprets that in a very nice and delightful way.

I am very pleased to see the back of the Stokes – Donalda, Frederick and Dash. However, I am way too hung-over to get involved, so Peter kindly offers to deal with their luggage in the morning. I am still in my dressing gown when the Stokes return after lunch to pick up their bags, so I hide in the living room and watch from behind the curtain. Donalda sits statuesque in the driver's seat, and by that I mean still, silent and stony, staring into the distance – quite terrifying – whilst Frederick, with a face puckered with worry, struggles with the gigantic suitcases. At one point he is on his knees, and Peter goes out and gives him a hand to push the thing into the boot. God knows what she's got in there.

I don't bother getting out of my PJs. It is a truly vicious hangover. I think I might be in shock from all the confrontation. I make bacon, bean and brown sauce toasties for what seems like hours. Franklin attempts to jump-start the car down the hill and, after he and Peter push it back up the hill twice, he steers it onto the drive and declares it dead. This is a worry, but he is soon on the phone and gets some bags and empties the vehicle of rubbish, which seems like progress of a kind.

I eventually crowbar myself off the sofa and go into Lavander Cottage to attempt the first pass of cleaning. A pleasant surprise greets me. There is a bin bag by the door, three bags of recycling split into cardboard, glass and plastic; the beds are stripped and the bedding folded into neat piles, with the windows open to freshen the place up. Everything has been put away, and the towels are stacked in the bathroom. The place is immaculate. Donalda is clearly a domestic goddess of the highest standards. On reflection, I decide that she would have been deeply disappointed had she come here and found that everything was perfect. How she must have crowed when she found those cigarette butts!

No problem, Donalda, you can have that one courtesy of Janet J.

. . . .

TIPS FOR RUNNING A B&B

Don't get emotionally involved with the guests.

Remember they're paying you for B&B only. Not therapy.

Accept that you can never please the Donaldas of this world.

CHAPTER 18

Booking No. 8: Simon & Bali – Mountain Bikers

Another week and another Airbnb booking. The cottage is full for a week from Friday with Simon and Bali, a young couple coming to check out Hebden for its mountain biking.

I'm on reception and don't want to draw attention to the fact that I'm moonlighting on the job, so when they ask over the phone is the mountain biking good, I just say, 'Yes, I hear it's good.'

At Valley Dental, we've had a couple of clients over the years come in with mountain-biking injuries. One very handsome young man lost both his front teeth coming down Stoodley Pike – the steep hill near the town of Todmorden – and had to have implants. Another chap got a tooth stuck into his cheek after he skidded on an easy downhill run and hit a tree. I wouldn't fancy it.

Since Donalda left Lavander Cottage cleaner than when she arrived, it's a doddle getting the place ready. Simon and Bali arrive at 3 p.m., loaded up with bikes, and ask if they can store them in the cottage. Of course I say yes, since it seems impossible to say no after they explain that their gigantic bikes are worth around £3000 each!

Their visit inspires me to get my old faithful Raleigh Wayfarer out and cycle into Hebden. *Reminder, I must get the brakes sorted.* Peter swears he could hear me slowing down from Hebbleroyd. Tonight, I decide to stay at Peter's rather than ride home in the dark. I don't have any lights, plus you get used to the smell of hot fat after a while.

It's strange having people in the cottage for a week. It's the longest stay we've had so far ,apart from the Croatians. You come to know their habits, what time they get up, what time they move upstairs. It gets a bit annoying when you know they've gone upstairs but they've left the downstairs lights on. Simon and Bali keep leaving the blinds open too so we can see them smooching. Maureen has taken to having her coffee and cigarette out the back of the kitchen, so she can watch them directly. I try and shoo her on, but she's not moving.

'Janet, they don't give a monkey's. They're young, sexy and oblivious to anything but each other.'

It's impressive watching them go out on their bikes in the morning, as I'm loading the car for work. As a cyclist myself, I'm in awe of the way they are able to balance on their pedals. Strong core, the sort of core I'll never have however many bums-and-tums classes I get to at the gym. They're both wearing what look like motorbike helmets, cool sunglasses, matching Lycra leggings with shorts on top, rucksacks that are absolutely filthy, probably from all the mud that's sprayed up on wet days, and grippy gloves. Off they go, and then as I'm pulling back into the drive hours later, head-to-toe in muck, they're back. It's a shame it's absolutely piling down with rain all week, not that Simon and Bali seem bothered. They're delighted when I dig them out the garden hose so they can wash their bikes down, and give them some old newspapers they can stand their bikes on in the cottage. They seem very happy and very in love, and it makes me fancy a cycling holiday (somewhere flat) in the sunshine.

Once they've strapped up the bikes to their car and pull away, I head into the cottage. It's not bad, six to a seven in terms of general mess. As I make my way round the cottage, I decide they've probably had sex everywhere – something to do with Simon's smug smile, as he's putting the bikes on the roof, and the balls of screwed-up tissues I find *everywhere*. It's none of my business, of course, what they get up to. I'm grateful for their custom, even if I do end up with bike rubber-tyre, black marks on one wall that take some cleaning off. Maybe I need to get some bike holder things for outside? Would they have used them though? Three thousand pounds. That's more than I paid for my car. I'll get a couple more bins for the bedroom and the lounge. *One thing at a time, Janet.*

I actually feel like I'm getting in the swing of this. I almost switch off and just get on with the job. Once the Marigolds are on, and I've got the spray and cloth in my hand, off we go. The sense of satisfaction is very real, as I whip from room to room with my list: bed changed, polish, hoover and mop. The kitchen is the trickiest. Little things catch you out, like inside the microwave or the tops of plug sockets. It doesn't take me too long – an hour and a half maybe – then I close the door to Lavander Cottage, nip home and give myself a massive big tick and a sit-down with a teapot of Earl Grey for a change, and a millionaire's shortbread for a job well done.

· ·

TIPS FOR RUNNING A B&B

Do you have somewhere to store posh bikes?

Don't forget to check the utensils jar for greasy spoons, and it's easy to forget cooker extractor hoods – they're a muck clinger.

CHAPTER 19

I'm now officially obsessed with Airbnb. I can't get off it. If I'm not checking the calendar or comments (*two nice reviews now*), I'm browsing the site for places to go. Ooh, if only I had oodles of cash. What I do have sits in my savings account like a tax grenade ready to go off.

Chloë had a moan today that she wants to go on holiday, and I realise we haven't been away properly for over a year. I make a snap decision and ask Tony for next week off. He looks flabbergasted. Dealing with staff enquiries – in fact, anything that doesn't involve staring into a gob, to be crude about it – is out of Tony's comfort zone.

'I've got thirty-six days of accumulated leave,' I remind him. 'I'm struggling to take it.'

'OK, yes. Yes. Can you sort out cover?'

So that's what I do. I ring round and organise my own cover for the week. Then I ring Chloë to tell her we're going on holiday.

'Where?'

'I don't know.'

'I've got a party Saturday night.'

'OK. Well, how about we go Sunday?'

'Where?'

'I don't know. We'll have to decide.'

'OK. Abroad?'

'I don't think I've enough money for abroad.'

'Ugh.' Groan. 'This isn't like where we go to Northumberland and walk along the empty beaches and read boring books, is it?'

'Not if you don't want to.'

'I don't.'

'OK.'

'Can we go to London?'

'OK.'

So that's the plan. I spend the rest of the day at work booking our holiday. By 4 p.m., I've spent over £700 on train travel and hotel and show tickets. *Wicked.* Again. Hurrah, can't wait.

It's wonderful to be away. Chloë and I get on great as long as she's had a decent lie-in, access to regular cheese paninis and plenty of Costa smoothies. I am so happy to see *Wicked* again – brilliant. London Eye – brilliant. Oxford Street – noisy. Tube – scary. King's Cross station is really something now. The biggest change to the last time I went to London is that the city seems a lot busier and there are many more homeless people everywhere you go. They all hold the same cardboard sign that says, in scruffy, black marker handwriting: *I'm hungry help me God bless.* I start to ask for change in shops, so I have some in my pocket to give them.

When Chloë and I get home to Hebden Bridge, I tell Maureen all about it. She gets really emotional and reminds me that she is currently penniless. Apparently, with me gone, neither she nor Franklin had the cash to buy essentials, and they've been surviving on frozen sausage rolls and lime cordial. I immediately apologise and give her the £40 that I have in my purse, and she sits at the kitchen table and weeps. It is pretty upsetting, and I decide not to hand over the *All I got from London was this lousy key ring* key ring. It's a rubbish old joke and Maureen is looking too sad for bad jokes.

Franklin hasn't been seen since we got back. He rang Chloë today to say he's got a job at a factory and will be collecting his things in the next few days when he can sort transport.

'What's happening about his car?' I ask, as a scrap man is winching it onto the back of his lorry.

Something about Franklin potentially moving on has motivated Maureen. She looks spectacular when she goes out tonight, to meet her man, in a jumpsuit and huge heels and her hair in a side ponytail style. I presume she's going to an eighties night.

She tells me, 'No, Janet, this is the height of current fashion.'

I congratulate her for looking so good in it, second time around. She gets quite snappy.

'Are you saying I look old?'

I have to spend twenty minutes reassuring her she doesn't. I give her £20 to buy some drinks, and she's very grateful and explains that she'll use the money for the week; she refuses to pay for anything whilst her bloke remains wedded to his wife. He has promised her a split, and she's hoping tonight might be the night. I don't want to say that I saw him arm in arm with his wife coming out of the butcher's only today whilst I was shopping in Hebden.

I get an early night.

I spend the morning in the garden while Maureen sits dragging on a cigarette and blowing smoke out of the patio door. She seems very glum. Not even Chloë with her cat dancing videos on Facebook can lift her spirits.

I don't ask.

It's another hectic start to the week. The phone in Valley Dental never stops ringing and there's a lot of frustrated clients coming to terms with Polly the hygienist's reduced working hours. I do feel bad when they're looking at two and three months before they can get an appointment. The problem is that Wendy, the other hygienist, just isn't as popular. Most people have tried her once and won't go again despite my best efforts.

When I get home, Franklin is on the drive filling up a van. I didn't realise he had that much stuff to take. I spot a colander and a chair from the cottage. When I challenge him, he begs forgiveness. He's found a flat, he just has nothing to fill it with, and please can he take some bits and pieces from the house. He asks if he can have the chest of drawers that was his mum's and that is now full of linen at the top of the stairs. Of course I agree, and then end up struggling to find homes for twelve duvet sets and endless cloth napkins. I don't think we've ever enjoyed a meal where we have actually used a cloth napkin. I even have wooden rings shaped like animals. I vow I will use them this Christmas to justify their drawer room.

Maureen and Chloë go off with Franklin to see his new place – a flat in the happily named village of 'Friendly' near Sowerby Bridge – and it feels odd to be left out. It's the first time in an age that I have been home alone. I fall asleep on the sofa watching a rerun of *The Hobbit: The Desolation of Smaug* and only wake up when Chloë slams the patio door as she returns with Greg. I thought she was with Franklin. Where did Greg come into it?

Anyway, Maureen had sent my daughter to tell me that she is

performing at the Spoken Word Festival in Halifax at the Grayston Unity bar there from 8 p.m. tonight if I want to go. I'm exhausted but think I've got to make an effort, as my sister has looked so rotten lately. I ring Peter, and we decide to catch the bus and go. Maureen is third in a group of five odd-looking people. She is wearing a very short 1960s leather dress with a zip up the middle and white tights and Doc Marten boots. She stands out, but she also kind of fits in. She does a funny thing about *Love Island*, with a very moving bit about never finding love herself. She performs it brilliantly, with loads of pauses and dramatic moments, and I find myself welling up listening.

I think it's because she's my sister and I know her, but then I look around and realise quite a few people are sniffing, wiping their eyes and looking for tissues in their bags. I go to buy her a drink afterwards, and when I get to the table, she's got four already lined up. She gives me the poem scribbled on the back of a flyer for a tree surgeon.

Why does Love Island never come to Halifax?
I've seen a few hunks in trunks at Gaddings Dam,
I've kissed some dusky strangers by the light of the Mixenden moon,
but it's like they're flicking channels for the next best show,
'cos I can never make them stick.

If Love Island came to Halifax,
I'd get my bits out no bother and splash about in Lumb Falls.
I'd try to persuade a gorgeous guy from t'valley
we could win the cash with a cuddle down Shay Alley,
but like spray tan and false eyelashes he'd soon be gone,
'cos I can never make them stick.

Love Island IS coming to Halifax.
I'm gonna be first in't queue, shouting 'Romeo, Romeo.
I'm here, where art thou, dear?'
'Cos I love to love and laugh and love;
I've a heart me, the size of Midgley Moor,
so why do I always lose and lose and lose and lose –
and then they go and then they're gone.

Love Island might be coming to Halifax,
but this time I won't apply
'cos like promises and engagement rings,
kindness and wedding vows,
I can never make them stick.

I tell her she is really good and how impressed I am, and Peter almost seems to get over his anxiety around her to say she was marvellous.

'Thanks for coming,' she says. 'It's good to know you two are here to carry me home.'

An hour and a half later, that's exactly what we are doing. We have to get a taxi, as she is so paralytic. I lie to the taxi man that Maureen has food poisoning to get him to agree to take us home. She has her head stuck out of the window for most of the journey from fear she is about to throw up. When her head comes back in, she is desperately searching for her cigs and a lighter, and mumbles, 'He's such an arsehole, he said he'd be there. He's not gonna leave her, is he?' repeated over and over and over again.

I feel so stone-cold sober sad for her. Maureen's love life is like an ongoing neglected motorway of abandoned relationships. It just goes on and on, every way you look; every kind of vehicle, bashed, broken, slung away or abandoned. From the moment she split with her childhood sweetheart Kenny Dolan at seventeen because she wanted some excitement, and then Kenny went on to win the pools and become a very successful local radio DJ who soon after married her most hated school enemy Dawn Bowker, well, nothing has been right since. It's like she chose wrong once and she's never forgiven herself or trusted herself to choose right again. Self-sabotage, they call it.

She told me that she went to therapy for a while to try and understand why she dumped Kenny's successors, lovely Sparrow and then clever Charlie and steady Stu. They were all half-decent in their own way. I think one or two of them could have made her happy for a while, if she'd given them the chance. Two and a half years was the longest relationship she ever sustained. Sparrow. Nice guy. Painter and decorator – desperate for her to have a baby. She broke up with him on New Year's Eve. I'd never seen her cry so hard.

I am feeling really sad for her, thinking about her romantic woes, when she gets the outside mixed up with the inside and blows a cloud of Silk Cut smoke into my face.

Later, I tuck her into bed after forcing a pint of water down her and situating a bucket close to her head.

'He's an arsehole,' she croaks. 'He's not going to leave her.'

'He's married with kids. No, he's not going to leave her.'

'But I love him.'

'Well, you'll have to unlove him. I'm putting a bowl here. You were brilliant tonight, Maureen. You're really good. Forget him. He's not going to make you happy. He's not going to. He's married, with kids. Concentrate on being a poet.'

'Spoken word artist.'

'Exactly. Yes, that. Goodnight.'

All whilst Peter was throwing a kettle of hot water down the side of the taxi to clean away the sick stains.

· ·

TIP ON NIGHTS OUT WITH SISTERS

Plan ahead and drive when you know she's going to be having a 'good time', in order to avoid falling out with cab drivers later.

CHAPTER 20

Booking No. 9: Sam & Elliott

For the first time in a while, Peter and I are planning to eat out. A new Italian, The Olive Tree in Napoli, has opened its doors in Hebden after what seems like weeks of getting itself ready. I've walked past it every lunchtime at Valley Dental and was intrigued when the newspapers finally came off the windows. It has a nice olive-green paint job, a lot of old Sophia Loren posters, and a two-for-one opening deal, and after trying to book for two weeks during breaks in reception, I've finally got us a table.

On the night in question, I have a lovely walk into Hebden along the canal, the fairy light strings all lit up and dotted along the barges and the wafted scent of syrupy sweet Himalayan balsam – an invasive weed and a total menace, but which smells delicious.

Peter meets me in the square; I note that he has put on a tie. It feels nice that he's made the effort. I am wearing a favourite summer dress I got for a wedding years ago, found on a Monsoon sale rail. It's a wonderful quality, baby-blue, heavy cotton, low cut and generous around the tummy – always my go-to when anticipating eating a bit too much. The place is heaving. I recognise six Valley Dental customers. Peter spots three overdue book returners, not that we let on to anyone. Being in public-facing jobs in Hebden, it doesn't do to say hello to everyone; we'd be there all night. I order an asparagus bruschetta starter that I'd never tried before and spot home-made cannoli with orange custard on the specials board that I order for dessert. I'm one sip into a delightful Sauvignon when my phone pings.

IMMEDIATE BOOKING. I show it to Peter to be sure I am seeing the right thing. Immediate booking. Someone has just booked the cottage for tonight. NOW. I am trying to decide what to do when the phone rings.

'Hello? We've just booked your place. I'm Samantha, but do

call me Sam,' says a friendly voice.

'Yes, I've just seen.'

'Is it OK if we come now?'

Gulp. I can see asparagus, on a plate, in the hand of the waitress heading toward me.

'Er, that's fine. I'm just out at the moment.'

'Don't worry. We're in the car. We're parked outside yours now.'

'Oh. You're there now? I'm in Hebden. I'll be there as soon as I can.'

Peter and I exchange eye-rolls. I ring Maureen. No answer. I ring Chloë. No answer.

'I'll go and get a taxi,' I say, standing up.

'What about your starters?'

Well, I wrap the bruschetta in a napkin and rush to Royd Rovers, the taxi firm in the centre of town. Where there is a queue!

'Why is there a queue?'

'Big opening of Oxygenic in Halifax.'

I ring Peter.

'I'm sipping my minestrone soup as slowly as I can,' he tells me.

'There's a queue for cabs.'

'Wait there, I'll drive you.'

'No, I've waited two weeks for that table. Stay there. Where's your bike?'

'It's in the alley. It's not chained up, but it's a bit cranky, so you'll have to be careful.'

It is an excruciating, bone-rattling pedal along the canal, with a saddle so high I have to stand up most of the way, and a single attempt at a gear change makes the bike grind as if the whole thing might fall apart. I tear along that canal at speeds I'll never match – a baby-blue blur past lovers and strollers, the geese bellowing as they leap into the canal to escape my wonky wheels of steel as if their lives depend upon it. I desperately try to remember what, if anything, I need to do in the cottage. Thank goodness it is prepped.

I am a sweaty wreck at the bottom of the street so jump off and wheel the bike up the hill, as I attempt to compose myself.

I am greeted by a friendly voice, coming from Samantha. 'Hello, that didn't take you long. Hope we didn't disturb you?'

'Not at all,' I lie. 'Are you visiting the area?'

'No, we live over in Riddlesden. Our daughter's having her eighteenth birthday party tonight. We were planning on staying at home, but it's so noisy already we decided we needed to get out of there.'

I go inside the house to grab the cottage key, to find Maureen warming up soup and Chloë stirring a Pot Noodle.

'Did you not see I'd rung?'

Blank expressions all round.

I call a different firm and organise a taxi to pick me up in ten minutes, then slice off some butter, pour out a jug of milk and dig out a packet of currant teacakes from the back of the freezer.

I leave Sam and Elliot in the cottage, whack up the heating and turn on the lights. They ooh and aah and are very grateful for the milk and teacakes but, by the sound of the glass bottles bouncing about in their Sainsbury's carrier bag, I probably didn't need to bother.

I am soon back in a taxi that is picking me up on a return trip from Halifax, then seated again in front of a creamy chicken rigatoni and a very merry Peter. He's finished off the bottle and two baskets of bread whilst he's been waiting. It was all worth it. The orange cream cannoli was to die for, and knowing I'd worked off a few calories on the fastest cycle ride I'll probably ever do in my life helps me enjoy it all the more, as I am completely guilt-free. What is also nice is knowing that, as we split the bill, tonight's treat is being paid for by Lavander Cottage.

Tonight, Janet Jackson is winning at life.

I bump into Sam and Elliot at half seven the next morning, as I am putting out the washing.

'Thank you, Janet, that was the best night's sleep we've had in years.'

'That's nice to hear. How did the party go?'

'Well, apparently the fire brigade turned up at eleven to rescue a girl from our monkey puzzle tree! So it disbanded after that.'

We all start to giggle.

Elliot scratches his head, saying, 'It must've bloody hurt. It's not like those trees are welcoming, are they?'

'How had she climbed up it in the first place?'

'It's by the back bedroom, so we reckon she opened the window and grabbed on to it,' Sam tells me.

'Drunk?' I ask politely.

'Well, that or stupid.' Elliot laughs.

'Or both,' his wife chimes in.

I hear the upstairs window open and Maureen sticks her head out, bleary-eyed and sullen.

'What time is it?'

I ignore her, telling the couple, 'I'm glad you had a good night.'

'It was lovely. We'll do it again. It made a nice change.'

They are off, leaving me to wander around the garden deadheading, memories of my own eighteenth birthday party drifting up. I'd already got together with Franklin at that point. There were three couples, all of us on dodgy motorbikes, and we travelled together, with two minor breakdowns, to Scarborough for the day. We ate fish and chips on the pier, got a bit wet paddling and ended up in the back of some pub dancing around to 'Ballroom Blitz' by Sweet, drunk on cider, surrounded by people dressed up as Dracula. Scarborough and Whitby are always a magnet to the goths. We crashed in an incredibly cold and noisy youth hostel, ate more fish and chips for breakfast and made it back to the farm before Mum and Dad had even registered I'd gone. A fabulous weekend.

Cleaning the cottage is easy as there is barely anything to do, so I sweep, mop, polish and change the bed in forty minutes. I find the backs of a pair of earrings and a lovely message in the guest book.

Sam and Elliot, escaping a noisy 18th birthday party, found peace, a comfy bed and a lovely hostess in Janet.

This B&B thing, I am enjoying it.

· ·

TIPS FOR RUNNING A B&B

If you can, always prep the cottage when someone leaves. You never know when someone will request an instant booking.

Try to find reliable people to help you run it if you need to go out or go away. (I haven't done either of these things, by the way, but it would be good if you could.)

CHAPTER 21

When the summer holidays end and Chloë is back at school, before you know it, it's the last day before October half-term and she arrives home, puffing and furious, with three carrier bags full of exercise books which she dumps around the house. She's complaining that she's stressed to the eyeballs about her GCSEs, whilst raiding the crisp basket and talking in a frenzy about how she needs to start revising now for her mocks which are in a few weeks' time. And for some reason it's as if it's all *my* fault.

'Where's the Monster Munch?' She says this with such accusatory venom I don't dare tell her Maureen had been down minutes earlier and taken the last packet.

'I'll get some more.'

'Thank you, yes, and smoothies. I need smoothies and raspberries and Mini Rolls.'

'OK.'

'And noodles. Can we have noodles for tea, do you think?' This, spat out as if I've deprived her of noodles her entire life, despite the fact that we go through four Pot Noodles and a Chinese takeaway most weeks.

After I've finished buying and cooking noodles for Chloë and heating home-made mushroom soup for Maureen, I get on Amazon and order a rash of multicoloured Post-it notes and a copy of *The Lazy Student's Revision Guide*. I pray she won't take offence; it has a lot of stars in the reviews.

Over the next few days, despite my stocking up on snacks and stationery, Chloë's revision seems to have taken a nosedive. She has Greg round playing *Red Dead Redemption* all the time. I don't realise he is in the house until I fall over his shoes at the bottom of the stairs. When I ask what they are doing in her bedroom, my daughter gives me a lengthy breakdown of *Red Dead Redemption* storylines – so much so I feel like I could enter *Mastermind* with it as a specialist subject, if I was so inclined. When I remind my daughter that her *Red Dead Redemption* habit might need to be put on hold whilst she concentrates on the small matter of exams, she flips out at me, accusing me of tyranny and a lack of compassion.

'Am I never allowed to rest?'

This, after two hours in which I have taken her three cups of tea, a snack box of cut up apples and grapes and Mini Cheddars, and a shepherd's pie and gravy, taken down all her washing and enough dirty crockery to completely fill the dishwasher and spent ten minutes recycling her rubbish. The whole while she is tucked up in bed with a geography textbook open and a PlayStation remote in her hand, music playing in the background and what looks like *Minecraft* on her iPad. Is this how they do revision these days?

I'm out at the shops future-proofing and buying more snacks for Chloë and the ingredients for a rigatoni when I spot mince pies for sale in Tesco. At first, I feel angry and disappointed. I really wanted to get all my Christmas shopping in the January sales, and wrap it and label it by Easter like I promised myself I would last year. I've failed, and now everything will cost the earth and it will be the usual frenzy. Back home, I cheer myself up with two lovely, warm mince pies and a tin of evaporated milk dated to expire on 19 December... *last year*. There is definitely extra satisfaction in using up an old tin. I've forgotten how good mince pies taste. I also put the prices up on the cottage on Airbnb for Christmas. It's Chloë's suggestion.

'Are we having people staying for Christmas? Won't that be a pain? How much are you charging?'

We go on and amend the website so it says £200 per night for Christmas Eve, Christmas Day, Boxing Day and New Year's Eve. It's a lot of money, but it will also involve a lot of effort and extra expense getting Lavander Cottage ready for Christmas, what with decorations and a tree and everything. Plus, you can fit four people in, and divide it by four, and then it's getting cheapish I repeat this to myself a lot before I dare make the amendments. I am humming and hawing and trying to justify the amount, bringing it down and putting it back up until Chloë, bright red in the face, grabs the laptop, presses the buttons and has it uploaded and saved in seconds.

'Done. Alan Sugar you are not. You need to think, Mum. *Holiday!*'

I can't think about holidays, not with Christmas looming around the corner. I dig out my Christmas box. It's full of Sellotape and wrapping paper and labels and cards. While working out money and Christmas and bills, I need two camomile teas and a flick through three old copies of *Prima* magazine before I'm calm enough to contemplate bedtime. I can hear Chloë shouting at Greg on her headset as I go past her bedroom. '*Get him, get him, get him, shoot him, shoot him, TAKE HIM OUT!*' Very relaxing. I pop my head round the door and tap my watch.

'Time to think about bed? It's school tomorrow.'

'I'm on study leave.'

Is she? I've no idea. Why don't I know? What sort of parent am I? An inadequate one, clearly. It's difficult when your kids are brighter than you. My daughter runs rings round me. I need to pull my socks up – I'll tackle it this week. Oh heck.

It takes another camomile tea and a *Prima* recipe before I can switch the light off for bed.

I'm busy on reception all day and have to call in at the Co-op on my way home for some essentials for tea. I'm planning on spaghetti and meatballs. I make it home for around five o'clock, having made record time through the roadworks. I rush to the loo and then briefly knock and inadvertently walk in on Chloë and Greg, both in their underwear and Greg with his penis in his hand. I take one look. A long look. I must have been in shock, because it's not something I want to stay and stare at. I am frozen by events. We are all frozen by events. Exactly as they show in the movies.

I eventually break the spell and say something like, 'Oh dear. Oh dear. Oh dear. I'm going to put the kettle on. Can you get dressed, please?'

I glide down the stairs as if I am on an escalator to Hell Town. Every hair on my body is electrified with acute embarrassment. I stare into the garden for several minutes before I scald myself on the hot-water tap trying to fill the kettle.

They both tumble into the kitchen, and I try not to look at them. It's almost impossible not to glaze over, as they begin hurriedly to explain themselves, with no apology and not nearly as much embarrassment as I am feeling. They are adamant that, to all intents and purposes, it's their first time and I have interrupted it. Hurrah. So pleased. Have absolutely no idea if I believe them. I am distracted by Greg's zip, which isn't done up. It sums everything up for me. I can't get them out of the house fast enough – I mean him, Greg. I ring my friend Victoria and tell her what has gone on. She is very clear.

'Get her on the pill.'

I come clean to Maureen, who laughs for quite a while and comes to the same conclusion as Victoria. I don't know what to do. Chloë has taken to eating in her bedroom. We haven't seen Greg all week. I daren't ask; I'm just too relieved. I walk into the hall, and the first thing I do is look to see if his trainers are thrown under the chair. Chloë says she's trying to revise. Revising is making her pretty nasty – she threw three pairs of dirty knickers down the stairs yesterday when I asked for her washing to be brought down. Once she's gone to school, I go in her room to collect cups and literally wade through a sea of clothes to retrieve used crockery.

I notice the revision guide is still in its wrapper.

. . . .

TIPS ON A TEENAGE DAUGHTER

Accept that your daughter/s will have sex. It's horrendous to contemplate. Sorry. I don't know how else to prepare you.

Accept they get very stressed whilst revising. It's your job to remain calm and buy snacks and Post-its in different colours. Again, sorry – that's all I have.

CHAPTER 22

Booking No. 10: Madrigal, Violet & Honey

Lovely lesbians Madrigal and Violet are staying in the cottage for the weekend with their three-year-old daughter, Honey. We have to plug their car into the mains as they're electric. I wonder how much it costs. Chloë walks Honey around the garden, which is terribly sweet, as they sniff at the last of the flowers one by one.

I enjoy watching them until Violet or Madrigal, I don't know which is which, says, 'Your daughter's brilliant with her; looks like you won't have long to wait for grandkids.'

My stomach curdles.

I ring the doctors and make an appointment to see Dr Rierdon with Chloë. It's for three weeks' time. I ask Chloë if she can wait that long, and she assures me they can. I hear her on the phone laughing and giggling to Greg. I'm no long sure they can wait. I ring and beg the receptionist for a faster appointment. They ring me at noon with a cancellation for a senior nurse first thing Monday. I bite their hand off.

I feel sorry to see little Honey and her mums go. They leave a sweet message in the guest book.

We have had the most relaxing time in Janet's wonderful garden. Lovely and peaceful break. Thank you, from Honey and her mums.

Cleaning the cottage after guests is almost therapy when you're worried about the sex life of your teenage daughter. It focuses the mind: there's a clear range of jobs, and I've now got the order down to a T. Kitchen first: fridge, surfaces, toaster, microwave, oven, windowsills, table, chairs, empty bin and any recycling (Madrigal and Violet left six bags of assorted plastics, glass and cardboard – I knew they'd be the types), sink, drainer, cupboard doors. They also left an interesting range of leftovers in the fridge. I wonder if they forgot to check? We've got three Alpro yoghurts, eaten by Chloë immediately; one unopened carton of oat milk – I'll give it a day or two, see if Maureen goes for it; six eggs – an excellent find; a barely touched vegetable spread I can use for baking; some rooibos mint tea that I'll leave out for Maureen, and finally, some oat biscuits that taste like they're doing you some good, especially if you dip them in tea.

I am upstairs changing the bedding when I find a teddy under the sofa. I'm just about to text them, to see if it matters, when there is a knock on the cottage door. It's Madrigal, looking desperate. She asks if I've found Arthur Bear.

'Honey kicked off when we hit the M62.'

I am delighted to hand it over and horribly worried that Madrigal is going to ask to go back in the fridge after I've already taken all the food over to the house and Chloë has demolished the yoghurts. Thankfully, she is so distracted by the teddy that she simply hugs us both and races back to their little electric car purring in the drive. I wave them all off and continue cleaning up. It's a good B&B lesson though.

• •

TIP FOR RUNNING A B&B

Don't be too eager with the leftovers. The guests might come back for them.

CHAPTER 23

Chloë is delighted to be now on the pill. I remind her that its contraceptive power will not kick in for three weeks and, as a precaution, I buy her Luscious Lips pineapple condoms, her choice. I take the moment to buy some baby oil and pick up my pill prescription. The one good thing to come out of this is that I am completely off food. At the moment, I feel like a trussed-up mannequin being wheeled into waiting rooms and doctors' rooms and pharmacies, nodding and compliant about my daughter being prepped for sex whilst secretly screaming on the inside. It's all so wrong.

But I am rolling with it.

In a bit of a daze all day, I go to get some milk this evening and do a detour down Fountain Avenue, where I am taken aback by the sight of an Egyptian mummy coming out of one of the gardens, with a Mrs Munster following it. Then it kicks in that it's Halloween. Of course! Hundreds of kids are parading up and down, buckets in hand, dressed up and knocking on doors for sweets. It's a 70/30 split on the avenue between the miseries who are all locked down in darkness and gloom, and the amazing efforts of the others who have bats on strings and coffin lids opening up and legs sticking out of the ground. I am disappointed in myself for being strictly in the unprepared misery camp. I must make more effort next year. The way I'm feeling at the moment though, it would not have surprised me to be taken for a ghoul.

Peter rings asking if I'd like to go for some dinner at his tomorrow. I say no, that I'm not feeling well. It's a lie. The truth is I'm not feeling happy. I've no capacity to be nice, and suddenly my relationship with Peter feels empty, hopeless and what's the point. He doesn't see through my lying, and I don't want to burden him with my problems. Deep down, I don't think he'd have the first clue anyway. He's lovely, Peter, but he has no life experience, not really. He's forty-six, with no children, and has never been married.

I always related to Rizzo in the film *Grease* and Peter's like Sandy before the makeover – sweet, innocent, and a bit naïve as to what life can throw at you.

Chloë is getting older and she's going to be gone soon. Then it will be me and Maureen in a death clinch and me desperately working to try and pay the bloody mortgage off while she gets increasingly booze-dependent.

When I get home with the milk, I ignore the couple of trick-or-treaters knocking on the door, as I've nothing to give them, and drown my sorrows in a cheap Rioja.

· ·

TIP ON LIFE

Being miserable from time to time is OK. Don't let it last longer than one bottle of Rioja though.

CHAPTER 24

Hebden Bridge is to get its very own Poet Laureate! Maureen's married man is in the paper, announcing it as chair of the arts festival. The chosen bard will be known as the Hebden Bridge Laureate and be part of the Hebden Bridge Festival. The winner will be revealed on New Year's Day, and the competition is to be held at venues around Hebden Bridge in the run-up to a shortlisted final on New Year's Eve at the Trades Club.

Well, I don't know whether to hide the paper or show Maureen. New Year with her can turn out to be a bit messy, on past experience. This competition has too much car-crash potential around it for my liking, a sense in no way diminished when my sister rolls in late tonight, carrying her own *Hebden Bridge Times* under her arm and slurring: 'I better get it or he's fuckin' dead,' as she stabs at the malt loaf with a spoon.

A letter arrives from the council today informing me that they are coming to visit the cottage to establish business rates. I nearly drop through the floor when I read the letter. Business rates?

I've been a nervous wreck all day. I have been adding up Airbnb takings and even though I've put £500 away for tax, with all the expenses of setting it up in the first place, I'm approximately £2,000 down. If I end up with a £1,000 bill from the council for business rates, on top of my existing £1,000 council tax bill for our house, plus a fine of, say, £500 for not declaring, then I'm really in trouble and may have to sell the house. I don't know how I'd break that to Chloë – and if we had to buy somewhere smaller, what would happen to Maureen?

I power through a Hebbleroyd maslin loaf. Maslin is a mixture of wheat and dark rye, and it's an amazing taste. I bought it from a new baker's shop that only opens twice a week: half-day Tuesday and a third of the afternoon on a Friday. Why do they bother? Maybe it's a business rates thing. Whatever it is, it's better for my waistline that it stays closed.

I've been a bit distant with Peter, I'm not sure why. Is it still that feeling that nothing's going anywhere? When he texts and asks me if I'd like to wander down to the cenotaph for Remembrance Day, it makes me realise what a nice man he is and I say yes. My poppy blows away on the walk into town, so I feel a bit cheap when I get there, though of course it doesn't matter really. What matters is I'm there. However, I soon regret it as we bump into Laura and Oliver Watson, who both look impeccable in smart red coats; Laura is wearing a black hat and veil that makes her look like she's impersonating a poppy. I turn to Peter to whisper this in his ear, but stop when she gives me one of her evil 'I hate you really' smiles.

'Hello, Janet. How's things?' She looks us both up and down, and it's the first time I realise that Peter has a bird poo on the shoulder of his jacket, and I've come out wearing my gardening knee pads.

'I'm fine, Laura. You?'

'Yes, we're t'riffic, *thank you for asking.* We were just talking about going away for Christmas to Stockholm to see some friends. What are you up to? You're too preoccupied running your business from home, I expect. How do you cope with all the business and Valley Dental and everything?'

I tense up. She's the one who's called the council on me, I just know it. The business rates letter is her doing. Why can't she just leave me alone? The evil bloomin' cowbag. Before I've a chance to really think about it, I open my big gob.

'All going wonderfully, Laura, *thank you for asking.* Once you get the entrepreneurial bug, it's *so* difficult to stop. One day Airbnb, next day you're calling the council offering to set up a homeless shelter. *Bye!*'

I can see the horror dawning on her face, as her mouth drops open. I nudge Peter into the crowd to escape her. He lands us next to two old ladies, who look so similar they must be sisters. I am feeling quite bad about using the homeless in that cavalier way and make a little apology to God and a promise to fill and put the charity bin bag, that was posted through the door, out for collection. The band crashes into action, and the two old ladies trill along together. It sounds as if they are in some sort of competition with one another.

It's a shame really because one of them really does sound like Vera Lynn, the other, *much* louder one, like Vera Duckworth.

The rain pounds down all day, I clear up in the afternoon after a nice Sunday lunch of roast chicken and the trimmings, and Peter goes off to see his mother. I am feeling a bit weepy watching the Remembrance Day service on TV when Chloë wanders in.

I look at her and she says, 'Don't start, Mum. I did it. I did a minute's silence off Snapchat.'

It makes me laugh and feel glad that she did remember. This opens the floodgates and I can't stop the tears when the Queen arrives at Westminster Abbey. It's as if she represents the living link to all those poor souls who perished in all these bloody horrible wars that never seem to end. Will this be her last Remembrance Sunday, I wonder? I have finally caught *The Crown* on Netflix, years behind everyone else. It is fascinating to see her so young and vibrant, and it brings so much understanding to her role. The programme should be on the curriculum at schools. I suggest it to Chloë, and she is in complete agreement. She reminds me later that she didn't take history classes, but if they do make *The Crown* part of the curriculum she plans to transfer, as she's already binge-watched it three times and thinks Diana is a hero.

. . . .

TIP ON LIFE

Make an effort to listen to the quiet voices. Just because someone is loud doesn't make them interesting, they're just loud.

CHAPTER 25

Booking No. 11: Nile & Reema

It's been a weary Tuesday of dental cancellations and miserable patients. Miles is looking very run-down at the moment. Apparently his marriage has turned into a battleground on the home front, according to dental nurse Judy. I offer him a supportive smile whenever he walks through reception, and I can see he is trying to lift his head out of the gloom with a weak, acknowledging lip curl in return. Come home time, he drags himself down the stairs with what looks like an overnight bag, as I'm putting on my helmet to leave.

'Cycling today, Janet? I'm thinking of getting a bike.'

'It's an easy cycle in along the canal, nothing to it really.'

He wanders out with me, locks up and takes a long look at my Raleigh Wayfarer up against the railings at the front of the building.

'When did you get your bike, Janet?'

'I can't remember, I think I found it.'

'It might be time to lose it.'

'*Excuse me*, it's done me proud!' I laugh, but it is getting on a bit.

'I'm pretty sure my dad had a Wayfarer. Hold on...' (he peers closely at the handlebars) '...I think it might be his.'

'Oy!'

He chuckles. I think the bike has cheered him up.

'Right, here we go. Have a nice evening, Miles.'

'Goodnight, Janet. See you tomorrow. Are you in?'

'Yes, in tomorrow. See you then. Bye.'

I feel a bit self-conscious as I wobble off, knowing he's watching me, but I'm soon away and picking up speed. I hear the phone ping a couple of times on the way home. It's either Chloë (*pick me up a Pot Noodle*) or Miles (*did we turn off all the lights?*). It's only once I'm home that I'm able to check.

IMMEDIATE BOOKING.

Oh no! Did I change the bed? I try to refuse it but get a heavy 'cancellation fee' threat of £100. So I rush around the cottage spraying polish into the air and throw some bleach down the loo. I'm still at it when I hear the rumble. It sounds like a heavy diesel train but turns out to be a peculiar, hand-painted car from what looks like the 1940s or maybe the 1970s, spewing out puffs of black smoke. It's old, that's for sure.

A tall, gaunt, dirty-blonde, long-haired guy peels himself out of the driving seat and, after a bit of bending and crouching, wanders round to shake my hand.

'Hi, I'm Nile,' he says, his handshake strong. 'And this is Reema.'

Reema elegantly emerges from the car, a tall, arresting brunette, her hair swings well below her waist and with startling, grey eyes, she sorts of floats her hand in my direction.

'Hi, welcome,' I say, still in a bit of a tizz at the speed of it all. 'Have you travelled far?' Oh dear, now I sound like the queen mother.

'From Iona in Scotland, we're on our way to Marrakech.'

'Amazing, what a journey.' I think the car looks like it might struggle to get them to the bottom of the street – but that's obviously not for me to worry about. Nile is literally hopping on one spot.

'Can I use the loo?' he says urgently. 'I've had the bladder on hold since Penrith.'

'Of course, of course, upstairs on the left.' I open the door to Lavander (with the emphasis on the 'lav') Cottage and he rushes past and thunders up the stairs.

Meanwhile, Reema wafts her pendant necklace in front of her before she enters, murmuring, 'I need to settle the spirits.'

'It's not had anyone in lately,' I say, hoping it might reassure her.

'Ugh, that chair.'

How rude! It's a nice leather armchair, so I'm not sure what she's on about, but she shifts it around so it's now facing the wall. Meanwhile, hyper Nile races past to their vehicle and returns with big cushions, a duvet and a washing-up bowl. He spots me looking.

'Reema likes her things around her.'

'Whatever makes you comfy.'

I leave the key in the door and I'm off. I catch sight of them later through the gaps in the blinds in the kitchen, and I can't be sure but Nile is standing with what looks like Reema's feet in his hands whilst she does a headstand. His eyes are closed and he's yawning. 'Freaks,' is Maureen's insight when she pops into the kitchen for a top-up to her wine glass. She knows this sort of people, so I don't disagree.

Reema's reaction to the chair bothers me all the next day when I'm stuck on reception. I remind Maureen that they should be leaving at eleven and text her multiple times to see if they've gone, but I don't get a reply until two o'clock when she texts back that yes, she's watched them bump the car off down the road.

When I finally get into the cottage after a speedy cycle home, the scent of joss sticks is overpowering, as is the temptation to shout at someone by the time I've finished rearranging every piece of furniture in the place. Cushions and chairs have been moved downstairs, the TV has gone upstairs, pictures have been shifted and even the kitchen drawers have had their contents swapped. As I open all the windows wide to let out the gusts of patchouli, I'm raging. I'm still raging an hour later when I'm back in the house, peeling and chopping veg for our evening meal.

'I mean, who do they think they are, rearranging everything?'

Peter pours me another glass of wine, saying soothingly, 'Obviously they were a very strange pair.'

'I mean, would you go into someone else's house and rearrange everything?'

'Absolutely not.'

'For just one night too. I'm going to give them poor feedback. I don't like to, but I wouldn't want anyone else going through that. And all the way to Marrakech?' I snort rudely. 'They'll be lucky to make Marsden in that thing.'

Midway through the lamb casserole, Peter brings up the subject of Christmas and how he's dreading it because he has to look after his mum and there's very little in the way of carers that day and he can't cook to save his life and... well, by pudding, I'd invited them, he'd agreed, and now Peter and his mum are coming to stay with us from the day before Christmas Eve through to the day after Boxing Day.

I don't know how I'm going to break it to Chloë and Maureen.

Maureen's idea of a good Christmas revolves around a smorgasbord of alcohol that begins with Buck's Fizz on Christmas Eve morning and finishes around 4 January with her prancing around in her underwear whilst downing a yard of Guinness. Chloë has yet to acknowledge that Father Christmas doesn't exist, which is useful, of course, when demanding unrealistic and very expensive gifts of the Apple/Pandora/Mac make-up kind.

Peter is very attentive after dinner. I wouldn't think anything of it, but he's *sooo* hyper-nice I can't help but wonder what I've let myself in for. In anticipation of the Christmas visit, I agree to go and meet Peter's mother next Sunday. While Peter is in the shower, I dip into a book I've got on the go about how to extend the planting interest into winter. It's always dogwood. I plan to put some hyacinth bulbs in some nice old clay planters at the weekend and silently pray they're not going to be the best thing about this Christmas.

Thank God it's a day off and I'm dressed. There's a bright, sharp knock at the door, and I'm expecting Jim performing a Jackson Five medley, but it's Shannon from the council. I recognise her bright yellow mac and this time with matching hat. She's wearing an uncompromising expression – and, boy, can she move! This time, not even the vestigial reek of Reema's joss sticks puts her off coming right inside Lavander Cottage and flying around, checking everything. I'm so grateful that I've got into the habit of cleaning up the moment the guests leave.

'Yes, right, it's just as I remembered,' she says briskly, making for the door.

'OK.'

'I'll be in touch.'

It's all happening too quickly. 'Can you give me any indication, Shannon?' I ask. 'I'm trying to decide whether to keep going. I've had a couple of guests since the planning passed. I don't want to get into trouble for doing something wrong, I wouldn't want to be fined... the money is such a worry.'

We are standing outside the cottage, and she looks at me then stares at the bathroom window where Maureen is draped over the sill, smoking.

'Morning,' Maureen drawls.

Shannon ignores her and points up at the thick, black wire that's connecting the main house with the garage.

'It's an annexe, love. An annexe. It's part of your house. You're fine to have people stay in your house; they're not regarded in planning as business premises. An annexe that's the key!'

Ready to explode with gratitude, I have to stop myself giving her a hug. All that I can manage is a raspy, 'Thank you.'

'I'll write to you confirming our conversation. Goodbye.'

As Shannon drives away, Laura Watson jogs out of her house, setting off for her morning run. In her lemon, Lycra one-piece and with her golden, waist-length hair plait, she looks just like Barbie. I don't know what comes over me, but I wave at her and, as she turns away, I stick two fingers up. She whips round to adjust something, and I have to pretend to be swatting a fly.

Everything is brighter since the visit from Shannon. Suddenly I'm full of Christmas spirit and looking forward to one of my favourite days of the year – 'Stir-up Sunday'. I get well prepared, with Christmas carols on the speaker, a tinsel halo on my head and my red mohair Christmas jumper on, though it is off again in half an hour once I get the oven heating up. I've made six Christmas cakes and a Christmas pudding, all before 9 a.m. I've decided these will be my presents for work, plus one for Peter and one for home. It has been a real dilemma knowing which recipe to follow. I did a Hugh Fearnley-Whittingstall last year, which went down well, though it was a bit heavy on nuts. I was tempted to go the Jamie Oliver route, but decided he can a bit heavy-handed on citrus. Nigella Lawson's I'd followed once before but must have got something wrong, because the mixture was like chewy toffee, and we were still scraping off the baking paper on New Year's Eve. So I opened up one of my trusty Delia cookbooks, comforted in the knowledge that her recipe would also be heavy – on the booze. I think it's going to be one of those Christmases.

This passing thought is intensified by meeting Peter's mother in Grassington. She is very sweet and very nice and very greedy. Joan Delilah Crouch, she opens a tin to show me some coffee cake and closes it before we have a chance to say yes, we'd like some. I swear she fakes forgetting when Peter nudges her about it twice.

Joan is a mixture of harmless old dear and ruthless assassin. We play dominoes and she wins three times. She slams down the double six just as if she is landing a punch. She also has Peter running around like an idiot.

Fetch that stool! Show Janet my tapestry. Where's the tea? Not that tin! Under the sink. Can you pull the blind open? Can you pull the blind down? Turn the radio down. Oh, I like this one, turn it up. It went on and on, and I could see Peter's sad face when I said I had to get off and sort out Chloë for school. I don't have to do that these days, not really. But I want to get back to my cakes, and there's only so much conniving, bossy old lady anyone wants to endure.

When I get home, Maureen is on fire, as it turns out that my sister has reached the semi-final for the Hebden Poet Laureate gig tonight. She is striding around the house shouting stuff out loud whilst I am making the gravy, and it's quite disconcerting. I try asking her what the laureate will do, and do they always need to be angry about stuff?

'Look at the state of the world, Janet, aren't *you* angry?'

I've six cakes that have risen beautifully and are a lovely golden-brown colour, *The Archers* is on and I'm enjoying a small sherry.

'Not really, Maureen.'

'Well, look out the window, honey, the sky's crashing down.'

She stomps upstairs, I stare out of the window, but I'm very pleased to see the dogwood is very striking against the fence. To add to my joy, the hyacinth pots I planted in October are all happily sprouting. When I look at the world, I see so much to wonder at and be grateful for. I guess I'm just not one of life's angry types. Maureen whooshes past in a cape covered in feathers and a pointy, fascinator-type hat with a tall feather that wobbles as she walks.

'I'm going to smash down the walls of certainty and absolutism,' she declares.

Not in that hat you're not, I think to myself.

'Right. Do you need a lift?' I say aloud.

'No, I'm being collected.'

'Good luck tonight. You look amazing, as always.'

'It's not about looks, Janet, it's about fire.'

'Well, you've got plenty of that too.'

A horn sounds and she whirls out, calling back, 'Don't wait up.'

'I wasn't planning on it,' I say with a sigh.

I am to open up the dentist tomorrow, so I need to be up and at it early. I'm exhausted. Five minutes with Maureen in protester mode is tiring. I hope she does well and then she can burn off some of her fire somewhere else for a change.

....

TIPS FOR A PERFECT STIR-UP CHRISTMAS SUNDAY

Preheat oven.

Turn up the carols.

Always cook on a lower heat for longer than the recipe says.

Ensure there is plenty of booze – for you, not the cake!

CHAPTER 26

Booking No. 12: Delicious Delia & Chums

A letter arrived from the council this morning, rating the property for business rates at £0.00! I'm so chuffed I get on M&S online, order myself two pairs of socks, then find a query for the coming weekend from 'Delicious Delia' – any relation to Christmas cake Delia, I wonder? She wants to know how many people we can fit into the cottage. I reply with six maximum, thinking two for the double bed, one each in the two fold-up singles and two in the sofa bed downstairs. She says that's wonderful and can she book for Saturday night? I say I don't want any stag do's or hen nights or a party. Delia responds, *It's a work recce and I promise we'll be well behaved.* So Delicious Delia and five friends are booked in.

When I tell Maureen and Chloë over our midday meal – very decent fajitas with fillings pulled together from the remnants of what was left in the fridge: two soft peppers and a box of overripe cherry tomatoes – Chloë immediately quizzes me.

'How much have you charged?'

'Normal price, £74 for the cottage.'

'But there's five/four extra people.'

'Yes, but there's not much extra I needed to do.' As I stupidly say this, I think of the three additional duvet covers, sheets and pillowcases that I'll have to launder when the guests have gone, plus all the extra hot water that will be used, and the extra clearing up.

'You're not gonna win any awards for Businesswoman of the Year, Mum.'

'I don't really know what to charge.'

'Email this Delia woman.'

'I will do.'

'Do you want me to do it?' she says in a resigned voice, as if she spends her entire life dealing with the wreckage of my appalling financial mismanagement.

'No, thank you, I'll email her.'

Maureen takes a big swig of her cider. It's cheaper than bottled water now, apparently.

' "Work recce"?' she quotes. 'What does that mean, I wonder? Very interesting, six of them. Is she working? Are they all working? Like a troupe? Fab. What time do they arrive?'

They arrive on Saturday at 3 p.m. Delia & Chums are the most interesting-looking bunch we've ever entertained. They consist of a bald-headed guy called Bojo, who must be at least six foot six inches tall, and five women of all shapes and sizes, with a rainbow of hair colours and attitudes. Delicious Delia seems to shop at the same place as Angel Strawbridge from the TV series *Escape to the Château*. She is wearing a long, orange cardigan that would suit Angel to a T.

The group have only been in the cottage fifteen minutes when two of them are outside blowing bubbles, and juggling what look like hot cross buns, on the lawn. Maureen drifts out into the garden wearing a cowboy hat and gold chaps, and manages to pop a bubble and catch one of the hot cross bun things coming in her direction, after which she disappears and we don't see her for hours, until she arrives back in time for the evening meal.

It turns out that Delicious Delia & Chums are a burlesque troupe who plan to take Hebden by storm. It all sounds good for business so I'm all for it, even though I can tell Maureen is secretly hoping I am going to be shocked and disapproving.

'Did you realise one of them is a ladyboy?' she says slyly.

'Oh, right.'

'Do you know what that is?'

'Yes. Chloë and I watch *RuPaul's Drag Race* together.'

'Oh, right. Burlesque. They're very kinky, apparently, full of S&M motifs.'

'Lovely. Are you stopping to eat with us or are you out?'

'What is it?'

'Omelette.'

'Yes, go on then. I'll stay and eat with you. Can I have cheese but no onion and make it heavy on the parsley? According to Polly, it's an Ayurvedic cleansing agent.'

'Righto.'

I wonder how Hebden will respond to burlesque.

The troupe are currently checking out venues and then will be back again next year. Ooh, it's lovely to think of Lavander Cottage having bookings next year! It's as if this is actually a business.

Later that evening, Chloë presents me with her Christmas list: Apple iPad Pro and Pencil are top of the list, along with new trainers; laptop; Mac make-up palette; Pandora ring; earbuds; iTunes voucher; Amazon fire stick; Bluetooth speaker; Benefit toiletries pack; Superdry parka; art materials; ghd hair straighteners; Tangle Teezer hairbrush; trip to London; and boohoo vouchers.

So far on the list I've got her a Tangle Teezer hairbrush.

Franklin pops round after tea. He's looking very smart, if a bit worn out.

His job at the cracker factory is going well. He's even got a promotion to foreman. He's working every hour God sends, what with it being Christmas. They've taken him on permanently, so he plans to get a mortgage as soon as he can. I'm very happy for him and tell him so. He says he'll be able to contribute to Chloë's enormous Christmas present list. I do a rough calculation of cost, and it comes to near enough two thousand pounds!

He offers to buy the ITunes vouchers and the earbuds.

As he's leaving, I stupidly ask him what he is doing for Christmas, and he hums and haws about his sister being away and his brother being off with his girlfriend and her family and, well, I feel sorry for him and now he's coming here for Christmas Day. I hope Peter won't mind.

Delicious Delia & Chums have departed. I drag myself into the cottage, to at least get the bedding in the wash, and find that they have left the place in very reasonable order. Nothing has been moved or broken, and the washing-up has been done and left on the drainer. I collect the towels, strip the beds, and check inside the wardrobe. Uh-oh. A gigantic red velvet catsuit glows on a hanger above a pair of equally gigantic ruby patent high-heeled shoes. Poor Bojo, he'll kick himself when he realises he's missing his Christmas outfit. It's going to cost a pretty penny in postage. I take the items over to the house, and shout Chloë down to look at me in the shoes. It's great fun strutting around in them until I fall flat on my backside, bashing my head on the kitchen table leg.

Janet Jackson, when will you ever grow up?

. . . .

TIP FOR RUNNING A B&B

Don't forget to check drawers and wardrobes.

. . . .

TIP FOR LIFE

Be careful in high heels if you're not used to them.

CHAPTER 27

Booking No. 13: Ryan & Francesca & Baby Soon

I'm due into work in an hour and pile up in my head the list of tasks I have to do, which starts with buying, wrapping and labelling sixteen cards and gifts for Valley Dental clients. I also have to buy and wrap a Secret Santa gift for Tony, which is the shortest straw in the whole building. He has everything money can buy. I've then to ice and decorate six Christmas cakes. I've got Chloë's end-of-term Christmas show to attend at school, and I haven't even started on my own Christmas cards, even though it's 14 December.

I'm giving my hair a speedy damping down with the straighteners when a booking pops up on my phone, for TODAY. Boo! The moment I read it, there's a knock at the door. I rush down half dressed in decent top half and PJ bottoms, open the door and it's Ryan and Francesca, booked via Airbnb. They're both slim, sporty, smart and well spoken. I'm sure they shouldn't just turn up, isn't there such thing as agreed arrival times? And, boy, do they know how to chat. They give me quite a grilling on primary schools in the area, bearing in mind they don't even have a baby yet!

'Best to plan ahead,' says Francesca.

I am so glad I've got the cottage ready, so I can let them in early and escape. Now I only have ten minutes to finish getting ready and then a manic drive to get parked and into work for nine o'clock.

That tricky start has gone on to become a difficult day. I am on a manic search on Amazon for possible gifts for Tony, and client card writing between appointments, when the electricity goes off midway through Mrs Kemp's extraction. I am charged with finding emergency lighting and manage to drum up, from the bike shop in Hebden, four head torches and an LED, solar Christmas tree. Standing there with a head torch strapped to my head whilst Tony huffs and puffs away on top of a squealing Mrs Kemp is not pleasant. I'm so grateful to get home and pull together a semi-respectable speedy meal of chicken and peanut stir-fry and veg spring rolls. Peter has invited himself round, which is fine, until he suddenly says to me that he is feeling a bit neglected. I try to listen, but I'm struggling with a mini plastic reindeer which is refusing to stand up on the third Christmas cake.

'You haven't even asked me what I'd like for Christmas,' he points out.

I am a bit put out by that one. I suppose I hadn't even really thought about it. I'm so focused on sorting out work and the cottage and Chloë's enormous list, I haven't spent a lot of time thinking about anyone else.

'I've bought you six things,' he says, and looks like he might cry.

I feel horribly guilty.

'I'm sorry, Peter, I have bought you a couple of surprises (*lie*). If there's something you'd like, please tell me.'

'I don't want to say. It feels a bit transactional now.'

'OK, well, do you want to make a list, and I can maybe pick some extra things off that? Then it might feel less... like that.'

'OK.'

He still looks sulky, so I take him into the utility room and give him a 'special kiss'. I then explain that one of the cakes is for him, and the atmosphere subsides.

Somehow, I'd forgotten that relationships need work. And the last thing I need is more work, not when Christmas is coming. Is this Peter thing working out? I can't tell. It's nice when it's nice. It's a pain in the posterior when it's not.

I can't avoid another grilling from Ryan and Francesca, who decide to stay for two more nights in their primary school search. They tell me they are stalking the school runs and talking to parents they've seen grumbling on chat rooms. I'm astonished by their commitment and their planning. I don't think I've ever planned anything in my life that wasn't a couple of months ahead. These guys are planning for years ahead. I can't decide if they're impressive or unbelievably naïve.

They leave the cottage immaculate, so perhaps they've got it all right and I've got it all wrong. I decide I must make the effort to plan at least one thing six months in advance and see if it works out – once I decide what that thing is. It's got to be important. I'm still struggling to think of the thing at midnight. Too tired to continue. Then wake up at a quarter past midnight and write down 'subscription to *Woman & Home*'.

Yes. *Plans.*

. . . .

TIPS FOR RUNNING A B&B

Talk to your guests. You never know, they might have some good Tips on Life.

. . . .

TIP ON ROMANCE

It takes work. How do you decide if it's worth the bother? (I'm looking for tips on this, by the way.)

CHAPTER 28

Booking No. 14: The Emergency Old Couple

I am enjoying my third cup of tea and reading in the *Mail* about how bottom lifts are the biggest surgery boom market when I receive two separate texts from women I know in Mytholmroyd asking about availability at the cottage. An old couple have apparently managed to burn their kitchen down and then have been flooded by the fire service, so their home is currently uninhabitable and they are now homeless.

One of the texts is from Hilary Mayhew – one of those school run mums who says hello one day then ignores you the next depending on who else she's talking to. I gave her plenty of room to be nicer, but after five years I stopped bothering. The other woman – Maria Lovell – never smiles; just a steady, thin-lipped line that never changes for anyone, day in, day out, and she was always more affectionate to her dog than her son. So I went back to Maria and texted *cottage free*.

Three hours later, Maria's forty plus daughter, Shauna Bryce, turns up outside our house. I actually had a run-in with her once when she worked in the Co-op: she insisted I pay full price for the last open box of Haribo. It was near Halloween and everyone was desperate. Today, she's sporting dirty fleece trousers and zero charisma. With her are two very frail, shell-shocked oldies in a battered Land Rover. They look around the cottage, making approving noises. Shauna can't get them in there fast enough. All they have in the way of luggage is two carrier bags.

'I'll have to go and buy some stuff for them,' she tells me abruptly. 'They've nowt at home.'

I'm showing them how to make a cup of tea and they're telling me everything in dramatic detail, one speaking over the other:

'I said, "Bill, the cooker isn't working".'

'She's never been able to work the ignition button. You have to double press it then release, *then* light.'

'It's never worked properly since he washed t'grill with Oven Pride.'

'She's saying, "It's not working again, Bill".'

'...and he's a rolled-up bit of newspaper, he's lit t'gas fire and – *kaboom!* – the whole bloody thing is on fire.'

'I'm trying to do the damp tea towel thing, but the bloody tea towel went up and I thought, *You're fucked here, Bill*.'

'I shouted, "Get out, Bill! We need to get out, Bill!"'

'Mrs Armitage next door rung t'fire service and they poured gallons and gallons in. It were like a ruddy swimming baths.'

'When I saw my bag of rollers float out into t'road, I said to meself, "Edna, we're in a right mess now".'

They are patting each other as they talk, obviously still traumatised. Then Bill pulls cigarettes out of their carrier bags and passes Edna a packet. My heart sinks.

'I'm sorry, you can't smoke in the house.'

They look at each other, confused, passing lighters between themselves, then Edna drops her packet of fags and struggles to pick it up, so I am on my knees, handing them to her as I say, 'I'm sorry, it's a no smoking space.'

'We're going to get insurance,' she says in a wobbling voice.

'Yes, I'm sure you will. It's a no smoking space. Do you want to try and find somewhere else?'

They look at each other, shaking their heads and nodding. I have just given them a cup of tea and Bill is biting into one of my home-made mince pies. He spits out a few crumbs as he speaks.

'No, we'll stay.'

'Yes, we'll stay, thank you.'

Edna sighs and opens and shuts her cigarette packet.

'Where can we smoke?'

So Chloë and I build them an improvised shelter outside the cottage door from an old garden gazebo and two garden chairs. They spend more time sitting outside in it in their pyjamas with fleeces on than inside. And Maureen and Chloë spend quite a lot of time staring at them out of the patio doors.

'How do they keep alive when all they do is smoke?' my

daughter asks, aghast.

'Their insides are like chimneys; this is what their bodies feel comfortable with.'

'That's rubbish.' She looks horrified.

'It's not rubbish. Your body grows accustomed, that's why you have to withdraw very slowly, so your body doesn't go into shock.'

'Eh? What, so something good for them, like an avocado, might kill them?'

'Exactly.'

'Bullshit.'

'*Chloë.*'

'Sorry, Mum.'

Apparently, while I'm at work the next day, Bill and Edna have a load of charity parcels dropped off at the door of Lavander Cottage. Maureen is on the phone to me, spitting feathers, as she tells me about it.

'I've helped them unpack the parcels, and you should see what they've got! Marks & Spencer rosé, whisky-infused Christmas cake, rosemary and sea salt crackers, Sainsbury's Taste the Difference fruit cocktail and a green wax Cheddar wheel. Then the clothes – all brand-new Sainsbury's Tu. You know what? I might burn down this place, Janet. I could do with some charity in my direction.'

I laugh at her, though I make a mental note that, before I go to bed, I will make sure all the matches are hidden and any candles are blown out.

We do Secret Santa after work. I don't know why I bother. I get a pair of funny rubber gloves and a funny washing-up brush. I'd spent hours trawling gift guides before I'd bought Tony his mini remote-control flying insect. He absolutely loves it. He assumes Miles has bought it him and has it flying round reception before it hits our new dental assistant, Willow, going up the stairs and it drops like a stone into the fish tank. That is the end of frivolities. Tony is in a foul mood and refuses to have a drink and he's gone.

I use Edna and Bill as an excuse to leave and find them in my own kitchen when I get home. Apparently, they can't work the cooker (history repeating itself) and have finished the Cheddar wheel and crackers and now have no more cold food. Chloë is feeding them spaghetti hoops on toast. She adds a second tin and makes me some too, so I can hit Amazon and rush through a few presents for Peter's mum, the postman and the binmen. Mustn't forget that Franklin is coming too, of course. I'll have to get him something from Chloë and me and Maureen, and I must try and think about something nice for Peter – a book perhaps?

I'm up early on the Waterstones' website for inspiration. As if Christmas isn't enough to cope with, it's Maureen's birthday today. She's forty-seven slash thirty-nine again and ready to party. She comes down for breakfast all done-up in a yellow, tent-type dress that goes down to the floor, with an open-to-the-bottom back, and gold, gladiator-style, up-the-leg sandals, and a yellow beret. She pops open a bottle of Prosecco before eating her breakfast – which consists of a raspberry. Harry is coming for her at eleven o'clock, and they are planning a day of bohemian excess, getting the train into Leeds and taking it from there.

I give her £55 in pound coins and a nice card about sisters being the chocolate chips in the cookie of life. Chloë doesn't manage to come down and sign her *Best Aunt Ever* card before Maureen gets up, so I take it up to her and have to refrain from holding my nose; the room stinks so badly and the mess in there is unbelievable. There is a crunch of broken glass under two consecutive footsteps, as I creep in. Greg is wrapped around my daughter in bed, and I have to more or less hold the pen, as I help her scrawl her name onto the card. Chloë always gives Maureen the same present – a Chanel Rouge Coco lipstick. She loves it, I take the thank yous.

I use my day off to go into Manchester for a shopping frenzy. Not sure what I've bought; it goes blurry around Boots 3-for-2 when the blood is cut off from my fingers from all the carrier bags. I order takeaway so I can continue to wrap late into the night. Peter comes round, but I send him to bed early so I can get some wrapping done. I've not seen or heard from Maureen and Harry though I know they're in the house when I spot one gold gladiator sandal, a pair of size 10 Reebok trainers and an empty kebab box on the doorstep.

I'm more than halfway through my elf workshop when there is a commotion at the door. It sounds as if someone is literally trying to bash the door down while screaming at the top of their voice.

I shout to Peter to come down, and he does, looking very scared and sleepy. We very tentatively open the door together, and two women barge their way in, one leading the charge and screaming: 'Where the fuck is he, the cheating bastard? I'll kill her!'

I don't require an introduction and shout up the stairs, 'Maureen? MAUREEN!'

I say it out loud, but I don't need to. The next moment, Maureen is out of her bedroom and she and the woman are pulling each other's hair at the top of the stairs. Harry, not a pretty picture – unclean, unshaven, in orange boxer shorts – is attempting pathetically to intervene.

'Hermione, stop! I'm sorry, I lost track of time.'

Hermione stops hitting Maureen long enough to start laying into Harry. I am seriously concerned that someone is going to hurt themselves on the stairs.

'Can we please come off the stairs! Someone is going to fall and break their neck.'

Maureen starts laughing, as the woman hits Harry on his backside and he hops about like an idiot. I have to intervene. I shoo Maureen away, wrap my arms around Hermione, who weighs less than a 25kg bag of compost, and carry her down the stairs to the hall. Harry stays safely at the top of the stairs.

'I'm sorry, Hermione,' he calls down, over the banister. 'I've been seeing Tish.' I was confused for a moment as to who Tish was, then realise he means Maureen. 'I wanted to tell you, but I couldn't.'

Poor Hermione is now bawling inconsolably. Maureen is kneeling next to Harry, patting his back. Hermione's friend, who is called Jemima, recognises Peter, it turns out, and they start chatting. Apparently, he told me later, she has *The Book of Nom* out on extended loan and it is two weeks overdue with a raft of people asking to borrow it.

'What's going on, Mum?' Chloë appears half asleep at the top of the stairs, looking confused.

'Nothing, love, go back to bed. Everyone's just leaving.'

Hermione and her mate take the hint and head for the door, and Harry, looking like a broken man, stumbles down the stairs in his boxers and out of the door after his wife.

Maureen goes pale and leans against the stairs. After an age,

Harry comes back in and hugs a hugely relieved Maureen, and everyone finally goes to bed.

Peter asks me if I am OK. I say yes, I just need another ten minutes to finish wrapping.

The Reebok trainers are gone when I get up, a bit late due to last night's shenanigans. I spend the morning cleaning and cooking. Peter has gone to get his mother. Maureen creeps down around one-ish, looking hollow-eyed and puffy.

'That smells nice,' she says, perking up.

I am lifting the third cauliflower cheese out of the oven, with two already cooling on the side.

'Would you like some?'

She wolfs down a six-person portion, half a Christmas cake and three mince pies, then says, 'I don't feel well.'

I don't see her for the rest of the day.

It's a classic busy Christmas Eve settling Peter's mum into the back dining room. She's quite hard work, but once she gets chatting to Edna and Bill after they come in for more warm mince pies – because they 'couldn't get the oven to work' – she seems to settle. There are bitter complaints from Maureen when the three of them take over the living room and dominate the television with something Christmassy when she wants *Love Island* reruns, or something.

'When did we turn into a bastard old people's home?' she whines.

Peter tells me to sit down about sixteen times. I drink half a bottle of Crianza Rioja wine and eat four mince pies and six mushroom vol-au-vents. I collapse in front of *Top of the Pops 80s Special* and I'm happily singing along to Jona Lewie 'Stop the Cavalry,' when Chloë decides to share some Airbnb comments that I hadn't realised existed:

Pleasant host.
Found an unwelcome cigarette butt, and mattress below par.
Generous welcome basket.
Awesome stay, deffo come again.
Loved it. Thank you for having us.
Fun and games in Hebden!

It was highly amusing trying to guess who said what, especially when Bill, Edna and Joan joined in, throwing in random names. Maureen, however, has barely raised a smile all day. She has been looking at her phone mournfully.

Christmas Day

I'm up at what feels like dawn, prepping Christmas dinner. Peter comes down to help but, once he's peeled some potatoes, he is best off out of the way. His mum keeps him busy, directing the bringing and taking away of footstools.

Chloë seems happy with her gifts. Her favourites appear to be, in order: iPad, boohoo vouchers; a load of smellies; some Mac make-up and a pair of PJs from M&S. Peter loves his chopping board, home-made biscuits, posh leather gardening gloves and Shelley Klein's latest hardback. Peter's mum loves her lavender bag and smellies from Boots. Maureen doesn't even seem to register her PJs and slippers from M&S and her Boots smellies.

Peter has bought me some racy, red underwear, which I stupidly open in front of his mother. She is looking at it pie-eyed, and I don't know what comes over me, but I wrap the red stockings around my neck like a scarf and she seems to calm down. Joan is flustered because she hasn't bought anything and spends the afternoon writing out cheques and handing them to anyone who passes her, *except Peter.*

Franklin turns up at two with a new girlfriend called Lucy, who must be thirty if she's a day. Chloë is not impressed at all, barely speaks to him, and goes out for a walk with Greg. This takes the edge off when Harry turns up, and we can all hear him and Maureen having a ding-dong up in her room. He eventually sits down for what I suspect is his second Christmas dinner, given how little he eats and the gravy stain on his shirt.

Bill and Edna come round for what they tell me is their second Christmas dinner but, given how much they eat, I doubt it – it's as if they've starved themselves in readiness. Shauna turns up between the main and dessert, and insists they go with her for a couple of hours, which is a welcome relief really, as there isn't a lot of room in the lounge once they get settled on the sofa.

Everyone seems to love Christmas dinner. Maureen and Harry

wash up – a first for Maureen. The crackers from Franklin are very good – Fortnum & Mason apparently, yielding a real pair of scissors and a laser pen that could bring down a Boeing 747, according to Franklin. He and Peter get on well, laughing at the cracker jokes and each other's company; just a relief from all the women, I expect.

I contemplate my presents – a load of gardening books, a pair of new gardening gloves, some seeds, a pair of wellies, a new hand food blender and a vegan cookery book from Maureen. I'm very pleased. Peter's mum is in bed for 8 p.m. having drunk almost an entire bottle of sherry, demolished a ten-pack of Prosecco cocktail chocolates and two Baileys coffees. Harry and Maureen disappear upstairs. Franklin leaves after dinner with Lucy, who might be very nice but is silent for the entire visit so it's impossible to tell. Which leaves Peter and me in the front room, having the place all to ourselves for what is a moment of absolute joy: a cuddle, a mince pie, a glass of pink Prosecco in my crystal pudding wine glasses I got as a wedding present off Auntie Nancy years ago.

I am on my second mince pie and double cream when we are interrupted by the door opening and the sounds of Chloë coming in with Greg and a lot of snappy conversation. She tells me later they are not talking, though I hear a lot of loud whispering about a Pandora bracelet he promised to buy her, and she's only got a Pandora locket instead. I hope Chloë isn't spoilt.

I'm woken at 3 a.m. to the sound of low moaning. I can't immediately ascertain where it is coming from and wander downstairs to find Peter's mother naked on the living room floor, clutching a tea towel. I ask her if she's hurt herself and she just breathes out, 'Pissed.' This enables me to feel quite confident in my attempt to move her. She's extremely slim, so no weight at all, and I more or less carry her back to the bed we've set up in the dining room. I tuck her in then get her a glass of water. By the time I return, she's got her mouth open and is seemingly not breathing. I'm gripped by panic and shake the bed a couple of times, then she emits a curdling, guttural, phlegmy gasp that evolves into a snore. After two more blood-chilling minutes, I realise this is how she actually sounds when sleeping and crawl towards the bedroom, where Peter is happily snoring away.

I am exhausted.

Boxing Day

Exhausted. Eat body weight in chocolate. Sleep badly.

Day after Boxing Day

Look at garden. Eat leftovers. Watch *Poirot* repeat, squashed on sofa with Edna and Bill. John Malkovich a bit miserable. Doesn't twirl his moustache once.

Day after day after Boxing Day

Finally, Peter takes his mum home. Hurrah! Thank God she only brought enough tablets to last until today. She's very demanding of Peter; I've barely spoken to him. I'm trying to decide what I can rustle up from the last of the turkey leftovers when Maureen appears through the patio doors, wet through and weeping.

'You all right? You're wet through,' I say, concerned.

'I've walked from Hebden. It's over.'

She sounds broken. She is broken. She doesn't seem to be able to stop crying for hours and then the night and then the next day and the next day. Nothing shifts the gloom, not even a home-made Prosecco cake with reindeer candelabra and the promise of a *Love Island Best Bits*. She is incredibly sad, and I'm so gutted for her. I daren't ask about the Poet Laureate final. The article is on the front cover of the *Hebden Bridge Times*, and she gets written up as 'in contention' along with a load of other names. Eventually, I decide it might cheer her up to know she's front-page material, and I take it up to her with a huge marshmallow and cream hot chocolate and a mince pie. I open the curtains in the bedroom and shuffle onto her bed with a tray.

'Maureen.'

'Go away.'

'Maureen.'

'I'm not accepting visitors.'

'You're front cover of the *Hebden Bridge Times*.'

'What for?'

'Sleepwalking naked.'

She turns and sits up. '*What?*' She grabs the paper. 'Ha, ha, very good. It's a no to jokes at the moment.'

'Look – you're front cover.'

She sits up properly and interrogates the paper. There's a two-second silence, then: 'Fuck it. FUCK IT! I am going to win that bloody thing.' She points at the hot chocolate. 'Has that got alcohol in it?'

'Not currently.'

'So what's the point?' She gets out of bed and comes downstairs.

A whisky shot later and Maureen is up and pronouncing long words, short words, rhymes and swear words. She goes on and on well past my bedtime, and I want to be supportive and believe I am being, until I wake up on the sofa dribbling with no Maureen around.

The day dawns bright and chilly, and I know she's serious about this, as I can hear her gargling upstairs. She accepts an offer from Peter and me to accompany her that evening to the Trades Club for the Hebden Bridge Poet Laureate final. Maureen is in a tight, body-con, scoop-neck dress with a hat-cum-veil, when she asks me what I think of her outfit.

I say, 'Sexy Michelle from *'Allo 'Allo*.' She doesn't look impressed and tells me the inspiration is Helena Christensen at Michael Hutchence's funeral. Same thing, I think, but don't say it.

The Trades Club is packed. Harry is there, mooching near the bar, looking sullen, and his wife, Hermione, is at his side. She is glammed up to the eyeballs in a tight red 1950s-style dress with major cleavage. She is glued to his side, her arm wrapped around his shoulders, which does not look at all comfortable. Maureen is very stoical all evening and doesn't once glance in their direction, though I can see Hermione beaming lasers from her eyes at Maureen's back.

My sister, surprisingly, remains very sober. She has one small red wine, until it is almost her turn to perform, when she turns to me and says, 'Shit, I've never done this sober. I need a vodka.' I rush to the bar for her and bring her back two shots. She necks them one after the other without flinching.

When 'Mitzi Jackson' is announced, I watch as Harry and his wife exchange looks and reluctantly take their seats at the judging table, along with a couple of other Hebden types with big hair and headscarves, who like to put themselves in charge of everything. Maureen has told me she was starting with Maya Angelou's 'Still I Rise', which gets a huge round of applause, and then it's her turn to do an original poem on any subject.

Maureen searches through the crowd and then stares right at me, smiles and says, 'For Janet, my one, true champion.' I am so shocked and proud. She looks luminous and beautiful under the lights. She takes a pause, then reads the following lines:

I Will Never Lose My Looks

I will never lose my looks, because my eyes will always sparkle,
I will never lose my looks, because my wild heart glows from within.
And as the cracks and creases around my eyes became troughs and furrows,
as life ploughs its way across my face, like it did at twenty-three, thirty-four, forty-five...
still, I will not tell myself I'm less, because I almost lost my looks.
I will be amazed at how tall I became when I stood back up,
and I will dazzle everyone with the return of my wicked smile.
And as the months reach over the days and the years take a tumble,
let me tell you what I'll know then too.

I will not lose my looks.
I will let my hair grow wispy, so the dye no longer sticks,
leave space for the moon to weave glitter through the threads,
and fashion me a tiara from the stars, that I will wear everywhere,
so that you, sister, can search the missing skies and find me luminous still.

I cry my eyes out. Everyone does. It's amazing. The room is pin-drop silent, and then it explodes. Triumphant. The crowd go bananas! Maureen stumbles a bit, almost as if she has been hit by the noise, or the vodka is kicking in. Anyway, she comes down off the stage and doesn't look at the judges, all of whom are standing up to applaud her, except Harry, who is wiping at his eyes, and Hermione, who is throwing a drink down and looks mightily annoyed.

Maureen reappears beside us. I give her a giant hug, and she then proceeds to get mightily sloshed, starting with my glass of red wine.

Finally, at two minutes past midnight, Harry coughs into the mic, stands up on a bench and declares that the Hebden Bridge Poet Laureate is Tommy Gunsmoke. Well, there is a smattering of applause and then some boos. Someone lifts Maureen up, and she is carried across the room like a crowd-surfer. It's amazing. There are loads of cheers and someone shouts, 'Mitzi! Mitzi!' which gets going like a chant. Then it all gets a bit cold and boring.

Peter and I are waiting outside for ages, as Maureen speaks to every single person in Hebden Bridge. Harry and his missus skulk past us without knowing. She is ripping at his elbow, and I can hear him saying, 'Sorry, sorry, *SORRY*,' with a fury that doesn't sound at all sorry.

Peter and I get a kebab from the town square, and we sit on the wall outside the taxi rank watching as person after person shuffles along the queue and makes their way home.

After an hour of waiting for Maureen to join us, I ring her and she answers, saying, 'Are you coming or what?'

'Eh? We're here waiting for you at the taxi.'

'I'm home. I've been here half an hour with Tommy and a bottle of champagne.'

We are so cold at this point we walk to Peter's, where it is actually colder in the flat than outside. It also stinks of cold fat.

Happy New Year!

We are up early and toddle back to mine along the canal. It's a lovely New Year's Day. I spend the whole walk back planning the big breakfast I am going to make, so much so that when Peter asks me something I reply, 'Poached eggs,' which has him laughing, as he's asking me what is my New Year's resolution?

When we get back in, Maureen looks like she hasn't yet been to bed and she's extremely giddy, as she has been asked and agreed to become Hebden's unofficial Poet Laureate. I don't know who decides that. Anyway, she's chuffed.

'Hebden's all about the alternative. Well, I am it!'

Tommy Gunsmoke, the official Poet Laureate, is very jolly if a bit smelly. His outfit is a lot of leather and denim that looks like it could stand up and hold a conversation of its own. He's a gentle, likeable type, though I notice he has his hand in permanent contact with a hip flask which I can't help but think is a bad sign. He and Maureen both manage a big breakfast then collapse in the living room. Maureen crawls up to her bedroom and leaves Tommy splayed out on the sofa for the rest of the day with his boots on. Chloë sprays him with perfume before she puts the TV on and watches a *Friends* marathon.

Edna and Bill join her for season eight, and I realise, as I'm feeding them the last of the Christmas cake and some cheese, that they have not paid me anything for the cottage yet. I reach out to their daughter to ask if the insurance has come through as they owe me near enough £800, and is there a plan with regards to payment? She arrives an hour later to collect them and take them to hers. The old couple seem convinced they are coming back, and I don't really want to be the one to upset them, so I simply wave them off with the Christmas cake wrapped up in napkins.

It takes me hours to turn the cottage around. Either they smoked in the bedroom or they just smelled so badly of smoke that it travelled with them *everywhere*. I have to leave the windows open all day and clean, clean, clean. Bit depressing, though Maureen's so happy she buoys me up with her endless singing and dancing. Harry texts her to congratulate her, and she sends him a rhyming voice note to the tune of 'Santa Baby' whilst impersonating Marilyn Monroe.

Thank you, baby,
Tell me what you're doing for tea?
Tee-hee,
I'm doing Tommy, Bill and Cody, that's three,
Three just for me.
Tee-hee, tee-hee. Teee-heee.

. . . .

TIPS FOR RUNNING A B&B

Try not to let guests into your actual house.

Avoid feeding guests if you can, since it encourages them in.

. . . .

TIPS FOR CHRISTMAS

Prime yourself to be exhausted and broke. Sorry, this isn't exactly a tip, more preparation.

Maybe try to get a few early nights in and save all your coupons for December.

CHAPTER 29

Booking No. 15: Lovely Thomas & Emily

It's early January and the new school term, and the pressure is on for Chloë. She's worrying so much about her maths that I'm paying for a tutor, which costs £16 an hour. I'm £300 overdrawn on my current account. Bloody Christmas! I could borrow from my ISA, but I'm trying not to.

It seems the Airbnb gods are listening, for lovely couple Thomas and Emily come and stay at Lavander Cottage for two days to do some winter walking. Emily works for a charity that looks after insects, and Thomas is a wildlife photographer who has had books published. I could talk to the couple all day; they're so interesting and nice. Apparently, this area is on a list for special scientific insect interest because of the carnivorous ants in Hardcastle Crags. I think I am probably overstaying my chat welcome when I realise they've got their coats on and Thomas looks at his watch for the third time. I can't help it, it's like having a real-life Chris Packham and Michaela Strachan on the doorstep.

They leave very early on departure day, again very nice of them, and I go in the cottage after they leave and it's spotless. They've even left me some chocolates and a thank-you card. They are my favourite Airbnbers, and I wish they could be my friends. They live in Oxford though, and I've not got their address so it's not looking likely.

I am trying to crawl my way out of the overdraft through old-fashioned thrift. The key is not to let anyone know. I turn the heating down by a couple of degrees and try not to use the tumble dryer, as it's so expensive. It means washing is slung everywhere and turning Chloe's PE kit around during the week is tricky. It makes me really sympathise with some of the really poor parents, everything about laundry is so expensive, how do they cope?

I try some food thrift; I make breadcrumbs out of an old loaf that tops a macaroni cheese and plan to use up the rest in home-made fishcakes using potatoes that are starting to sprout and a teeny bit of haddock in the freezer. Menu planning is a very relaxing and satisfying task when you get time to do it. My plans for stew and dumplings using every last vegetable and some frozen beef are thrown out of whack though when Chloe insists on veggie burger, chips and salad three nights on the trot. I think she might be premenstrual by the demands for chocolate and the permanent scowl, so I daren't refuse. I make the stew anyway and heat it up for lunch over a couple of days.

It's quite a relief when Peter suggests we go for an early-bird meal at the Thai Flower. Being careful with money all the time is tiring. I hum and haw about whether I can justify it, but then he tells me he's booked it anyway, anticipating they'll be busy, and that's the decision out of my hands – which I really like. When we get there it's more or less empty, and when the starters arrive the spring rolls are limp.

I must have grumbled about this loudly, because the only other couple in there who are a few tables away pipe up: 'My pad thai is greasy. I've heard the chef's gone back to Thailand.'

Well, what with the food not being very good and me joking to Peter that I quite fancy Donald Tusk, the night is a bit of a disappointment. Peter spends a lot of the date talking about European politics, of which I know very little and care even less. I think this becomes obvious when I yawn loudly over the limoncello meringue pudding that is oversoft, with a puddle of what I think is warm lemon curd. All in all, not the best night ever. It's twenty pounds each and, as I hand over the cash, I have to really stop myself doing a mental shopping list of what I could buy for that money, especially knowing we've run out of kitchen roll and garden peas.

I am woken up in the middle of the night by a very excitable Peter telling me he wants to go to Europe. I am initially quite excited too, then slightly thrown, and then when he starts whispering in French I get back into it, until I hear the word *gare* and think, *Did he mean to say station?* Anyway, it went on long enough for me to think about all things European, and I decide I quite fancy a city break to Belgium.

CHAPTER 30

Booking No. 16: Malky

Today there was a last-minute Airbnb request for the cottage. The place is immaculate, mainly thanks to Thomas and Emily, and so I accept it, even though Malky has no reviews. Got to think of this overdraft.

When he turns up on his motorbike and parks in the drive, I get all of a flutter, wondering what I'll do if he is a raging maniac with a chainsaw, and then realise I am mixing him up with Meat Loaf in *The Rocky Horror Picture Show*.

Malky is rugged and handsome and explains in a lovely, deep voice that he is in the area to meet his long-lost brother, Tim, from his dad's side, who lives in Luddenden, just west of Halifax. It all sounds very romantic, and I wish him well. Maureen is out doing yoga stretches around his bike in her gold chaps, but he doesn't seem to notice, and she comes back in looking crestfallen. I try to placate her.

'I think he's got family issues.'

'He's definitely got issues,' she snorts. 'No man, straight or gay, has seen me do downward dog in these beauties and not blinked.'

Malky spends some time in the garden in the evening. I wander out and offer him a slice of home-made red velvet cake and he offers me a glass of Chardonnay. Why not? We get chatting about his allotment – he's growing potatoes, garlic and Jerusalem artichokes currently, with a plan to branch out to salads if he can get the bed organised in time. And once we've talked gardening, he relaxes enough to tell me quite a bit about himself. Malky is long divorced. Married in his twenties, he was working away a lot as a diver welding underwater oil rigs; with too much time apart, his wife left him for the postman! He enjoys being on his own, he tells me, with no one to answer to, no drama and especially no in-laws. We laugh about that. He's been all over the world, welding oil rigs. The Middle East pays the best, apparently, and there's nowhere to go, as you're kept on-site for safety, so you rack up the cash. He has no mortgage now and is looking for his second home, maybe in Lanzarote maybe in Thailand, or maybe Florida.

'What's wrong with Scarborough?' I say, and we both laugh again.

It's getting quite late by the time we go in, and when I ask him if he has everything he needs, he gives a big sigh and says, 'Some arms to cuddle up with' – and looks me straight in the eye! I'm quite shocked and go a bit weak-kneed, I have to say. I break out into a sweat on my forehead, although you wouldn't know unless you were looking – and that's the main reason I have always had a fringe.

I pick up the red velvet cake plate and smile, saying, 'Better get going. I've an early start. Delicious wine, thank you. Good luck for tomorrow, Malky. Let me know how you get on.'

I go quickly back inside the house and close the curtains and lock the doors, mainly to stop myself from running back out and throwing myself into the arms of Malky. What is wrong with me? What is right with Malky? I feel so guilty replying to Peter's text: *Goodnight, lovely* that I send him a kiss emoji. What a flaming hypocrite. Am very wound up all night, tossing and turning, contemplating what it would mean for my character if I was to go and knock on the cottage door. *Who would know?* I ask myself. Then: *Why am I restraining myself?* Has living too long with Maureen's amoral approach impacted on my moral values? Is it OK to just fancy someone?

In the morning, I put on a low-cut blouse and tight pencil skirt and heels, and once the curtains open on the cottage windows, I go and put the bins out. Malky comes outside.

'What do you want me to do with the recycling?' he asks.

'Just bag it up into cardboard, plastics and glass.'

He brings a tiny bag of rubbish out and hands it over. I don't know about him but that bin bag is electric.

'You look nice,' he says, and clears his throat.

'Thank you.'

'I'll let you know how I get on.'

'Yes, I'd love to know. Good luck, Malky.'

'Have a good day, Janet.'

Way too much eye contact, way too slow closing the doors. Melted cheese Louise. I've got a crush on Malky. I'm thinking about him most of the day, in his leathers, me in leathers, me on a motorbike again, flying down to Scarborough...

When I get back, Malky has left, the cottage is empty and tidy, and there's a big smile emoji in the guest book. I'm feeling so disappointed; all the thrill and the excitement evaporated in an instant. I begin tidying up to distract myself then I hear a bike in the drive. It's Malky, with a bottle of wine in one hand and some flowers in the other. I open the cottage door with a smile, and he approaches, beaming.

'Any chance I could crash another night?' he asks. 'I don't fancy the drive back tonight, it's been a tough day. I'll pay cash?'

'No problem, I've no other bookings this week.'

'I couldn't resist these beauties.' He is holding a glorious bunch of pink roses that smell wonderful.

'I'll get you a vase.'

'They're actually for you, Janet,' he tells me. 'I was hoping for a bit more of that red velvet cake and maybe a partner in crime.' He holds up the wine.

There is a pool of Janet on the floor.

'I think that can all be arranged.'

I warm up some home-made lasagne and take round the last of the cake with ice cream. The wine is delicious and, as we drain the bottle in Lavander Cottage, Malky pours out his day.

His brother Tim turned out to be an arsehole, just like his dad. Tim has three kids he doesn't see – blames the ex-wife and the kids. Poor Malky then confides in me that he himself only has one testicle and it doesn't do sperm of sufficient quality to have kids, so it's quite a sorrow to him. I'm absorbing this, just as Chloë knocks on the cottage door. I answer, feeling extremely guilty and tipsy. Thank heavens she seems completely oblivious.

'Can you put some money on the lunch app? I had to borrow an apple from Jude.'

'Of course. Sorry love, I didn't realise. I'm just chatting to Malky here.' They exchange greetings, then my daughter turns to leave.

She says, 'I'm going over to Rachel's for a study session, Mum.'

'Don't be back late. Text me when you're setting off. I'll walk on and meet you.'

'No, it's cool, Greg is walking me home.'

Seeing her brings me up sharp. The bottle is empty and it's time I made my escape.

'I'm sorry it wasn't what you hoped,' I say to Malky.

'It's something I needed to do. I've made the best of it, Janet, and there have been definite highlights.' He then looks into my eyes and says, 'Can I kiss you?'

I don't resist, I lean into his kiss and we have the most outrageously good snog. It goes on and on and on. He takes my hand, and I know he wants to lead me upstairs. I wrestle with the urge, landing another kiss on his lips, and then another for good measure.

'I'm on mum duty, you're on the back of a tough day, let's take things steady.'

'I understand.'

He wraps his arms around me and pulls me close. He has a way, a smell, a heft that is near enough intoxicating. We share another long soft kiss and then I wriggle free, pick up the dirty plates and head for the door.

'Lovely evening, Malky. I'm truly sorry about your brother.'

'I'm not, Janet. It closes the book. You've been a delight, an amazing cook and a fabulous kisser.'

I giggle like a froth of a girl, whether from nervousness, too much wine, the sheer thrill of it, I can't tell any more.

'Sleep well.'

I'm out of there before I change my mind, and take in a deep draught of the night air, stepping into a huge stream of moonlight beaming down like a West End spotlight on me, Janet Jackson. Sometimes, I decide then and there, it's about grabbing the moment. So I knock on the cottage door, call out, 'Malky...' and let myself in.

I'm up spectacularly early and slip back into the house, where everything is where it should be, there are no disasters, though I feel different, everything else is safe. I'm putting a wash through when I hear the rumble of the bike kick off early. For some reason, I don't rush to say goodbye. It feels better to leave it enigmatic; not too needy, not too final. He has my number. I wander over to the cottage and find £100 on the table under the flowers with a huge smile and a heart scrawled on the back of the recycling information.

Thank you, Janet, for making an old man very happy. I'll be in touch soon.

I am giddy with the sheer naughtiness. Maybe Maureen is rubbing off on me? That old man, one testicle or not, had everything going great guns and he made this old woman very happy too. Thank you universe for a night of a lifetime.

I make a decision to start a cash savings pot and put the notes in an old Ringtons tea tin and hide it in the cleaning cupboard where there's absolutely no fear of Maureen finding it. I lie down for a while on my bed and am woken up by the alarm at 7 a.m. I decide the whole episode was down to hormones and wine on a school night, and promise myself I'll never think of Malky again.

• •

TIP FOR RUNNING A B&B

Avoid flirting with the guests. It can lead places. Unless that's what you want, of course.

CHAPTER 31

Booking No. 17: Seamus & June

Harry and Maureen are back on. I notice his Reebok trainers lying by the back door this morning. Maureen explains she'd been doing an alternative Valentine's night at the White Lion and he'd come in to find her.

'Before we knew it, Janet, we were outside, against the wall, looking out at the waterwheel and doing cartwheels of the mind and body.'

I went to mop the bathroom at that point.

Peter has got access to a Costco card, and we decide to make an afternoon of it. We go mad on tins of chickpeas and cannellini beans. I've decided I don't eat enough beans, and they are very cheap when bought in trays of eight. I can always remember how my grandmother had a curtained-off area in the bedroom; when the curtain was pulled back, it revealed hundreds of bags of sugar. I buy a pallet of six bags in honour of that memory, followed by eighty toilet rolls, fourteen tins of tomatoes, eight tins of tuna in sunflower oil (on special offer), and kidney beans – two tins.

Peter reveals he has a thing for tinned pears, so we buy six tins of those. Baked beans – a dozen tins. Six Lockwoods tinned mushy peas. By the time we reach biscuits, the fever has set in. Flour – three bags each of plain and self-raising. Six packets of fig rolls. Six packets of chocolate digestives. Ten bags of Bombay mix, though I think we are overreacting at this point. Three jars of olives, some baklava and two packets of dried mango. I have completely lost any sense of budget. We spend more than £148 at the till on food, and I absolutely love it.

Once home, since Peter is staying here more or less all the time, we struggle to find cupboard space and, while we're unpacking, Peter and I both get very excited in the pantry, which I put down to the wild abandonment we'd shown at the checkout. We have just finished being rather outrageous, with Peter's zip snagging on his corduroys, when Chloë walks in complaining there is nothing to eat in the house and she is starving. Fortunately, I have some Pringles at hand to distract her from Peter being caught in his zip.

Work tomorrow.

It's a quiet day in Valley Dental, and I enjoy it after all the excitement of the last couple of weeks. I find a really good recipe for easy tarte Tatin and think I'll make it tonight because there's at least three apples going off in the fruit bowl. I pick up a newspaper one of the patients has left behind and see that Janet Jackson is going to tour the UK this year. I might go. I'd love to get her autograph and a signed photo: *To Janet Jackson, best wishes from Janet Jackson.*

Miles wanders down at lunchtime, and we have five minutes discussing the chilli pepper plants he's trying to grow on the windowsill of the hotel he's living in temporarily. He's a different man without his wedding ring. From my own experience with Franklin, I understand the shaking up you have from divorce. When you're married for a long time, it feels like 'forever' is a given, and then when it's not, well, the ground beneath you moves like in those movies where worlds collapse under everyone. It's all such a shock. It's as if an earthquake has hit you full force and you're left clinging to a tree stump, not sure how much of you and your life is left standing as the storm subsides.

I talk about my tarte Tatin plans and he almost drools. He explains that he's had every takeout Hebden has to offer except the grilled cheese booth. He's saving that for the weekend.

Talking of earthquakes, we've had a flood – one along the lines of what Noah had to deal with. Well, nearly. Chloë and I go down to the bridge to watch, as the river rushes by. It's risen so high that it's touching the beam that holds the bridge! The power and speed of the water is breathtaking. Todmorden is shut off, apparently. Someone moans about the amount of time the flood defences are taking. People are forming lines and throwing sandbags about. Someone else says it's peaked, and then they start talking about depression and pressures and south-easterlies. Well, it's obvious they know what they are talking about, so we leave. But not before doing a very sneaky Poohsticks. Sneaky, because apparently, it was a build-up of wood backed up under the bridge that caused Hebbleroyd to flood last time, since the water couldn't escape and get past the 'dam'. I don't imagine two lolly sticks are going to cause a flood, but it might be like the butterfly effect thing. One little thing. Gosh, I hope not.

It's Saturday, and it's St Patrick's Day. Airbnbers, June and Seamus, are staying in Lavander Cottage. They are wearing the only two large Guinness hats in Hebden: it's easy to spot them coming out of the railway station. I fear that the couple will be disappointed in Hebden, since there's not a single shamrock in sight.

The next morning, I note that Chloë seems very stressed. When I ask her to wash up the jug, bowl and two pans she'd used to make an omelette, she screams at me at full volume.

'*I'm doing my art project!*'

I make the mistake of wandering into her bedroom to drop off some washing and see she's doing a collage of my face from photographs all cut up into pieces.

Back downstairs, there's another shock. Harvey has taken to leaving the entrails of small animals near the back door, and the sight of what looks like a little bladder attached to other stringy bits before breakfast has me gagging.

I watch Seamus and June wander out of the cottage bleary-eyed at 11.45 a.m., still in their Guinness hats. I give them a wave and decide I'd better go out and be friendly.

'Hope you've had a nice time?'

They seem happy enough, if a tad the worse for wear. They have a wonderful Irish accent, but it is hard to tune into, and they speak quickly. I pick out 'Christmas', 'great' and 'slept by logs'. I nod, smile back and say 'Great, thank you,' and then they're gone.

The cottage is barely touched, which is a relief. The thought of a huge cleaning job on a Sunday makes my heart sink. As it is, I'm soon in the swing of it and go through my mental checklist. The kitchen and the bathroom are always the things I dread, and by the number of Guinness cans and pizza boxes there has been zero cooking, which is great, and the towels are untouched, so they've not bothered showering either. I find a pair of gloves, one sock and a leaflet for gong healing that I stick in the guest book.

I'm done in an hour and turn the key. Knowing it's all set up for the next guest or guests is so satisfying. I make myself a frittata from leftovers and sit outside in the watery sun that can't decide if it's coming or going. Everywhere I look there are buds. Every pot, every bed, has something interesting peeping from it. Spring is definitely coming and sipping this cup of tea from a lovely mug, taking a bite of well-seasoned frittata and watching the narcissus dancing in their frilly, yellow skirts while the birds are singing away for pure joy, life is good.

• •

TIPS ON LIFE

Prep for larder space *before* a trip to Costco.

Enjoy the little moments.

CHAPTER 32

Booking No. 18: The Algerians

I'm forty-five today. I don't know if it's connected, but I hear a creak as I get out of bed. Chloë has made me a card. The outside features a portrait of me knelt down in the garden, with my bottom looking huge, and inside is a hand-drawn picture of a slice of cake. Can't help but think the two are related. Decide I am looking a bit on the tubby side and commit myself to diet once today is over with. Peter brings round a caterpillar cake from Tesco and a delphinium, and Maureen gives me a tub of Nivea body cream and a three-pack of Ferrero Rocher, both of which she has tested on my behalf.

Hurrah, we have a booking! A lovely family party arrive comprising two brothers, one wife and two small children. I have put out all the beds – I think one brother is sleeping on the sofa bed downstairs, with the family sharing the big bedroom with a double bed and two singles. They are lively, fun and jolly. I am a little hung-over, so it's hard keeping up with their giggling and stories. They immediately ask for a cash discount, and I have to explain that unfortunately I can't as the money is already with Airbnb. They tell me they are going to York for the day tomorrow and then a big wedding fayre in Harrogate. I try to say York's quite far away, but they're not having it. They've never been out of London before and keep saying it's so beautiful here. They run a wedding business apparently.

I'm woken up at 6 a.m. by the sound of a car alarm being abruptly brought to a halt. Again and again and again and again. After the fiftieth time, I realise that it probably isn't a car alarm. Maureen staggers into my bedroom half an hour later. It's a very rare sighting for her to be up at this time in the morning, and I have to say she is almost unrecognisable.

'Will you tell those little bastards to shut up?' she snarls. 'Some of us are sleeping. It's bloody Sunday.'

I creep into her room and peer over the windowsill through a slit in her lace cobweb, tie-dyed window thing. The two children are playing outside Maureen's window with a bouncy, illuminated rubber ball thing that is emitting the piercing car alarm noise with every bounce. They are having such a good time I haven't the heart to stop them. When I go back into my room with a plan to try and placate Maureen with a promise of £20 from the proceeds of the Algerian stopover, I find her already asleep and snoring, in my bed.

The family are soon out and setting off for the day, so we see *or hear* very little from them for the rest of the day. I'm putting the recycling out in the evening when they pull up on the drive. The car doors fly open and the family pour out. The two smiley brothers approach me in an instant.

"Allo, lovely place. We love it. We think maybe we come back Christmas? You booked up already?'

I gulp, a bit on the hoof. 'That sounds nice.'

'Does it snow here?'

'Ah...' I think ahead to the prospect of Maureen, rich on Christmas spirit, being woken up by the sound of excitable Algerian children and the plethora of noisy toys they would inevitably be opening on Christmas Day, despite being Muslim. I picture her vicious Scrooge antics, and it gives me The Fear.

'No. No snow here, I'm afraid,' I lie. 'You have to go up. Up, up, up to Scotland – the Highlands – to guarantee snow at Christmas.'

'Ah, we take your number though, eh? Contact you direct next time.'

'Lovely,' I say. 'It's 07902 501980,' (*one digit wrong*). I feel so bad. Though imagining the look on Maureen's face when I tell her the Algerians are back on Christmas Day... No, I can't face it.

Someone – it must be Jenny, the other part-time receptionist – has alerted work it was my birthday yesterday, so when I get in I find a nice plant and some fabulous nutty chocolates from everyone. I have eaten half of them by noon and waddle around the park at lunchtime rather than eat anything else. Miles is floating around after lunch when there is a filling no-show, asking questions about Lavander Cottage, and I make him smile with the story of the Algerians and their early alarm call. I am starving when I get home and demolish the last of the caterpillar cake. Think I might have an eating disorder.

Maureen is reading Greta Thunberg's book again and is going on and on about climate change and taking action to do with climate rebellion. She is mid flow, writing one of her spoken word poems, performing it at the same time:

'*Twice the Earth asked the people, and twice they turned their backs.*'

I am half listening whilst I hoover around her, having already made tea, done two loads of washing, tidied up and cleaned the bathroom. When I ask if she would mind emptying the bin in her bedroom, she harrumphs and talks about women and the pursuit of art in the face of domestic drudgery. Having pulled her long, black hair out of the bathroom plughole and scraped her nail varnish stains from the wooden floor in her bedroom, I'm not feeling remotely sympathetic.

'I might have a poem in me myself,' I say bitterly, '*if* I had a moment to do it. As it is, I struggle to make time for a poo.'

She laughs, but I don't. I'm telling the truth. She finally takes the hint and empties her bin and piles her dirty bed linen by the washer.

'I'll do my bed,' she says, as if she is saving me work rather than piling another load of washing on my to-do list. I'm not usually bothered. I don't usually even notice. Maybe it's time for more HRT.

I get an email tonight from an Italian family who live in Lucca. They want to rent the cottage for a couple of weeks whilst they look at the area for schools. They wish their children to learn English and think they might move over here for a year. I'm very encouraging, of course, but I can't help but wonder, how do they afford it? I would never dream of living abroad. Where do people get all their money from, to do these things? How do they feel so free? It's like I'm trapped by an invisible anchor in Hebbleroyd. I know these days I'm doing really well, having a nice house with the garage conversion and everything, but it did take five years and every spare penny to do it.

I've done an audit and work out I owe £54,000 on the mortgage. I've got fifteen years left to go on it. I'll be sixty. The way things are at the moment, I'll be lucky to pay it off. At the moment, I'm struggling to settle all the bills. I'm saving £20 a month into an ISA and £60 into a pension. I bet there'll be no state pension by the time I get there. I really need Maureen to start contributing. I don't know how to have it out with her or even if it will make a difference. What's *she* going to live on when she's old? Muggins here, that's what.

I brace myself and drop a big hint over breakfast. 'I need to have a chat with you about money.'

She's very distracted and turns up the radio to listen to the news, saying over it, 'I promise you, I am thinking about what job I can do.' She then disappears upstairs, comes back down with a heaving rucksack and leaves. I can't decide if I feel sad or glad.

I always try to give it a couple of days with Maureen before I worry where she is. It's like an unspoken rule between us.

Anyway, true to form, end of day two, I get a text.

Yo, sis, I'm in London tackling climate change. Struggling to get home. Can you buy me a ticket or BACS me some cash? I'll pay you back promise. x

I ping her £75. Surely that will be enough.

Two days later, she's back, dirty, exhausted and elated. She has a two-hour bath, wafts into the garden and climbs the magnolia tree. Apparently, she's been hanging out a lot in trees in London with a lovely guy called Squat. She insists Chloë take multiple photos of her in various poses up the tree to send on to her tribe. She's lying full length along one of the branches with her leg exposed when the branch snaps.

'Why are you being so callous?' she groans, miffed, as I ignore her and try to bandage the tree whilst she rolls around on the ground.

'I am restraining myself here,' I say tersely. 'I actually feel like bloody killing you.'

At that, she leaps up and scuttles off into the house. I stare at my poorly tree through the kitchen window, as Maureen shows off her comment on the BBC website on her laptop.

'One climate protestor told the BBC: "The Earth has asked us twice, let's not turn our backs again."'

Chloë pulls a face and asks: 'When did the Earth ask us the first time?'

Maureen rolls her eyes and disappears off to her bedroom with a maxi-pack of Twiglets. I feel like snapping every one of them in half.

• •

TIP FOR RUNNING A B&B

Always remind yourself that even noisy guests are gone quite soon.

• •

TIPS ON DEALING WITH RELATIVES

Whatever it is, nip it in the bud; money, tidiness, not pulling their weight in the house. Don't be too soft, or you might grow to resent it.

CHAPTER 33

I want to be in early to do some new online training and get it done before the rush starts. I am hanging up my coat at work when Miles walks out of the downstairs loo in his pyjamas.

'Morning, Miles.'

I note he has a toothbrush stuck in the corner of his mouth.

'Morning, Janet. I'm... uh... running a bit late.'

'No, it's me, I'm here early,' I explain. 'I'm doing some training.'

'Oh good. Do you mind not saying anything about this?' He looks down at his pyjamas. 'I'm trying to save some money and got sick of the hotel. My wife's determined to ruin me if she can.'

'Mum's the word.'

I rush behind the desk, where it's safe, and switch on the computer, rattle some papers, rearrange the pens in the pot and feed the fish, all the while pretending nothing's happened, in the hope it allows Miles to go away and get dressed. Instead, he stands there rooted to the spot, staring into the distance.

'She loved me once and now she wants to ruin me. How does a marriage go so wrong?'

I'm not sure if he is actually asking me or pontificating, that type of thing.

I pipe up: 'I think people sometimes need to hurt someone else when they're hurting themselves.'

'You're right. I tried so hard to make her happy, Janet. I did try – for years. Nothing worked. Yet I made sure she didn't want for anything.'

'People get disappointed with their life, Miles, it's not your fault.'

'I did sleep with the nanny, Janet.'

'That would upset her.'

He gives a big sigh. 'Well, I'm paying for it now.' He pulls up the blinds on both windows and lets the light in. 'It's Tuesday, right? Let's get on with it.'

I receive a call from Chloë at school at 9.45 a.m. screaming that she's left her art book at home, and her life is over and her exam is ruined unless she gets it delivered immediately. When I tell her I am at work and already busy, but that I could nip out at midday and collect it if I go for an early lunch, she says that will be fine and to bring it to student services, and slams the phone down.

At 10.50 she rings me again, screaming, 'Where are you? This is urgent and school are going to call you to give me permission to leave school to fetch it.' The phone slams down then school immediately rings.

'Can Chloë be allowed to leave?'

'Yes, of course. Has she got her door...' phone slammed down, '...key?'

By 11.20 a.m. Chloë is now crying hysterically on the end of the phone. She can't get in; she doesn't have a door key.

'Stay there. I'll be as fast as I can.'

I speak to Miles mid extraction and tell him I need to take a very early lunch – it's a Chloë emergency. I race home, definitely breaking the speed limit, and walk into the kitchen to find the neighbour's ladder propped up against the window: all I can see are feet up the ladder at ceiling height. I walk round the back and there is Chloë, distraught, at the top of the ladder. I tell her to get down then drive her back to school with her art book in complete silence.

I make her favourite macaroni cheese for tea and, as I am clearing up, I am dying to say, 'Are you prepared for tomorrow?' However, I daren't risk it and text her at 9.48 p.m. instead. Twelve minutes later, she responds with a praying hands emoji.

The next day is our one-year anniversary dinner according to Peter, who suggests we go to the new Indian restaurant in Hebden. It's very nice. I have tikka fish and rice. I'd completely forgotten about the anniversary until he reminds me. Bad girlfriend. I make up for it by being a very naughty girlfriend round at his.

I wake up extremely early and walk home along the canal feeling very down about the perilous state of my finances. I can't understand why the Airbnb bookings have dropped off. There must be a reason. Once home, I get onto the calendar and discover I have inadvertently blocked out half of April and May. I have no idea how I've done it, but I'm relieved and spend a couple of hours updating pictures and amenities and feeling altogether better about everything. After all, there are some nice reviews.

Chloë is revising all day for her exams, and I provide an endless supply of snacks and drinks. Two dishwasher loads of crockery come down from her bedroom. I'm so proud of her for knuckling down and sincerely hope she does well; she deserves to.

Peter brings round the first cut flowers from his allotment and two tickets for Chelsea Flower Show at the weekend! I make a rather spectacular jam roly-poly in celebration, and we get high on life and some leftover botanical gin of Maureen's. Life's not all dollars and dimes.

After making sure Chloë is OK with what she has to do re exams and that there's plenty of 'easy' food in the fridge, Peter and I set off to the Chelsea Flower Show. The Grand Central train from Halifax zooms us down there and, after serious consultation with the Tube map, we manage to get ourselves to Sloane Square. Then Peter gets all excitable and suggests we jump into a bike taxi. It's actually very good fun, and we are roaring with laughter as we hit the kerb and two potholes in quick succession. When we jump out and the taxi man stabs his fingers at his phone to do calculations and then says we owe him £40, well, that wipes the smile off our face.

Peter starts fumbling in his pockets for his wallet, and I grab his arm and point-blank refuse.

'Forty quid for a two-minute cycle?'

'Three minutes,' the young man says, cool as a cucumber.

'Well, we're not paying it.'

'You should've asked before you got in.'

'We're not born yesterday. Thirteen pounds a minute? I don't think so.' I pull a £20 note out of my bag and shove it into his hand. 'Come on, Peter.'

We don't stop to get his reaction. We run across the road and join the trail of old people in cream linen shuffling towards the gate.

Peter, all buoyed up by our cheeky escape, spots the champagne bar once we are in.

'Let's have champagne!'

His face on his return is that of a broken man. His hands wobble, shaking the two small glasses in his hand.

When I ask him what is up, he doesn't reply for quite a while, then says, 'Thirty pounds.'

Having only just escaped being ripped off once, we are ripped off again in short order. Welcome to Chelsea.

It's an interesting day, full of the most beautiful dresses, enormous begonias, and crowds and crowds of people, so you struggle to see the gardens – though the Yorkshire garden bit that I saw through the crowds was best by a long way, naturally, amazing giraffe sculptures and waterworks and loads of twisty, silver stick things that everyone has bought to prop up stuff once they get home. We watch a woman almost take the eye out of a man behind her with one.

But the price of everything! Who can afford all this? Where do they get their money from? If I work every day until I die and hold a second job on top, I'll never have enough spare, not even for one of the baby giraffes. I can only just afford one twisty, silver stick thing and some begonia seeds.

As we walk back to the Tube we buy a *Big Issue* from a lovely man who is doing an analysis of the people who buy his magazine. It turns out that Lancashire and Yorkshire folk are among the best customers, with the Scottish the best of all. Londoners, he says grimly, are the worst. No doubt they're all broke from the cost of living down there.

I go through the Chelsea programme on the way home and find lots of things we didn't see. A bit of me feels all mixed up – as if I almost wish I hadn't come to the flower show. There was so much to love and be proud of, but it's as if the best of everything is really only for those who already have more than enough. Still, I snitched a couple of sneaky cuttings into mini plastic bags and pray I can keep them going once I get them home.

After the thrill of Chelsea, everything's feeling back to normal when a postcard pops through the door from Malky. The message says: *Hey Janet, fancy a ride out?* He's written a phone number and drawn a smiley face. On the front there's a picture of a stunning beach and the words *The Glorious Northumberland Coast*. The thrill is unbelievable. I'm transported to the night in the cottage and the heady feeling of going to Scarborough as a teenager, arms wrapped around Franklin, as we flew up the A roads. I sneak the postcard into my bag and spend the day at work pulling it out and rubbing my finger over the image of the Northumberland coast. Of course I shouldn't go – what about poor Peter? Would I like it if he was wrapping his arms around someone else and flying off to the coast with them? I would not, but then, I'm not sure where Peter and I are going. If anywhere. He's lovely. It's lovely. It's been a year. I'm happy, aren't I? Maybe Chelsea is as good as it gets. Malky on a motorbike, now that's living. I call my very wise friend Victoria.

'Janet, my love, you were married for decades of your life, from being very, very young. You're free to have fun. Don't apologise and don't bloody tell either. Try it out for size. Yes, I know I said that! I mean it! Maybe Peter is the dream ticket, or maybe he's Mr In-Between. The fact is, you're excited and you want to. Bloody hell, woman, you're forty-five. Have some bloody fun!'

I text Malky. He's picking me up next Friday after work.

I'm a dither with the subterfuge. I organise for Chloë to stay at her dad's that weekend and then I batch cook sixteen cheese and onion pasties and a carrot cake to calm my nerves. Chloë eats three pasties and two slices of cake. She'd forgotten two technical terms in her media exam and is now predicting fails. I try to reassure her that two missing phrases won't make or break a result, but then she reminds me that she hasn't finished her film and in her last exam her pen ran out. I try to put on a brave face, but she isn't fooled and storms off with the crisp basket.

I'm immensely relieved when Peter tells me he's off visiting his mum this weekend. The dogs are playing up with the neighbours again, and he thinks he'll have to take the snappiest one of them to the RSPCA. I'm trying to summon up a lot of guilt, but I'm not really feeling it. Sometimes Peter goes on and on without realising the conversation has become very one-sided. It's also a little bit on the boring side listening to someone explain their favourite plot twist in a new book I've no interest in as they do all their washing-up.

After I finish the call, I go up into the loft where I rummage through the old boxes and dig out my leathers. I haven't tried these on for at least fifteen years. It's a thrill to see them again. I'm convinced they're not going to fit, but with a bit of persuasion I squeeze into the jacket, though the trousers are a complete no-go. When I unzip the jacket, my boobs explode out as if they've been kept prisoner for weeks and the zip gets stuck at the bottom. I eventually manage to wrestle out my arms, but I'm trapped in the jacket round my waist and have to come down from the loft with it on. I'm sweating profusely by the time I'm at the bottom. Maureen saunters past and quizzically raises her eyebrows. I don't let on; I can't cope with conversation whilst I'm forty plus degrees. After having to engage my pinking shears to cut the jacket open, I spend the evening on Amazon; I already have Prime, so I can get some replacement leathers in time.

Typical! An immediate booking for the Friday comes in. Thankfully, I have been doing bits and pieces of recycling rubbish and bed-making across the week, so I manage to get Lavander Cottage turned around first thing before work and agree I'll meet the guests at lunchtime to hand over the key and talk them through it all.

CHAPTER 34

Booking No. 19: The Ropers

I know as soon as I see them that they are going to be trouble. She is holding her baby protectively, as if I'm about to snatch it. Her nose wrinkles at the cottage from the moment we walk in. He looks broken, as he carries in bag after bag through the door and she commands him with her outstretched finger where to dump it.

'No dishwasher?'

These are the only two words I get out of her before I leave them to it. As I am about to fly out of the door back to work, I catch a fleeting glimpse of Maureen drifting up the stairs with a coffee and force her to agree to oversee the cottage until I am back on Saturday afternoon.

'I think Mrs Roper's going to be a problem finder,' I warn my sister.

'OK. I'll make myself available for moans. Where are you going again?'

'I told you, I'm going to Bamburgh.'

'Bamburgh. Right. With Peter?'

'No, not Peter – a friend.'

'A friend? Which friend?' Her antennae are up, and I do not want to tell her anything, not whilst I don't really know what I'm doing either.

'Someone you haven't met. Could you please do me this favour and watch the cottage for twenty-four hours is all I'm asking?'

'Consider it done, no problem.' She gives me a very sly grin.

Needless to say, when Malky picks me up from the house after work and I'm strapped into new leathers that are straining at every seam, Maureen is out with a big smile, waving me off.

The trip is amazing, up to the services on the A1. The sun is shining; we weave in and out of the rush hour traffic. It's so exciting to feel the wind in my face again, and the motorbike is gigantic so I don't feel my bottom is creeping over the seat. It's like a very comfy office chair. I am eighteen again and anything is possible. Except getting *off* the bike. Twenty years ago I don't remember ever thinking about it, but this time *it's a thing.* I'm so stiff when we pull up at the services, I slide one foot onto the ground and inexplicably have to lift my other leg so high to balance it on the seat that tendons that have not been asked to perform this position in a great many years scream with the effort. I have to use both hands to help the leg down then stamp about a bit to try and retrieve some feeling in the foot and return the leg tendons to normal service.

Malky is so busy fiddling with panniers and oil checking that he doesn't seem to notice, or if he does he's kind enough not to let on. It is a stressful loo break, as I struggle to open and close a thousand poppers and a stiff, industrial zip on the new leathers. As I'm washing my hands, I realise I've a huge flappy bit of leather unsecured on the jacket which detains me for a further five minutes trying to decide where to tuck it in.

After this, the rest of the trip to Bamburgh is a painful blur. Rain on a bike, at speed, is like angry hail. You're very sorry for whatever it is that you've done to deserve it.

I keep my head down and my eyes closed, so when Malky shouts, 'Check out the sea,' I open one eye for the briefest of seconds to see a slug length of grey stuff at a distance, shout, 'Yeah!' back, and squeeze my eyes closed again, for what feels, to my aching back, like eternity.

When we finally reach the hotel – a small, grey faux castle with turrets, on a high street, with a way-too-squidgy bed and a musty smell that only grows when we attempt to pull on the acres of red velvet curtains – Malky and I share a glass of champagne and have a kiss on the bed, which is all very lovely save for the fact that both arms seem to be stuck into a rigid, bike-hold position. It's a surprisingly useful pose for cuddling someone and then sitting down for the meal looking perfectly normal. It's only strange when I'm trying to get changed later and the arms refuse to go above my head.

The next day, we enjoy breakfast in bed, which has to be one of the highlights of the trip. Breakfast is so hard to get wrong, even for the chefs here, who overboiled and burnt everything on the plate last night. It's fortunate for me I prefer my toast, mushrooms and tomatoes well-done and it is, after all, very tricky to pull off a soft poached egg. Who knows, maybe they were perfect in the kitchen, but they were squidgy, vinegary bullets by the time we were having a go at them. But Malky and I are way too preoccupied with the papers and the springy bed and everything else to care.

It turns out Malky is *so* interested in bikes that we spend the morning talking about his favourites, followed by his biking adventures. I'm half listening, half preoccupied with when I can discreetly use the bathroom. I make an excuse to leave the room and end up in the loos in the bar downstairs. I'm pulling my face together with make-up as best I can in the creepy, flickering half-light when I get a call from Maureen.

'Toilet's blocked.'

'What?'

'They've blocked the toilet.'

'How?'

'I don't know, do I? What do you want to do?'

'And I don't know, do I? What can I do from here?' I think frantically. 'Ring a plumber.'

'I don't have any numbers.'

'Let the Ropers use our loo if they need to, and go look for a plumber.'

'I'm not even dressed for ringing round.'

'Join the club, I'm on holiday.'

'How's it going?'

'Wonderful until two minutes ago when you told me about the toilet.'

It sort of spoils things, as I spend the next forty-five minutes ringing round and eventually sort a plumber to come this afternoon. Malky fiddles with his phone, but he's staring out of the window, and I can tell he's not best pleased we've been hijacked by B&B worries. We wrap up and have a stroll around Bamburgh. The weather isn't great, and we end up sheltering in doorways to escape the wind tunnels.

Malky has a good stare in the bike shop, and I try and look interested, but I'm much more taken with the florist next door. We quickly run out of shops either of us like and agree to set off back. I am so stiff that I clamber back on the bike like a reluctant toddler. My back is aching and it wasn't the best night's sleep, so I'm feeling much the worse for wear, trapped inside this helmet, and once the rain starts it's like a bad dream. I more or less slide off the bike to the ground at the services. I can't face all the unpopping and unzipping and avoid all liquid, only opening my mouth on the way back for a few drops of icy rain to relieve how parched I am.

The weather brightens up as we drive back into Hebbleroyd. I spot Chloë with Greg loping along beside her down Lupin Drive. I'm keen to avoid an introduction, so I don't waste any time saying goodbye to Malky. Unfortunately, he wants to use the loo and then Maureen is keen to have a chat about cylinders, and before I know it Chloë is on the drive looking shocked. To be fair, my hair is half monsoon wet and half dry helmet shape, I've unzipped the jacket and struggled out of the arms with it still zipped around the waist, and I'm in a too tight, biker chick T-shirt from the 1980s. All in all, it's not a good look.

I do the briefest of introductions and only when I'm sure Maureen, Chloë and Greg have all gone inside do I give Malky a peck on the cheek and say, 'Thanks for a great time. Sorry about my plumbing emergency.'

He grabs me around the waist and insists on a much longer lip plant. He's an excellent kisser, and only when I disentangle myself do I realise that Maureen, Chloë, Greg, a stranger holding a bin bag – *and Peter from the driving seat of his car parked on the road* – are all watching us.

My knees go weak and the ground wobbles, then I realise Malky has kick-started the bike and, with a dramatic wheel skid, he speeds off down the road, leaving a whirlwind of dust and emotional carnage in his wake. Peter gives me the most plaintive look that makes me feel absolutely terrible. He has a dog bouncing around on the seat next to him and it starts yapping. He looks like he might put his window up but stops midway, then he makes to get out of the car, then decides against it and reverses down the entire street in the most awkward and wonky way. I turn around and everyone has disappeared except the stranger holding up the bin bag.

'How do. Nice bike. Tommy the plumber. Fifty-two dirty wet wipes, what do you want me to do with them?'

So the Ropers left a complete mess; stains on the rugs, food crumbs and greasy handprints everywhere. All complimentary shampoos and soaps gone, every tray in the oven covered in grease. What were they eating? And the review very quickly posted a snidey:

Clean, well-stocked/I wouldn't call it a cottage – odd position between houses... but then I am fussy. Host a bit too welcoming.

Her private feedback: *Mattress hard. Sofa hard.*

Chloë is reading the review with me and restrains me from leaping in with some return comments, and I have to change the password so Maureen definitely can't get access.

After the deepest of baths, I wrap myself up in my fluffiest and biggest dressing gown because it's the nearest I'm going to get to a hug. I go downstairs planning a huge crumpet and cheese supper for more comfort. When I go in, Chloë is sitting on the side in the kitchen playing with her phone and eating from a gigantic bowl of popcorn. She doesn't look at me and simply pushes my phone towards me.

'Peter called.'

My stomach drops to my boots. Why have I been such a bad person? *ONCE.* And everyone knows. People get away with things for ever. Not me. Not Janet Jackson. I've hurt someone who doesn't deserve it, and now I'm going to hell in a basket.

I'm too tired. I head straight for bed, hungry as punishment, and don't ring him back.

• •

TIP FOR RUNNING A B&B

Keep a list of tradespeople you can call on in an emergency.

• •

TIP ON LIFE

Do not try to have two boyfriends at the same time. What are you thinking? Or if you are, be smarter than me and keep them well separated.

CHAPTER 35

Booking No. 20: Romeo

It has been raining for four weeks now. The lawn is awash and resembles a meadow. I've been awaiting my chance to get out there, and every time I have an hour free, it's raining. The drizzly stuff, the soak-you-to-your-bones stuff.

I keep trying to persuade Maureen to pop out and mow the grass whilst she's at home and when it's dry, but she reminds me that the last time she cut the lawn, I complained it was 'uneven, half-done, don't bother if you can't do it right', so she refuses to do it on the grounds of avoiding getting into my bad books. There's a logic in here somewhere. I've often thought Maureen is a wasted politician. Someone in the surgery told me *Question Time* is coming to Halifax and that you can apply for tickets. I'm keeping very quiet about it in case Maureen sees it as her *Opportunity Knocks*.

I am going into the library today to confront Peter. After Malky dropped me off and Peter was witness to a kiss, he's not been accepting my calls – and who could blame him? I'm awash with guilt after he left the message on Sunday '*You should've told me you were seeing someone else, Janet. We are over.*' I baked him two cakes and left them on his doorstep. No response. I sent him a letter apologising and trying to explain that I was being badly behaved for the first time in my life and that I was so sorry, I didn't mean to hurt him blah, blah, blah. No response. My goodness, the excuses Franklin came up with for cheating! Eventually, I seem to remember, he blamed my parents for chronic neglect that had affected my brain and my ability 'to attach'. I found that odd, given I was very attached to him: *he* seemed to be the one struggling to remember he had a loving partner.

I sneak into the children's section, knowing that Peter avoids preschool like the plague, and sidle through the popular DVD section onto *True Crime, Horror...* then get slightly distracted in

Cookery. I pick up a Jamie Oliver – *Five Ingredients* – hold it in front of my face and arrive at the desk.

'Can I take this out, please?'

I put the book on the desk, and Peter looks at me. I can see his face drop off a cliff and then he pulls it all back together and clenches up.

'Have you got a library card?'

'No, sorry. Can you set me one up?'

'I can give you a form, if you want to GO AWAY and fill this in and come back later.'

'I'm sorry, Peter.'

'Me too. You're holding up the queue.'

'There isn't a queue.'

'There will be soon if you keep standing there.'

'Peter, please talk to me, let me try to explain.'

Peter speaks in the angriest of whispers. 'You wanted fun on a motorbike with a biker. Hope you enjoy your exciting new life, Janet.'

'ONCE, Peter. ONE silly mistake.'

'Shush, please. Keep your voice down!'

'I'm whispering. Look, it was a chance to be eighteen again. I jumped at it. It was stupid. Just for once I was really selfish and really stupid.'

'I'm forty-eight, Janet. I'm comfortable with middle age, and I prefer to be with someone who is too.'

'Don't you think things were getting a bit boring, Peter? You must admit it.'

He bridles. 'No. I was very happy.'

'Can't we be friends?'

'Janet, I'm not interested in FRIENDS.'

I don't know what comes over me. I'm stuck for the right words, exhausted from the effort of whispering, full of remorse but also super frustrated. I start to sing!

I realise I've blurted out the first line of the *Friends* theme tune at Peter, not thinking. After the first words tumble out, I start to get into a rhythm and sing the rest, and really get going, building up to quite a tempo. Where I don't remember the exact words, I sort of make some up. Peter looks like he is about to explode with embarrassment, and everyone in there is looking over now. I get to a point where I can't remember the lines, so repeat the chorus, loudly, and then sort of skip out of there. Ah, well. I came. I sang. I tried.

Chloë finished her GCSEs today. I offer her a celebratory lunch in Hebden tomorrow, but she mutters vague things through closed lips which, according to Maureen, translates as 'she's getting pissed with her mates.'

I'm so glad the exams are over. School is over – sixth-form college next. What a milestone of effort. It's so strange. Can't imagine what this next stage is going to be like.

Wonder if I can get her to mow the lawn if she's off next week?

This morning, I wake up to a last-minute booking email. From someone called Rob, for tonight, six people. I'm gutted. I was so looking forward to a relaxing weekend in the garden, and now *six* people are arriving. Lavander Cottage can accommodate six, but only just. I send an email: *Can you let me know the make-up of your party, please*? The reasoning behind this is that, if it's six lads, I might say sorry, no single-sex parties over four, and cancel the booking. It's my place, I'm allowed, I decide. I can't face a riot of mess on Sunday.

While waiting for a reply, I turn the cottage around and do some last-minute preparation. There's no reply to my email, so I text Rob about the numbers again, all the while hovering over the 'cancel reservation' button.

Rob calls. His voice is like velvet pouring down the phone. It's the strangest thing. So easy-going, so pleasant, so lovely, so nice. I'm actually flirting down the phone. We have quite a chat about why I'm in touch and, of course, he understands. It turns out there are only two of them. They are colleagues, they'll need two beds please. He's jet-lagged from travelling so he didn't press the right button. He's pressing all *my* buttons. It is so strange – as if we are destined to speak, as if we've found each other. He calls me later to say he can't get in, then later again to say he's found the key. The calls go on and on. It's so nice.

I'm at a loose end after the evening meal. I've washed up and wiped the kitchen surfaces; the laundry is done; there's nothing to watch on TV and I'm mooning about a bit in the garden watering and deadheading and feeling a tad lonesome. That's when I wonder if I should go and say hi. I resist. It's sheer nosiness and I'm nervous about what might happen, given my current moral breakdown and the chaos that has caused.

I put myself to bed early, but it's a mistake, as I'm restless and up in the night, which I attribute to eating too much linguine. In the morning, I check my phone, wondering if it has rung and that's why I'm up, and there's a message alert from Rob at 12.03 a.m.

Can we smoke in casa? No worries if we can't, plus glass of wine on offer.

Thank God I was asleep, and thank God Maureen isn't in charge of bookings.

• •

TIPS FOR RUNNING A B&B

Buy individual packs of butter. It saves you a fortune.
Remember guests come and go. Don't make the cottage part of your drama. Even if life is a bit dull.

• •

TIP ON EX-BOYFRIENDS

Sometimes you have to accept you've got it wrong and say sorry. How many times is enough? I don't know.

CHAPTER 36

Booking No. 21: No-Show Glenda

I've been prom shopping for Chloë. It's an exhausting rush around what was Debenhams in Bradford. We are looking for dresses when Chloe spots some gold shoes she loves. So we are now looking for a matching gold dress. I know, ludicrous decision, as if this wasn't hard enough. We then try Next – where there's 'next' to nothing, get distracted by accessories in New Look then drive over to the White Rose Shopping Centre, a midsized shopping precinct on the fringes of Leeds our nearest biggest city. Chloë tries six dresses on in a boutique there, and the one that looked the best on her she rejects – simply because it's a size 12 when she is a size 8. A bit knackered now, we trail off to TK Maxx in Halifax on the way home, where she tries on three dresses and we buy one. Then, once we're home, we sit in front of the computer and order six dresses from boohoo.

When we're done, I'm 'boohoo' all right, from the £276 I've just spent, although Chloë reassures me that we can send them all back.

The next day, there's a pre-prom dress-up session. Chloë likes one of the boohoo dresses but needs the side taking in, the neckline adjusting and a split making in the side. I spend the rest of the day unpicking and picking and attempting to invisibly sew things together. I am immensely grateful when Maureen gets up at 3 p.m. and takes over. Fashion is her thing.

When prom day finally arrives, I'm glad because I didn't think I could take any more teenage tension and build-up. Chloë's friends call for her, as they've planned to take a taxi all together, and they all look so gorgeous. I send a photo to Franklin, he texts back : *She looks beautiful. I'm so proud.*

I don't know what comes over me, but I shed a tear. We did it. We got her here.

As the taxi pulls up, I hear Maureen call out, 'Girls, d'you want a joint to loosen you up?'

I'm about to intervene when I hear Chloë say: 'I hate smoking, Auntie Maureen. Weed's boring, and we don't need loosening up, thank you.'

I high-five her in my mind. Maureen comes into the kitchen with a face like a pickled fist and swigs the dregs of a red wine bottle I've been using for cooking.

I struggle to wrap up all the other boohoo dresses and sneak them into a parcel before Maureen catches sight of them.

Tonight, on TV, they're showing Glastonbury highlights from previous years, and my sister is watching every minute of coverage. She has put a small camp together in the living room, with a patchwork blanket, bottles of cider and lots of crisps. She shouts me in to watch Janet Jackson, who is dancing with her Rhythm Nation troupe and big shoes.

'She's faking the voice. It's not her voice. She's cheating the voice,' Maureen insists on repeating throughout the five minutes of her set.

Standing in the living room in my wellies, grubby shorts and gardening gloves, I get in position and say, 'Mitzi bitch, shut yo' dirty mouth. This is Janet Jackson,' and I do a very reasonable shuffle approximation of her Rhythm Nation dance moves. Maureen howls with laughter, but I can tell she is a bit impressed. We watch Lizzo later in a purple leotard that shows off everything. She's a big girl, but she's proud as punch of her figure, and there's something lovely about her confidence.

I spend a couple of hours this morning recleaning the cottage after an age of no bookings. It's all nice and fresh now, ready for Glenda from Glyndebourne and her two friends who are walking the Pennine Way and are due to arrive at any moment. I wait and wait until I know I'll be late for work if I hang around at home much longer, but although they have paid in advance, the threesome never arrive. The weather's not great, so I hope they're OK. I contemplate putting the Calder Valley Search & Rescue Team on alert but don't actually know if the women have even set off so resist.

On the way to Valley Dental, I recall everything I managed to get done this morning. After I'd refreshed Lavander Cottage for Glenda and Co., I flew around at home like a whirling dervish, emptying the dishwasher, pegging out washing on the line after putting another wash in, as well as emptying bins, mopping the kitchen and wiping down all the surfaces, and all before I've headed out of the door. I can't help but feel a swell of resentment.

I decide to have a drink after work with my friend Victoria to discuss the Peter incident. She's unrepentant.

'He can't be good for you or you wouldn't have contemplated the bike ride.'

She's right, of course, but I'm finding it difficult to reconcile loyal, kind Janet with badass, cheating, biker Janet. They're a world apart, plus Peter is lovely and, even if we're not Romeo and Juliet, he deserved a nicer send-off.

Victoria has multiple daughters, and she describes how she is desperately trying to encourage her eldest daughter, an ex-art student, to get part-time work. One day, in a shop selling paintings, she got so carried away telling her daughter how easy it would be to create some art to sell that she invented a range of paintings she could do called *Paradise, Mist* and *Hollow Morning*. Overhearing her, the shopkeeper asked her about her artwork, as it sounded interesting. So Victoria, trying all the while to engage her daughter, went to Home Bargains, snapped up three canvases for £3, picked up a paintbrush and palette and painted all three. After allowing twenty-four hours for the oils to dry, she duly covered them in bubble wrap and carried the canvases to show the shopkeeper, who took them on. After which, Victoria went on to develop a range of nature-inspired abstract pictures that she sold at £40 a time to the shop where they were framed and sold at £100. But it wasn't long before my friend got fed up, declaring that the commerciality was killing her artistic instincts dead and she had to stop.

Her daughter is currently studying to be an accountant.

This evening, after a pleasant meal with my daughter and sister, who for once helped out and cooked us a very nice shepherd's pie and apple crumble, I'm going through my very blank diary and realise it's Peter's birthday tomorrow. So I ring him and unexpectedly he picks up.

'Hello, Peter, I wanted to wish you happy birthday for tomorrow.'
'OK. That's kind, thank you.'

'I wondered if you'd fancy a trip to Harlow Carr?' It pops out. I have a day off tomorrow and feel the need for a getaway – and why not? The Royal Horticultural Society gardens in Harrogate are always a delight to visit.

'Um... er...'

'The weather is meant to be nice,' I encourage. Then – oh. 'Have you anything else already planned?' Maybe I'm taking things for granted here.

'Um... er...'

Which means 'OK, let's do it.' So, that's it, we're going to Harlow Carr. I don't quite know myself what I'm planning, but I fancy a day out with someone who knows something about plants. If Peter gets too Dramarama I'll go into the Bettys Tea Rooms there, buy one of their deservedly famous Fat Rascal scones with a funny face – and give him that to chew on!

It's a chilly but bright day, and I'm glad for my M&S down gilet, bought in last year's sale. As we're walking round the beautiful gardens, I think I see the gardener and broadcaster Sarah Raven herself (big thrill) making notes near the wild meadow. Peter takes it upon himself to steal a cutting from one of the perennials beds – I think he's trying to impress on me that he does live life on the edge.

Once we've been to Bettys, and I've paid out £60 for our birthday celebration ginger biscuits, pots of tea and egg and cress sandwiches, I feel that we should *both* have taken a cutting. It's actually very nice with Peter – after all, we do get along. When I drop him off in Hebden later, he reaches over for a kiss and, not really knowing how I feel, I make it a peck. That way, if it turns out we are friends, he can't say I was encouraging him unnecessarily, and if things do develop, maybe it signals the start of things. Either way, it was a lovely day.

Though I wake up at dawn, worrying about money, I try to get on to my bank's website but online banking is 'down for essential repairs.' I have a horrible feeling it's a fraud thing. All the bills are due to arrive soon, and I'll be plunged into debt and forced to sell the house and Lavander Cottage, and put Maureen into sheltered housing. She won't be able to stand the old people and will end up committing suicide.

I make myself a peppermint tea and vow to avoid egg and cress sandwiches going forward. I've decided all my angst is down to indigestion from bolting the gorgeous food at Bettys whilst worrying about the cost.

• •

TIP ON DAUGHTERS

Beef up the bank balance for prom dresses.

• •

TIP ON EXES

Try to be friends, it's much nicer.

CHAPTER 37

Booking No. 22: Trevor & Phillip

Fortunately, Lavander Cottage was still immaculate after No-Show Glenda, so I didn't have anything to do for Trev and Phil, two carpenters and joiners who were doing work locally, apart from putting in the usual milk, butter and a crusty loaf. They were booked in for three nights. The lads turned out to be nice enough. They were away at 7.30 a.m. every day and returned about 6 p.m. with bags of takeaway. Having gone to the bother of introducing recycling boxes into the cottage, I was gutted when they left a bin bag out every day by the bin, and it was always full of cans and at least a hundred chicken bones.

Whilst at work today, I get a call from a random number and daren't ignore it in case it is a new booking. I need every penny I can get at the moment.

'Hello, can we stay for the next three weeks every Monday, Tuesday, Wednesday? And can you do us owt for cash?'

'Hello, who is this?'

'It's Mike from Crombie's Tiles and Flooring. We're doing up your railway station and need accommodation. I've seen you on your dot-com thing. They're good lads, can you do it?'

'Can you give me a minute, Mike? I'll just work it out.' Bringing up the calculator on my phone, I do a quick bit of maths and mutter to him over the phone: 'Lavander Cottage is £35 per person per night, so that makes £105 per night, times three is £315 per week. And the total for three weeks would be... £945. Er... how about I knock off some and then it will come down to £850?'

'Done – see you Monday.'

Mrs Wrighton took a small handful of Fox's Glacier Mints plus a free sample tube of toothpaste for sensitive teeth before she calmed down and realised I wasn't talking to her.

As I pull into the drive, I see the elderly couple Edna and Bill standing on the doorstep with a younger woman, their daughter. For a moment, my heart sinks, but when I get out and say hello, to my amazement they hand over a cheque for £1,200 for the accommodation last Christmas. I am both shocked and *sooo* pleased. They are very happy in their new place, the old couple tell me, and are very apologetic about how long it has taken for them to pay me what they owe. They tell me that they miss my cooking, and I promise to make them a Christmas cake.

Feeling over the moon at the prospect of being in the black again, I go back out and buy a load of artisan bread and three types of cheese, and then I come home and bake a coffee and walnut cake. It's a fabulous, long, sunny evening and I have a blissful moment all to myself, sitting in the garden getting roasted, listening to the birds and drinking some lager I'd hidden in the shed so Maureen wouldn't see it.

I am really enjoying the peace until Chloë comes down in her bikini and tells me this is global warming, and the planet is now technically on fire. I giggle, obviously a by-product of the lager. It's stronger than I thought, and she isn't impressed. I end up falling asleep and burn my nose, so I suppose it serves me right.

I've had a busy morning turning the cottage around from Trev and Phil's stay so it's ready for the tiling and flooring chaps. For two burly joiner types, Trev and Phil left the place clean and tidy and I have no complaints apart from the bin bags. They are both well-trained husbands, I decide.

There's another surprise. Delicious Delia has turned up again, just as she said she would. She is back with a plan. She and Maureen go round six local venues, and she has now booked the Hebden Bridge Picture House for a burlesque festival this coming October. Delia tells me that she will be back later in the year with all the artwork. Lavander Cottage is booked for the entire week whilst she preps and brings everyone together from across the world! I've agreed to fetch in two extra fold-down beds for the crew.

It's quite exciting! Though when I walk around Hebden later, picking up a seeded tin loaf from one of the posh bakers, I inadvertently get caught up in a 'Radical Feminism in the Age of the Influencer' queue outside the town hall – and see a lot of severe fringes and Doc Martens. I wonder if Hebden is ready for sexy, burlesque-y stuff...

CHAPTER 38

Booking No. 23: The Crombie's Tilers

The Crombie's lads are lovely. I chat to the three of them when they get here and reiterate my rules: no smoking inside the cottage; please try to recycle; and please be quiet after 11 p.m. They're smiley, friendly and up and away for six o'clock every morning. I discover this when I'm hanging the washing out in my scruffiest dressing gown, wellies, no make-up and hair looking like the Hair Bear Bunch. They are very cheerful and don't let on, so I pretend everything is perfectly normal too. One look in the mirror, though, and I am mortified, and I bet they're laughing at me in the van. There is a bigger one who always has a pizza box, a shorter one who is always on the phone and seems to be the organiser, and another younger lad who's as skinny as a wire and is always carrying the heaviest-looking toolbox.

As they're only here every Monday, Tuesday and Wednesday night, I have to turn the cottage around as soon as they leave every Thursday morning, just in case I get a booking before they get back the next Monday. It's really hard work, changing three beds, and sanitising the place, and I'm praying we don't get a booking, as I'm feeling worn out with all the working at Valley Dental and the cleaning and the washing for both the cottage and the house.

Chloë has been invited to go away with Greg's family for a week in Fuerteventura. She is so excited, and we spend a lot of time choosing new bikinis for her from Amazon. Why haven't I booked a holiday, I wonder, and secretly feel absolutely heartbroken when she sets off a few days later with her brand-new suitcase and her bumbag and her £300 in euros. I'm proud I can contribute and that finding the money for her is not the issue it might have been earlier in the year, though I'm glum that I spend all my time working, and that to get a holiday she has had to go away with strangers.

. . . .

TIPS FOR RUNNING A B&B

Remember that you are 'front of house', even at 6 a.m.

Don't become so tied to your B&B that you don't have a life yourself. When did you last book a holiday?

CHAPTER 39

Booking No. 24: The Italians

It's been a whirlwind. The flooring and tiling guys go after their third week and leave a gorgeous message in the guest book, all in capitals. It says: *Cleanest place we've ever stayed in, Top work from CROMBIE's flooring!*

Then it's all stations go to prepare for the Italians, the Rossi family – mum Carmela, dad Tommaso, and their small sons Edoardo and Gabriele. The two little ones will sleep upstairs in the big bedroom on the fold-up beds, next to the double bed. I even get Maureen on the case, insisting she help me make up the beds and give me a hand with cleaning the kitchen and doing the polishing. She dresses up like Cinderella to do it, wearing a headscarf and raggedy dungarees. We just about finish as the Italians arrive. They are lovely, their English is amazing and the children are like little dots. They fly around the garden, curious about everything. After they snap off two of my agapanthus though, I have to step in.

They've been here two days when we get awful news. Carmela has looked the wrong way crossing the road and has been knocked over. She is in hospital, with a broken leg, some bruising and a few cuts; the staff want to keep an eye on her for a couple of days. Tommaso and the children look so upset that I invite them round for a meal that evening and make a big dish of pasta, tomato sauce and Parmesan. As they're eating it, all the while looking shocked – the youngest boy, in particular – I realise making pasta is a big mistake. It will remind them how much they miss their mummy's cooking.

A day or two later, Carmela is home. The ambulance driver and Tommaso carry her upstairs. I take her over a load of DVDs and a cake. She has a bad break, apparently, and is wearing a huge, heavy cast and must get around using a walking stick. The family's plans have been turned upside down; they now need to extend their stay by up to three weeks so Signora Rossi can get signed off by the hospital. Luckily, I only have two short weekend bookings for August, so I contact the people with the news and give the Italians a big discount. I get a very grumpy response over email from one of the wannabe August guests and then I realise at the end of the email *that it was Donalda*. A lucky escape! And how astonishing that she had wanted to return to Lavander Cottage after her carping, and when the whole set-up was so far beneath her high standards!

When Carmela is settled and comfortable, and the kids understand that their mamma is OK, and that they can draw a picture on her cast, I am free to drive off to Manchester Airport to pick up Chloë. She comes through Arrivals at 2.10 a.m. looking beautiful, relaxed and very 'scarfy'. There is one round her neck, one over her head, what looks like a scarf around her chest, and one wrapped around her waist. All of them seem to have little bells on them, so she's quite the noise generator. It's a good job, as I need something to keep me awake, as I'm lost for what feels like hours trying to find my way out of the airport's one-way system.

The next day, it's exam results day. Despite her very late night, Chloë is up at six thirty, which must be a shock to the system. I'm used to being alone for a good three hours at that time of the morning, but she's stomping around, banging doors, in a dreadful mood. She shouts at the suggestion of having some breakfast, shouts that she has no clothes to wear because everything is dirty from the holiday, shouts that she can't find other clothes because they're hung up in the wardrobe, shouts at Harvey for miaowing on the stairs, shouts that her trainers are thrown in the cupboard where she left them, shouts when I offer her a lift to school to pick up her results.

We arrive outside the school at 8.30 a.m., and she runs in with her hoodie up and is out ten minutes later with a large, brown envelope. I realise my heart is pounding, not least because the tutor for maths cost me nearly £500 last year. She rips it open to find her grades. Here I shall explain, to those who do not have teenage children, that the top grade is 9, and the lowest is 1. She has lots of Grade 5, a couple of 6's in geography and art, a 4 for maths – hallelujah! – and one 3 for home economics 'because the teacher was a dick'. She's done terrifically. I prompt Franklin, whilst she's in collecting the results, and he calls her on the way home to congratulate her.

We have a quick change, a bit of breakfast and then it's off to Burnley College to enrol for her A levels. She wants to do three art subjects but is persuaded to take English literature, art and design, and textiles.

Greg calls. He has six GCSEs at Grade 5, which is OK for him to do his BTEC in plumbing.

We celebrate with pizza from Marco's on the way home, and the promise of last-minute tickets to go to the Leeds Festival at the weekend. Of course I agree, but on reflection, why do I have to pay for Greg's ticket too? They cost £130 each! It's a lot of celebration.

I dare to raise it with Chloë and she tells me, 'Don't worry, you're not paying for Greg's. His mum and dad are loaded.' Hurrah, I can look at the bank balance again without my chest tightening and my stomach curdling.

A few days later, I endure four hours of traffic hell dropping Chloë and Greg off at the Leeds Festival. When I eventually arrive home, Maureen shows me a social media post she's just received from Chloë on Snapchat that shows her looking happy and smiling by a tent, Greg's head lurching out from the tent zipper. I have to say I wasn't delighted to see she had a hand-painted sign on her inner thigh which said the word 'cock', with an arrow pointing at her groin, in lipstick and glitter. I want to add a comment, but the post has gone, so I can't, according to Maureen. Instead, I text Chloë to let her know I'm safely home, and don't get a response for two days – until five minutes before I'm collecting her and Greg on the ring road, which is when she sends me a thumbs up emoji.

By the time I have dropped Greg off in Savile Park, it's the posh bit of Halifax, a Georgian square full of giant, detached houses in between the grammar schools. When we arrive home, my daughter is fast asleep. I wake her up and insist she immediately has a shower. I get all her washing into the machine, and she's tucked up in bed by seven o'clock in the evening.

Maureen borrows twenty quid off me so she can go and protest about something in Cathedral Gardens, Manchester. It's throwing down buckets as she's leaving. I ask her if she wants a lift to the station, but no, she doesn't. Harry is picking her up, thanks. She hasn't mentioned him for a while. To be honest, I was hoping he was well out of the picture.

Peter gets in touch to tell me he's got a cold and can he come over? I gently put him off by saying I'm feeling tired, but the truth is, not only do I *not* want to catch his cold but, for the first time *ever*, I got 14 on PopMaster, the Radio 2 daily pop music quiz on the Ken Bruce Show, and I'm having a good time bouncing around the kitchen to the 1990s bonus tracks. I fancy a ginger, soy and honey salmon and I've only one piece – and sometimes doing everything, for everyone else, all the time... well, it's just lovely to be alone.

• •

TIP FOR RUNNING A B&B

You need to be flexible. Sometimes guests have problems leaving.

• •

TIP ON TEENAGE DAUGHTERS

Don't overpromise rewards around exam results. You end up doing daft stuff like the drop-off *and* pickup at Leeds Festival. (Insert other festivals as required.) The traffic *will* be a nightmare.

CHAPTER 40

Booking No. 25: Delicious Delia Returns

Today the new term has begun at college, and my daughter is due there at nine o'clock in the morning.

At 6 a.m., I put all the lights on, make her two cups of tea and a bacon sandwich, then open every curtain and window in order to rouse Chloë and get her up for the first day of college. Welcome to the new regime.

Today, the Italians are leaving and flying back to Lucca. Poor Carmela is still on her crutches, though the cast is now off, and she wears a softer cloth splint thing. I'm sad to see the family go but, blimey, I have to get on it as soon as they are settled in the taxi. I'm so glad I took the day off, as the cottage is in quite a state. So much oil! It's like they splashed it on the wall for a joke.

Delia is due to arrive at 2 p.m. but then texts to say she'll be here at midday. I am sweating cobs when she turns up. I'm barely halfway through the big clear-up. Luckily, Maureen is around and drags her into the house.

Delia's artwork for the burlesque festival is quite something. The poster she has designed shows her in a champagne glass wearing a turquoise corset and turquoise fishnet stockings, and popping a cherry in her mouth, with a bubble that says:

Hebden Bridge, pop your burlesque cherry
Friday 11 October
Burlesque Festival
Hebden Bridge Picture House

It's quite risqué, and I don't know where it comes from, but a bit of me feels a frisson of something staring at the poster. I put it down to the excitement of the whole thing. Maureen is going to write and perform a cheeky rhyme to open the festival, apparently, and the pair of them plan to spend the weekend spreading the news, which means walking around Hebden Bridge in corsets and suspenders.

They down a bottle of Prosecco, and I drop them off at the market with a handful of flyers. I feel bad leaving them, since it looks as if it might rain.

The next day, Delia tells me the flyer-ing has been a brilliant success, though she lost Maureen in the Shepherd's Gate. I am feeling a bit worried after texting my sister repeatedly, asking her to let me know she's OK. Shepherd's is the posh country pub on the outskirts of Hebden, and it can be a bit notorious for late-night lock-ins.

I don't need to worry for long.

Mid-afternoon, I'm up to my eyes in weeding as Delia drags her suitcase down the drive to get collected by a taxi. At the very same moment, a flashy yellow sports car skids to a halt, and Maureen steps out of it in a full-length fur coat. She kisses the grey-haired bloke driving it and, as he drives off, she flashes him what she's wearing underneath. It becomes apparent, when she turns around, that she has only her underwear on from yesterday. I try to stay composed, but I'm struggling.

I let her say goodbye to Delia with me, but once the latter has jumped in her taxi, well, I turn on Maureen and snipe, 'Thanks for letting me know you're OK.'

'What? Oh, sorry, phone dead.'

'Who was that?'

'What?'

'Banana car, penis extension.' I am foaming mad. I can't help it. A wave of anger has come over me.

'Carl.'

'Carl. Right. Another prick to add to the list.' I'm not proud of my language, but I was seething with her.

'What's up with you?'

'Parading round town in your knickers and you pull a bloke, big surprise! Flashing him as he's driving off, when you've known him two minutes and you've been who-knows-where and no one knows if you're safe! He isn't spinning you home 'cos he's a gentleman and he likes your bloody poems, is he? Oh, I don't know, Maureen. At your age, a bit of bloody common sense would not go amiss. You owe me a bloody fortune, and I don't want you dead in a cellar, tied up by some red-faced monster *before you've paid me back.'*

'Oh. Right.'

'The heating is on, if you want a bath. I'm weeding.' I'm also boiling with rage.

I clear three beds of weeds, pull apart six containers that are looking tired and rip out the clematis that has got too wooden and stringy on the gazebo. Peter comes round, but I am incandescent and he doesn't know what to do with me. He goes home after a couple of hours with an excuse about meeting his mates.

I don't know what to do with myself. I end up finishing a bottle of Rioja on my own and having a little weep on the doorstep. I can't decide what's up with me. Do I need stronger HRT or a more sensible sister? How have I ended up in this situation? What do I do with her? She's wrapped herself around me like a leech, no responsibility, no care, so selfish, and I've allowed it to happen and I'm an idiot. I know what they call this. We're co-dependent. I encourage it. By allowing her to get away with it, I don't help her or me. Give me strength. Give me courage, to knock some sense into her or kick her out if she won't get it together.

The next morning, Maureen brings me a cup of tea into the bedroom and says sorry for being a worry. It's like she's read my mind. She says the grey-haired man's name is Carl, he's divorced, a builder, has two kids and a good sense of humour. Wearily, I wish her well. She' about to leave when I muster some of yesterday's fierceness.

'You need a job, Maureen. I'm not prepared to fund you doing nothing any more. You don't like to clean, you don't like to cook, well that's no help to me. You need to get out and do something. Things can't go on as they are. I'm not happy about it.'

Maureen listens quietly and then gets up and wanders to the door looking solemn.

'I am going to try harder. I promise.'

I shrug, are these just words? How do we make them real? I'll give it a week or two, I decide, then I'll need to make things more concrete.

Meanwhile, I've had to get more flyers. I put the burlesque ones out in Valley Dental today and they've all gone. When Miles takes one, I notice that he's looking a bit rough around the edges. The divorce is taking some sorting, according to Jillian the hygienist, and the ex-Mrs Miles, or soon-to-be ex, is now seeing someone else who happens to be very rich, so she's happy to drag out the lawyer's bills. After lunch, I ask him how he's doing.

'Awful. One step after another, Janet.'

He looks so gaunt that I then ask him if he's on a diet.

'It's the sorry-for-myself and no-one-to-cook-for-me diet. I'll pile it all back on when things have settled down, I'm sure.'

I decide I'm going to make some parkin tonight and bring some in for Miles.

At home this evening, I cry with laughter at an episode of *Celebrity MasterChef*, when an unknown 'celebrity' makes a healthy, raw brownie. It is so dry that when John Torode cuts into it with his dessert fork it explodes and almost blinds him with brownie dust.

'I think it's missing a bit of something to bind it,' he splutters.

Maureen pops her head in to say she is on her way out with Banana Car Carl *again*. She is wearing a very revealing, lacy playsuit, and I feel like saying something, but I hold back. Unkind? *Moi?*

Malky texts me tonight, asking do I fancy a trip out to the Dales? The timing's not great, as Peter and I are talking again and off to the Gordon Rigg Garden Centre for plants for my border, which is looking a bit underwhelming. I text him back with: *sorry have got plans, love to another time*. Though my heart sinks, I'm being good, I'm doing what's right, but where is the fun in that?

On our way back from the garden centre, Peter and I pop into Morrisons in Todmorden and there's a 'die-in'. First thing we know about it, we are walking round Gary Lovestock (who I recognise from Valley Dental – bridge – very painful landing on a kerb as a child) and a lady I don't know, who are laid in the middle of an aisle with some other people dressed in red looming over them from behind whilst everybody tries to get past with their trolleys. It's quite a commotion for Morrisons.

'Pick up some halloumi and cherry cider, will you, love?' one of the red people whispers to me as I walk past. I think it is part of the event until I look a bit closer and realise it's Maureen who spoke to me.

I ask Peter if he understands what it's all about. He doesn't know – thinks it's something about red meat. Anyway, it puts us off buying some chops for dinner. I do spot one of Delia's posters up on the noticeboard as we make our way out: someone has written *I would*, with an arrow pointed at Delia.

Chloë has stayed at Greg's three nights in a row, and I'm getting very cross about it. We exchange grumpy texts, and she turns up at 8 p.m. with hair like a rat's nest and a pile of dirty washing shoved in her school bag. She goes on to raid the freezer, eats two garlic baguettes with a mountain of chips and a jar of pitted olives. Given I've just washed up, I'm a bit gutted but hold it all back, because I'm actually pleased to see her. The house has felt strange this week, with her away and Maureen off with Banana Boy, presumably. This must be the future. Somehow it makes me think, *What will I do when Chloë goes to university and Maureen finally gets her act together and I'm all on my own?*

Peter offers to pop round. We are semi-officially back together now, I suppose. We've sort of fallen into it. It's not unpleasant, and he's lovely, and I like having the romance and regular sex in my life, though I'm holding something back, I can tell – a piece of me that doesn't want to commit. I make an excuse about being too tired for company, because I just want to enjoy the sound of Chloë being here and sharing a few moments with her alone, even if it is only so she can complain about the quality and lack of quantity of the snacks. It's reassuringly 'us'.

. . . .

TIPS ON SISTERS

Try not to judge – even when you disapprove of everything they do and say.

Remind yourself that life would be much more dull without them.

· ·

TIP ON DAUGHTERS

Treasure them whilst you have them, as they'll soon be gone.

· ·

TIP ON BOYFRIENDS

(your own, not your daughter's)

Kiss a few. Life is short.

CHAPTER 41

Booking No. 26: Delicious Delia & Chums

It's a nightmare to park in Hebden (again). I race into work on Friday morning. As I pass the newsagent, I notice the sign outside: '*No to Burlesque Fest!*' I rush in, buy a copy of the *Hebden Bridge Times* and am desperate to read it all morning. I don't get a moment until lunch, when I have to cut short a conversation with Julie Lovell about her new orthopaedic insoles. I must remember to pick it up with her though, as my feet are bothering me. I don't know what it means, but I'm thinking fallen arches.

The front page is all about Delia's concert. Apparently, a letter of complaint has been received and the town council has panicked and refuses to go ahead with the event. They are quoted as saying, '*There have been issues raised that this event may be demeaning to women, and it also raises issues of gender equality.*'

There is a photo of Delia and Maureen in their stockings and suspenders, and Maureen on her own, holding a baguette for some unknown reason, standing by the packhorse bridge, with a quote underneath from Delia saying, '*This is about freedom of expression. Feminism is the freedom to be who you want to be. Burlesque is art and art is meant to provoke.*'

It goes on to say, '*Delia, seen here with Hebden's unofficial Poet Laureate, Mitzi Jackson, who had her own thoughts to share, is quoted here from @MitziJackson1 social media account:*

Save Our Show

Dropping our drawers,
Doesn't make us whores!
In fact, showing our knickers,
Is good for jump-starting old tickers!
Life's too much fun,

To never show your bum,
Get on it, get busy –
Let's make Hebden Burlesque City!

It actually makes me laugh out loud. Miles gives me a suspicious look, as he slopes past me in his Lycra gear to go and do his new routine of a five-mile lunchtime cycle in the rain. No wonder he's miserable.

Maureen calls me over lunch. 'Have you seen the paper?' she asks.

'Yes, I'm reading it now. I like your poem.'

'Ah, thank you. So... big ask, is anyone in the cottage? Only Delia needs to move in so she can be around for her campaign fightback.'

'Oh. Ah.'

'And she'll need mate's rates – by that, I mean free. She's skint with all the outlay for the festival. If it doesn't go ahead, she's broke.'

'Oh.'

'Fact is, she's on her way here. I've said it's OK.'

What could I say to that? How about: 'And if I don't get some rent soon from *you*, I'*ll* be broke!'

Instead, I hear myself sigh, 'All right.'

When I get home, I am immediately pulled into a toilet blockage by Chloë, courtesy of Greg who has himself apparently been 'blocked up' for a few days. To clear it takes a full bottle of Fairy washing-up liquid and seven buckets of very hot water poured from a height whilst stood on a chair. Oh, the delights of being a mum.

Delia and Maureen are very hyper all evening. They're setting up an online campaign, a 'kick-starter something', ringing round other venues and doing a petition that I was the 832nd person to sign. When I ask where all the signatures came from, they look a bit sheepish. I don't ask any more questions: the twenty different coloured biros on the kitchen table give me my answer.

Chloë is delighted with some new feather pillows I ordered for her from Amazon after her anti-allergy ones had collapsed into flat pies. When she tells me Jeff Bozo made a squillion last year and paid zero tax, it did put me off. Damn Amazon Prime for making it so bloomin' easy to buy stuff.

I receive an update on the burlesque situation. There has been an emergency council session. If six councillors send letters tabling amendments, the decision has to be reconsidered, so Delia is telling me. Lavander Cottage is a hive of activity as people pull up, drop off, go in, and come out.

Delia wanders over at eight thirty, asking, 'Do you have anything I could eat, Janet? Maureen's on her second bottle, I can't keep up.'

I give her some cheese and onion pie and peas, bread and butter and a slice of Bakewell tart and a cup of tea. She wolfs the lot down.

'Thank you for your hospitality, Janet. I really appreciate your generosity.'

She takes my hand and kisses it. I don't know where to put myself, but I am floating for a while. Just being appreciated is such a nice feeling.

The news comes in the next day: the council have agreed, by a majority of two, that the event can go ahead. Delia and Maureen are ecstatic and, this time, both are merry by the time I get home. They are still merry at 11 p.m. when I go across and ask them to turn the samba down.

The cottage is hectic with comings and goings down the drive. Owning a B&B can be exhausting. On Sunday night, I am in bed by 9 p.m. with Jamie Oliver's veg cookbook. He makes it look so easy to not eat meat, so why am I then up and out of bed half an hour later, slapping together a juicy ham and pickle sandwich?

That ham sandwich helped me to go off to sleep, but I am up at six o'clock getting Chloë off to college. It's an exhausting hour persuading, cajoling, bribing and eventually waving her off. I get lost in chores on my day off, and it's coming up to lunchtime, and I'm sticking some washing out when a taxi pulls up and out gets a very tall, beefy bloke called Shadow. He's part of Delia's troupe and has just flown in from Berlin especially. Shadow is an American, but he left New York 'when it lost its edge'. Berlin still has it *just*, but it is 'on its way out'. I nod away, feeling quite the fraud, given the nearest I've got to New York is eating bagels, and Germany has never appealed, I think it was being forced to watch too many war films on a Sunday afternoon.

As we are chatting, I become aware of a lot of noise round the front of the house. I go through the patio door, sneak into the front room and peep round the curtains, and there is Laura Watson, fronting a group of ten to fifteen people, mainly older women, who are holding aloft a banner that says:

Not Naughty,

Not Nice,

Not in my Town

I am paralysed for a minute or two, then go into the hall and shout up the stairs. '*MAUREEN!*'

She comes hurtling down, complaining, 'How many times do I have to tell you? It's *Mitzi...* What?'

Mitzi is half dressed in what looks like a technicolour mermaid outfit, with a sponge cut in the shape of a shell sellotaped over one nipple.

'Look!' I gesture frantically at the group of enraged ladies outside.

My sister catches sight of them and bursts out laughing. Then her expression changes and she gasps: 'Sweet Je-esus – *Delia!*'

Covering up her exposed bit, she races round to the cottage, just as Chloë turns up with Greg, fighting their way through the throng.

'What's happening?' my daughter demands.

'What are you doing home?' I ask in the same breath.

'I forgot it's a training day.'

'Oh, right. I think it's a protest. Will you ask Laura if she wants a cup of tea?'

Chloë refuses, so I wander out with a big pot of tea and a batch of home-made Eccles cakes. Laura is shirty at first, but when I bring Lilac Fielding a chair because her knees are playing up, things calm down. That is, until Maureen's Carl turns up in his work's van with three heavy-looking lads. They muscle through the crowd, and Maureen flies out of the cottage, down the drive and jumps into his arms. He spins her around and, I have to say, they look very enamoured with one another. He puts her down and turns to me.

'Right, what do you want me to do with them, love?'

I was in shock. 'Nothing. It's not up to me.'

'It's your house though, isn't it?'

'Yes, but...'

'Well, they're trespassing on your drive.'

At this moment, it all gets a bit confusing. Delia erupts out of the cottage with her troupe of merry types, all half made-up and looking mind-bogglingly weird, shouting the words to 'Freedom', the George Michael song, so out of tune that I am glad for everyone's sake that they aren't a musical act.

This seems to catapult Laura and her gang into action, and they march down the drive shouting the lyrics to 'Respect', the Aretha Franklin song, but they soon forget the words and so Laura, at this point, shouts, 'RESPECT OUR WOMEN! Respect our town!'

To which Delia responds with, 'RESPECT our right to choose who we want to be! You don't get to approve us! Offence is not a sacred right.'

'Don't you dare use the word "sacred",' shouts an old bloke from Laura's side, in response. I'm sure I've seen him complaining in the post office.

That's it, then. It all gets shouty and loud and pushy. I have no idea whose idea it is, but there is a bloke with a camera and Chloë and Greg are on their phones. Anyway, it's all a big mess and yours truly is stuck right in the middle of it. I have gardening gloves on and a trowel in my hand and am feeling way too menopausal to cope with the body heat of twenty or so lady pensioners and a half made-up burlesque troupe.

Clapping my hands together above my head, I bawl at top volume. 'STOPPP! Stop this right now. *STOPPP!*'

Even if I say so myself, I can be loud when I put my mind to it; fifteen years of shouting livestock in across twelve acres does that for a girl.

They stop. They all stop. Long enough for me to say, 'Laura, can you take your protest off my drive, please? Go on, shoo. Delia, can you please return your troupe to my cottage, thank you? NOW!'

At this point, Carl wisely herds his lads in the opposite direction, silence falls and the whole thing melts away.

I make some fresh tea, crack out the emergency biscuits and things calm down enough for me to get changed and for Peter to arrive.

Around 6 p.m., Delia and the gang emerge from the cottage and reveal themselves. They look INCREDIBLE. One of them is green, one of them is gold. It brings up memories of when Chloë was really into *Barbie: Mermaidia*. Anyway, they look a treat, as they pile into a people carrier from Valley Cabs. I could tell Nick, the cab driver, didn't know where to put his eyes.

Laura and her posse have pretty much disappeared, leaving only a couple of stragglers, who accidentally wave at Delia and the gang as they pull away.

Peter and I are in front seats at the concert. It's AMAZING. Maureen is very funny. Carl brings Peter and me cocktails. I spot Laura and her gang shivering in the foyer with their placards. Someone gives Laura a cocktail, and I see her watching from the back. Delia and her gang are incredible performers; lots of dancing, quite athletic on occasion, quite naughty on occasion, very suggestive. I see Miles in the audience and quite a few clients from Valley Dental. Peter comes back with everyone, and we drink more cocktails. Shadow is a wonder with a shaker. Someone cranks up their Spotify playlist and we dance around, everyone dressed up in bits of stuff. Maureen has Carl in a jumpsuit of Shadow's and, with his muscles and everything, he looks very interesting. Peter drags me off the kitchen table at one point, and we have lots of fun with one of Delia's blindfolds.

I'm back at work the next day, and the rest of the week fades into a long hangover and the usual routine once Delia and the troupe leave. The cottage is a mess, but they have stripped the beds, which helps, though the amount of glitter, red paper love hearts and false eyelashes I find *everywhere* beggars belief.

Carl and Maureen seem more smitten than ever and are never apart, though her face one night when he drops her off is a picture. Apparently, he had introduced her to his kids, and without any warning. There are three of them: eight, twelve and fourteen – two boys, one girl. My sister goes straight up for a bath with a bottle of wine. When I ask her about it through the door, she says she is channelling Baroness Elsa Schraeder from *The Sound of Music* and is looking into boarding schools.

The *Hebden Bridge Times* flops through the door on Thursday, as always. It comes out once a week, and I always get it as it's full of useful information about somebody who's done something and somebody else who's raised money baking brownies, and when

Potato Day is, that sort of thing. Only today, to my complete horror, on the front cover is a photo of me pushing Laura and Delia apart, with my trowel almost poised to go up Delia's nose, and with the headline: '*To the BURL... RESQUE*'!

I flush from head to toe and my insides curdle.

It reads:

Burlesque gets nasty as the controversy boiled over outside Lavander Cottage, home and headquarters to the Delicious Delia Burlesque Troupe last week, after the council granted a last-minute reprieve to allow their performance at the Picture House to go ahead. Landlady Janet Jackson, pictured here, stepped into the fray and peace was restored. The show did go on and hundreds packed out the Picture House for a night of spectacular performance and racy spectacle. An eye-watering success!

Inside are lots of photos of the night itself and Delicious Delia of Delicious Delia & Chums is quoted as saying, '*We're thrilled the wonderful folk of Hebden Bridge were able to enjoy our burlesque experience and look forward to an even bigger and better show next year.*'

I have been pointed out by twenty-two people as the front cover star of the *Hebden Bridge Times*. Miles asks me if I really was part of the burlesque troupe. I say yes, and that I'll be handing my notice in next Monday so I can travel the world as Janet J, the Dental Dominatrix. That shuts him up!

When I get home, Delia has sent me flowers and a Marks & Spencer hamper. I book tomorrow off, since I can't face any more looks or questions. Bloody B&B, what have you got me into?

• •

TIP FOR RUNNING A B&B

Never be tempted to pop a deflated balloon indoors. You never know what is inside. Such as a thousand red paper love hearts – that go EVERYWHERE!

CHAPTER 42

Booking No. 27: The Fitties

Carl is round for Sunday dinner. He's very loud and domineering. I don't get the impression he does it deliberately, he's just used to bossing people about in a noisy environment. He's very straightforward, which I like, and he's very affectionate with Maureen, which I also really like. He tells us how he got started.

'At first I was a labourer, worked my way up to brickie, then I began saving, bought a couple of wrecks and did them up, now I've six houses around Hebble Valley and I'm on with buying some land. I'm gonna build a set of maisonette flats in Ludd.'

He keeps an arm around Maureen all the time and tells her she's gorgeous every two minutes. She glows in his warmth, and he's obviously smitten with her. I make way too many Yorkshire puddings. I think, *Don't worry, Janet, you can freeze them.* But it turns out that won't be necessary. I don't think I've ever seen anyone eat as many. Maureen watches in awe, as Carl demolishes everything on the table while she picks at her carrots. He is very complimentary about the food, giving it lots of 'Brilliant grub, Janet', and 'This is first-class scoff, this, Janet.'

At bedtime, Peter is restless and fidgety, as I'm trying to read my *Good Housekeeping.* I ask him if he is OK.

He turns round and says to me, 'Do you realise what a loser you've got in me, Janet?'

I am a bit upset at that and give him a hug and a kiss.

I say, 'Don't be daft. Having a couple of houses does not make you a winner in life, Peter. I like a man who can catalogue paperbacks and grow a good dahlia.'

Which seems to placate him, because he is snoring soon after. I, however, lie awake for a while wondering if it does matter, and if I do want a man with more prospects than a part-time librarian? I don't expect anyone to look after me – I'm used to being the one who does that. I want someone to treat me nicely, go out for the odd meal with, and maybe go on a city break. That's nice enough, isn't it? I wish he'd do something about it though, if he's not happy with himself. It's quite hard work propping people up all the time. Chloë likes Peter. She was annoyed with me over the Malky incident. I suppose I still think about Malky. It was fun, it was a bit cold and I wouldn't want to be looking in bike showrooms every weekend, but the excitement was what I needed. Malky doesn't have angst, he's been through the fire and he's at peace with himself. He's relaxed, confident and resilient – and that's very attractive.

At my age, maybe I should be thinking I'll be lucky to get anyone. And yet I don't feel that desperate. Watching Maureen tonight, she falls so hard; her eyes never leave Carl's face at the table. Even with the prospect of his kids, she seems so in love. I remember how I felt about Franklin, the passion, the excitement, the feelings of love that went on and on. With Peter I feel like I'm passing the time in a nice way, and part of me believes that's what I should do because I'm older, but I'm only forty-five and when I look at Maureen and see the way she looks at Carl, deep down I worry that I've given up.

Peter's birthday arrives. I bake him a Genoa fruit cake, which he loves, buy him some really good gardening gloves and a set of secateurs and lots of seeds for next year. He's really chuffed and gives me a bag of strappy underwear he wants me to try for his birthday treat. I'm not really feeling it, as it's a nightmare to get into. I don't know which bit goes where and, of course, as soon as I *am* in it, Chloë shouts for help.

'Mum! I've spilt tea! Help me, quick, I need to turn the mattress.'

I dig out the oldest, full-length, winter dressing gown to cover everything up. By the time I've made her bed, I am sweating cobs. When I get back to my own bedroom, Peter arrives with two glasses of Prosecco and gets very excited helping me out of the dressing gown, which I am actually very grateful for, being completely shattered. All round, Peter is very preoccupied and doesn't seem to notice that I am both clammy and tired. We have some fun, and he tells me again and again that this is his best birthday ever.

The cottage has been quiet since all the shenanigans with Delia's burlesque do. It's getting me down, as I'm still overdrawn at the bank. Maureen is not inspiring confidence with her lack of work ethic. I'm giving Chloë £30 a week to go to college, and she is looking a bit miserable today; she and Greg are not getting on very well. She blames the pressures and stress of modern life. I try not to be too judgmental, but how stressful is her life? She has her food delivered to her bedside, her washing taken away and returned, plus she has no job and no bills to pay. I hate to think what's coming down the track at her and how she'll cope with life.

And then, just as I'm really feeling worried, there's a booking. Hurrah! Two nights, four guests. A camper van and four lads all running in the Leeds half-marathon turn up this afternoon. Even Maureen, besotted as she is with Carl, pops her head out of the patio doors to say hi to them. They are all very suave in their Lycra kit, matching headphones, especially when they start to do lots of sprints, stretching and speed walks.

Peter turns up just as they are all coming back in looking sweaty and dirty from a test run, and we give them an impromptu clap. He joins in but seems subdued. I don't want to, but feel I have to ask him why. He says he's a bit intimidated, having had a bad day in the library. Apparently, he got puffed out chasing a five-year-old who had run off with Jilly Cooper's *Mount!*. He's also convinced he is now addicted to the Blue Baker's cinnamon buns, a growing problem since they opened the shop opposite the library six months ago. I said I hadn't noticed if he had put on weight and I wasn't bothered anyway. Although, having Maureen regale me with the athletic exploits of her and Carl, asking do I have any Canesten, 'we're at it so much I'm getting chapped', while I make Peter and me a pot of peppermint tea, makes me wonder, do I really, *really* fancy *fancy* Peter? Gulp. I know he fancies me, he tells me all the time. I feel *so* bad. What's wrong with me? Why can't I just be happy?

Maureen is on one tonight. She constantly checks the time. She's expecting Carl and is draped over the sofa in a bizarre, crochet, batwing, gold dress and those gladiator bootie heel things watching the news when Carl arrives with a Hammad's takeout and still in his work gear. She takes one look at him.

'I thought we were going out for a drink?' she snaps.

'We've had hell on knocking out three ceilings in the old barn up Cragg. A nest with two dead birds fell on Sprog when we were doing it. His face was a picture.'

But Maureen does not laugh, and I hardly dare to.

She wheels back round to the TV, saying meanly, 'Carl, I'm not interested in bloody Sprog. This is the Environment Minister. I missed the question there. Turn it up, Janet.'

It feels rude to turn the TV up, so I only raise the sound one notch.

Chloë gets up. 'This is boring. I'm off out. See you later.'

'Where are you going?' I say immediately. 'Make sure your phone's charged.'

'Shush, Janet, I can't hear the question.' My sister reaches for the remote and up goes the volume again.

Carl shouts over it, 'Maureen, who's in t'camper van?'

'One of the lads doing Leeds marathon.'

'Good on 'em.'

Maureen is agitated and rears round, hissing, 'Ssshhh!'

Carl either doesn't hear or doesn't care, and he certainly doesn't have a volume switch, so he shouts quite loudly: 'Anyone want some ribs before I neck 'em all?'

Maureen whirls round again, this time with a full, dramatic skirt swish, and her legs come off the arm of the sofa.

'Carl, no, I do not! I want to listen to the Environment Minister, but it's obvious you've no interest in the future of our planet, so I'm off to bed.'

'I thought you'd never ask.'

I can't help but burst out laughing at that one, which only inflames the situation. She is steely and furious.

'Well, I'm *not* asking, because I will not be sleeping with an Earth-destroying Tory.'

'Eh? You nutter! Who's a flaming Tory?'

'Nutter?'

There are door slams, people running up and down the stairs, and then fifteen minutes later I hear Carl's van speeding off down the road and Maureen wailing like a baby.

Peter sits in silence, rocking his cup of tea backwards and forwards. Eventually he comes out with: 'It's like Mum and Uncle Alistair on Brexit.'

I'm left feeling there isn't enough passion in our relationship. The nearest Peter and I get to a disagreement is whether or not to treat use-by dates as gospel. Having come down heavily on the side of 'ignore the use-by dates', it feels like Russian roulette dipping a breadstick in some caramelised onion hummus at bedtime. Halfway through the breadstick, and with a slightly curious taste in my mouth, it dawns on me that this is what I currently do for excitement.

I'm sad waving off the fitties the next day, such lovely lads. A couple of them are bright as a button having achieved PBs (personal best they explained when I asked), one of them is limping – a toenail has dropped off apparently – and one of them is under the weather having overplayed it early on and ended up in a St John Ambulance. I take out the bedding and the rubbish; it's not too bad for a group of lads, not really. Let's face it, Chloe's bedroom is much worse and, once I think about that, I end up going up to her room and tearing it apart – sometimes life is chores.

· ·

TIPS ON RUNNING A B&B

Try to keep on top of cleaning in your own house. It soon piles up when you're not paying attention. What's the point of having a clean cottage if your home is a bomb site?

· ·

TIPS ON LIFE

Don't get so fixated on being right that you end up being ill in the night with a gippy tummy.

Hummus does *not* keep.

CHAPTER 43

Booking No. 28: Julian from Cunningham

Christmas is on its way. To my delight, I find some old champagne cognac at the back of the cleaning cupboard. I must have secreted it there so Maureen wouldn't find it. I get stuck into Stir-up Sunday and make three Christmas cakes to the Nigella recipe; very rich, very boozy. Peter comes round asking if I fancy a walk up to the Robin for Sunday dinner. I don't, because I'm too engrossed in the cakes and enjoying listening to the *Archers Omnibus*.

He hangs around for a bit and says things like: 'Right, well, I'll get off and leave you to it.'

I obviously don't say anything very encouraging, because he does eventually leave. I feel bad, because that shows I'm not a good girlfriend, really. Sometimes I just want to listen and do my own thing. I also want to avoid the 'can my mum come and stay for Christmas' conversation cropping up. Not this year. She's deteriorated a lot apparently, and she wasn't well last time. I think Peter might dump me soon. It's been two weeks since we had sex.

Chloë passes through looking incredibly glamorous and announces that she is going to meet Greg for a 'final goodbye'. I ask her if she'd like a lift, and she says no, she needs the walk to compose herself. I tell her I won't drink so I can pick her up after. She says thanks, she'll let me know. Carl turns up washed, smelling very strongly of ladies' deodorant and with a dozen bottles of Stella that Maureen immediately gets stuck into. Well, we are all very jolly and having a bit of a laugh when my phone starts beeping, with the message: *Immediate booking*.

Then my phone rings.

'Hello, love, can I come in the next half hour?'

'Er...'

'I'm desperate, the missus is gonna kill me. Cut a long story short, she's caught me in flagrante, if you know what I mean.'

I know what he means. There is a crash in the background of his call.

'Seriously, can I come now?' He is sounding desperate.

'Yes, of course. You know where we are?'

I fly round the cottage, which I stupidly haven't tidied properly since the exit of the fitties. Maureen comes and helps – I think she's trying to impress Carl. We set to changing the double bed and putting away the others, seeing as how our guest is presumably on his own. Then, while Maureen is running round with the hoover, I'm upstairs in the bathroom, pouring bleach down the loo, spraying the shower and putting clean towels out and more loo rolls. Then both of us tidy the kitchen. I get a jug of milk together, some butter, and dig out a panettone I'd bought as an early Christmas treat. We haven't finished before Julian is round, banging on the door. He is probably in his early forties, very agitated and very grateful.

'Thank God for Airbnb. You don't get too many spare beds in Hebden.'

I am tempted to say something about how he's clearly found at least one spare bed, from the sound of his wife's fury, but it doesn't do to judge anyone these days, not with my tarnished record. Plus, he's obviously ready to hit the booze by the sound of the chink of bottles. His phone is going berserk. He opens a can and slurps from it then puts the phone on speaker so we can clearly hear.

'*...she's twenty-four years old, of course she's chilled and gorgeous. She's not got three screaming kids and doesn't have your miserable face to look at every day.*'

Maureen and I quickly finish what we're doing, wish our 'immediate booking' well, and leave him to settle down in front of the TV while he phones for a takeaway. I am very happy to close the door on that drama. Thanking Maureen for her help, I throw off my grubby clothes and collapse into bed with a hot-water bottle to read the *Good Housekeeping* Christmas showstopper dessert recipes and find it flat on my face when I wake up at half past midnight to hear a text from Chloë: *Can you come and get me?*

I quickly knock back two strong coffees to wake myself up, pull tight my dressing gown under my winter coat and drag on my wellies. When I arrive at Greg's, Chloë is outside on her phone smiling and very upbeat.

'Yeah, it's done.'

I'm so relieved she's all right. Her first big relationship break-up.

'Very proud of you, darling,' I tell her. Then: 'You seem very OK with it all. Was Greg all right?'

'He cried.'

'I'm sorry, poor Greg.'

'Yes, I hugged him and told him he would realise it was for the best in a year or two.'

'Very mature.'

'Yes, well, I've done a lot of thinking about it, assessed my feelings, researched relationship theory and long-term compatibility, and decided we weren't right for each other.'

'Wow, you know your stuff.'

'Yes, I think I want to be a psychologist.'

'Amazing.'

'We're fundamentally different attachment types; it would be too much like hard work.'

'Interesting... By the way, what attachment type am I?'

'Er, you'd need to do the theory test. My instinct is that you're the anxious type.'

'What about Peter?'

'No idea, Mum. I don't really know Peter.'

'Any advice for me and Peter?'

'Why are you asking?'

'I'm not sure what to do. I think I want to be single again. He's nice, he's just...'

'Not the one.'

'He's nice, he's just not...'

'Your soulmate.'

'He doesn't set me alight. He's lovely. He's nice.'

'OK. That's the third time you've said nice. If you're talking nice-friend zone, you have to tell him. The sooner the better.'

'But maybe I won't get better than Peter, and I'll regret it forever and wake up lonely and bitter when I'm seventy.'

'Anxious – thought so. No, you'll be fine. You need someone secure – and don't worry, Mum, with those knockers, you'll never be short of admirers.'

'Eh?'

Well, we laugh at that, especially when I remind her that she has inherited them. The drive past all the gorgeous Christmas lights on the quiet roads is lovely, and I feel quite emotional. I've got advice from my little girl, who's not a little girl any more. I feel a bit delirious from lack of sleep and, as we pull into the drive, Chloë gives a big yawn.

'Can you lend me some money to do Christmas shopping this weekend?'

'OK, how much?'

'Fifty quid should do it. I've Dad to buy for too.'

I gulp, but then decide not to panic. To myself I say, *Everything is going to be all right. You have a wonderful daughter who is going to do brilliantly, and a roof over your head, and Maureen has a Carl who can presumably fix the roof should the worst happen. It's all going to be OK.*

I'm soon in bed and asleep, but wake up still exhausted when Harvey scratches at the door before dawn breaks.

I've done a wash, got stuff on the airer and even managed some ironing by 7 a.m. I'm now up so early I decide to cycle in to work to keep the momentum going. I put my lights on in the gloom and, as I wobble off down the road, I notice a lot of yellow planning notices attached to the lamp posts and, after I spot my third, I pull up to read it.

Notice of planning application
Larkspur House, conversion of garage into self-contained holiday flat

Well, blow me down. Laura Watson, getting in on the action! I can't decide whether to laugh or cry. I cycle slowly into town and chain up the bike in the safe storage at the station so I can walk through the park to work and check out the flower beds on the way. It's a bitterly cold day, the hollies are lathered in berries and the dogwood's vivid, burgundy spikes bring a bit of jazzy colour along the whole run of the bed. But my mind is still on Laura. I can't get over what she's done – and what's more, she's bound to go upmarket. Well, at least she can't complain about my business if she's running one herself. I decide that I won't object; I'm not going to be petty like she was.

I'm stewing on how unexpectedly things turn out, when a snowflake lands on my nose. I look up, and there's a million of them tumbling from the heavens. It's one of those special moments: a hold-your-breath silence blankets the world and I take in nature's magic, and I marvel.

I, like everyone who comes into Valley Dental, have my eyes fixed on the skies. 'Will it stick?', 'Are we due more?', 'There's a freeze due tonight apparently', 'I'm putting money on a White Christmas.'

I chat to Mrs Fowler (scale and polish four times a year). She is admiring my cottage card on the counter and tells me she has two holiday lets and who do I advertise them with?

'Airbnb.'

'Oh, no,' she says. 'No, no, no, not enough eyeballs. Booking. com, love. Booking. com. You can thank me in March.'

I spend as much time as I dare having a look at Booking.com whilst trying to be efficient on reception. I'm signing and sealing the last of the Christmas cards for Valley Dental Denplan customers when Miles approaches the desk looking very furtive.

'Janet, can I have a private word?'

There is no one in reception and no one due in.

'Yes, of course.'

He looks around. 'Now?'

'Do you want to go somewhere?' I go to get up, I've no idea why.

'No, here's fine. Look... it's about your B&B.'

'OK.'

'Are you booked up for Christmas?'

'Er... no, not yet.'

'Could I book myself in? It'd be for two weeks. Right across Christmas and New Year, from December the nineteenth. I think the change of scenery will do me good.'

I'm gobsmacked. Miles. Next door? *Think of the money, Janet.*

'Right. Yes. Of course, I could do a discount if you like, since it's for so many days.'

'No. No, I don't want a discount.' He gives a long pause. 'If there was any chance of the odd meal...'

I look at him properly for the first time in weeks, months

probably. He is skin and bone, washed out, grizzly from a lack of shaving and a full ice cream swirl of grey hair in need of a cut. His clothes are OK, hidden under his uniform, though that hangs off him like he's picked up a size too big.

'I'll block that out for you, Miles, straight away, and I'll make sure that you get one home-cooked meal at least once a day.'

He looks me directly in the eye with a puppy-dog expression that has my stomach unexpectedly flipping, and then he puts a hand on my hand. It's warm, strong and my heart races.

'I'll pay extra.'

'No, no, it will be my pleasure. I always cook too much.'

He gives me a giant smile, the first I've seen in a long while. Then he skips up the steps, and I am taking in what having Miles next door will mean. I'll have to get him a little Christmas tree, make Lavander Cottage nice and homely, maybe invest in one of those fake log burners. I'm very grateful that Maureen has a current beau, so she won't be buzzing around, trying to ensnare him. I'll just have to ensure that her relationship with Carl keeps going until the New Year. It's only three weeks. I'm fairly confident she can do that.

At that point, I jump onto the Airbnb calendar and block out the whole two weeks. It is so satisfying to mark out those dates. Booked. Booked. *Booked.* And with *Miles!* I feel a little bit giddy when my phone buzzes in my bag. Sighing, I dig it out. It's probably Chloë after some more money.

It's not Chloë, it's a text from Malky!

What you doing Boxing Day? Fancy a run out to Skipton?

There's a picture of a trike, one of those enormous three-wheeler motorcycles with a very comfy-looking seat like a leather throne. Well, I don't think too much about it, but reply immediately, *Yes, sounds great.*

It does sound great. Skipton isn't too far away, so there will be less risk of cramp, and it's ages since I've been there. I wonder if they do a market on Boxing Day? *Yes! Seize the moment, Janet.* I'm feeling unnerved by my recklessness. Maybe it's the weather? Or the out-of-date Marmite I had on my toast this morning?

I'm desperate for a calming cup of tea and take a moment to brew up a strong one when the reception door swings open, and Peter stumbles in wrestling with a giant poinsettia.

251

'Two for a fiver at Aldi. I thought you might like one.'

I do like it, I love it. At that moment, I also realise with complete conviction that I don't love Peter.

'It's lovely, really lovely, Peter. Thank you. That's so kind and thoughtful. You are kind and thoughtful, you're lovely.' And then I blurt it out. 'Can we just be friends, Peter? I don't think I'm ready to be steady with anyone. I really like you, as a friend. I'm just not ready for anything serious. It's too much for me. It's not what I want at the moment.'

His face crumples, and I feel so mean. He puts the poinsettia on the desk so we can hardly see each other between the leaves.

'Of course, if that's what you want, Janet. I'm always around if you ever decide, you know... differently.'

I put my fingers through the leaves so he can see me.

'Thank you so much, Peter. You are lovely.'

'I'm not sure about that. Can I have a hug?'

I wander round the reception, and he gives me a big, clingy hug, his head settling into my cleavage. It's getting to the point where I'm praying for someone to come into reception. He eventually seems to take the hint after I cough, and he slowly unfurls himself.

'Thank you,' he says huskily.

'No, thank you for your understanding, Peter.' I scurry back round the reception to avoid more contact.

'You can keep the poinsettia.'

'Are you sure? That's very good of you. I'll give you the £2.50.'

'No, it's fine.'

'Thank you. I'm so glad we can still be friends.'

'Yes. Although I don't know if I can cope with friends right now, Janet. I might need some time.'

'Of course. I am sorry, you know, but I'm just not ready. I was married for a very long time and it has all taken its toll.'

'It's all right, I understand. You don't need to explain. Anyway... I'll get going. Bye, Janet.'

Then, with a stumble and a sneeze, he's gone. The rest of the day rushes by. I spend most of it putting together a new Booking.com listing from my Airbnb listing. I'm incredibly proud of myself and FaceTime Chloë so I can show her round it. She is super impressed and gives me the go-ahead. By half past four, I'm live on Booking.com!

At five o'clock promptly, Miles comes bouncing down the stairs and gives me a huge beaming smile on his way out.

'All good, Janet, for the nineteenth?'

'Booked in, Miles.' I give him a thumbs up.

'Wonderful.'

'I'll send you all the details in an email.'

'Righty-ho.'

It's my turn to lock up tonight and, having remembered we need milk at home, I wobble my way back on the bike with the carton in my hand. The snow arrives in occasional flurries, so I go at a snail's pace in case of skids. The stretch of canal boat fairy lights is like a sparkling constellation tonight to guide me home. I can't decide if I'm happy or sad, an idiot who's just said farewell to a good man, or a forty-five-year-old woman who won't take second best.

Once home, I get cracking and cook up a comforting minestrone whilst Chloë dashes in and out of the kitchen for snacks and drinks with new friend Ben. The *Mamma Mia Soundtrack* CD has me bopping around as it blasts out on the speakers. It's past six, and I'm mid stir when Maureen crashes in through the patio door in the arms of Carl. They're both giggling, and she is wielding a bottle of champagne that looks near enough ready for recycling.

'JANET, JANET, JANET. Say hello to the soon-to-be Mrs Pringle. We're engaged! Is it OK if Carl moves in? We'll probably have the kids Christmas Day.'

I'm taking in the triple bombshells when the phone buzzes loudly. It's Booking.com with an immediate booking.

TOMMY from Bristol, tonight for three nights, two guests. We're working local, job running late, we do IT solutions, sorry for late notice. Non-smokers.

I unwind my apron ties and put the minestrone onto low, plant a kiss of congratulations on Maureen and Carl, then pull on my Marigolds.

Clasping a nine-pack of toilet rolls, I say, 'Congratulations. How lovely. Let's think about Christmas. We'll probably need to get out the bain-marie. Excuse me – immediate booking.' And off I head to the cottage, a spring in my step.

Janet Jackson, coper, cooker, baker, gardener, receptionist, cleaner, mother, sister, lover and proud B&B owner. Into Lavander

Cottage I go, for a fast turnaround.

. . . .

TIPS FOR RUNNING A B&B

Always buy extra toilet roll, you'll need it.

Be prepared for the unexpected! Embrace it. Life's never going to be dull with a B&B.

. . . .

TIP ON LIFE

Try to be brave now and again.

. . . .

TIP ON GARDENS

Dogwood; good for winter interest.

ACKNOWLEDGEMENTS

I would like to thank Joan Deitch for her terrific editing and serious encouragement to a wobbly debut writer. Nicola May for her generosity with tips and advice. Hannah Dyson for her meticulousness. Sara @Simdesign for her wonderful cover design, Margaret for being the first and most generous reader, Steph for welcoming quite a few guests over the years, Matthew for the lino, Gaz for sorting the hob and Graeme for drains emergency cover!

A big thank you to all the guests who have come and gone from the garage cottage over the years... you make my world an altogether more interesting place.

BP

Printed in Great Britain
by Amazon

16308393R00154